Day Trips® Series

GETAWAYS APPROXIMATELY TWO HOURS AWAY

DAY TRIPS®
FROM RALEIGH-DURHAM

by

Ralph Grizzle

The Globe Pequot Press

GUILFORD, CONNECTICUT

ISBN 0-7627-2280-0

Manufactured in the United States of America
First Edition/Second Printing

 **To Marjorie**

Help Us Keep This Guide Up to Date

Every effort has been made by the author and editors to make this guide as accurate and useful as possible. However, many things can change after a guide is published—establishments close, phone numbers change, facilities come under new management, etc.

We would love to hear from you concerning your experiences with this guide and how you feel it could be improved and kept up to date. While we may not be able to respond to all comments and suggestions, we'll take them to heart and we'll also make certain to share them with the author. Please send your comments and suggestions to the following address:

The Globe Pequot Press
Reader Response/Editorial Department
P.O. Box 480
Guilford, CT 06437

Or you may e-mail us at:

editorial@globe-pequot.com

Thanks for your input, and happy travels!

CONTENTS

Introduction ix
Travel Tips xi
Using this Travel Guide. . . . xiii

Day Trip 1
Williamston 2
Windsor 5
Edenton 7

Day Trip 2
Halifax 14
Murfreesboro 16

Day Trip 1
New Bern 21
Oriental 27

Day Trip 2
Washington 31
Bath 34
Aurora 36
Edward 37

Day Trip 3
Smithfield 40
Selma 41

Goldsboro 42
Kinston 44

Day Trip 4
Morehead City 49
Atlantic Beach 53
Swansboro 57

Day Trip 5
Beaufort 61

Day Trip 6
Bailey 69
Kenly 69
Wilson 70
Farmville 73
Greenville 73
Tarboro 75

Day Trip 1
Wilmington. 77
Wrightsville Beach 86
Carolina Beach 88
Kure Beach 89

Day Trip 2
Southport 93
Bald Head Island 97

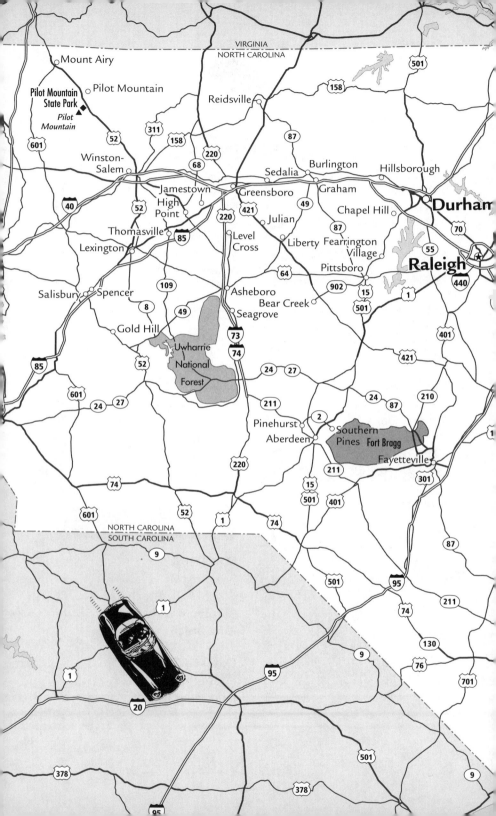

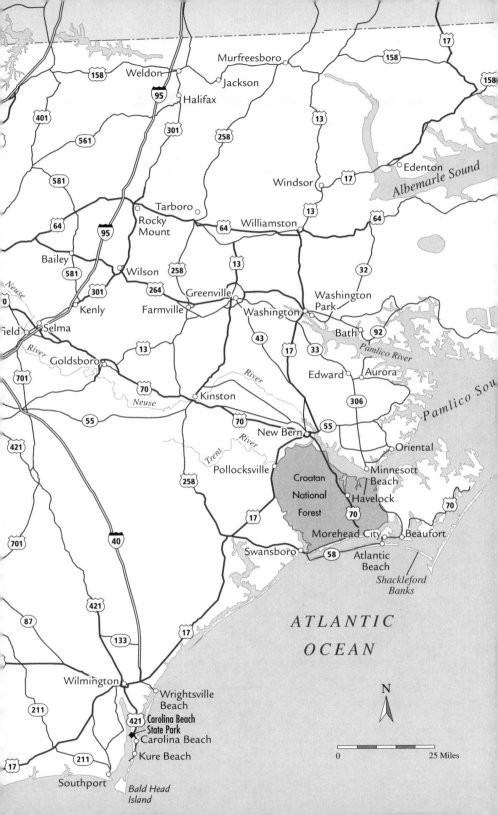

Day Trip 1
Fayetteville 102
Fort Bragg 107

Day Trip 2
Pinehurst 111
Southern Pines 115
Aberdeen 118

Day Trip 1
Chapel Hill 119

Day Trip 2
Pittsboro 129
Bear Creek 134

Day Trip 3
Hillsborough 137

Day Trip 4
Burlington 143

Graham 147
Reidsville 149

Day Trip 5
Greensboro 151

Day Trip 6
Winston-Salem. 167

Day Trip 7
Mount Airy 177
Pilot Mountain 181

Day Trip 8
High Point 183
Thomasville 188
Lexington 189

Day Trip 9
Salisbury 193
Spencer 198
Gold Hill 199

Day Trip 10
Level Cross 203
Asheboro 203
Seagrove 207

INTRODUCTION

North Carolina automobiles once bore license plates that displayed the tagline "Variety Vacationland." Those words have since been replaced with "First in Flight," in honor of Wilbur and Orville Wright, two brothers who on December 17, 1903, launched the age of human flight from Kitty Hawk, North Carolina. Still, North Carolina remains a variety vacationland, and our 78,000 miles of blacktop (more paved roads than any other state), put our state's varied attractions within driving distance for all.

Raleigh-Durhamers are particularly blessed. Within about a two-hour drive, they can reach country and coast—and even the edge of the mountains on the western end of our state. Nearly every type of touristic diversion beckons to capital-area travelers seated behind the steering wheel.

To the east, day travelers can point their cars toward the more than 301 miles of coast edging the Atlantic Ocean. Dotting these shores are exquisitely charming fishing villages and islands where local residents, descendants of English settlers, sound as though they just stepped off a boat from Britain. A day trip to the North Carolina coast can be not only culturally enlightening but also invigorating for mind and spirit. Be sure to breathe in deeply the salt air and sea spray from the Atlantic Ocean.

Your taste buds needn't go unrewarded as you travel the blacktop. Point your car in any direction, and you're bound to find a memorable meal. Leaving Raleigh, NC 70 east is known as the "Barbecue Highway." We've scoped out the best of the barbecue joints for you, so be sure to leave home with a full tank and an empty stomach.

A little farther inland, good roads will lead you to our Colonial past, which lives in perpetuity in towns like New Bern. There, glorious Tryon Palace, although rebuilt in the 1950s, looks much as it did when it was home to two royal governors in the 1770s. Nearby Bath, settled in 1705, boasts North Carolina's first church and the three historic homes that comprise the historic site at "North Carolina's First Town." Pardon the pun, but you'll want to immerse yourself in the history of Bath and other towns that reflect our heritage and our eventual break with the British Isles.

Heading northeast takes you to Halifax—where the Halifax Resolves, signed several months before the Declaration of Independence, represented the first movement for independence in our nation—and to Edenton, another of the three Colonial capitals where the King's appointees once ruled the Carolinas. You'll learn a great deal about who we once were, and who we have become, on day trips to these destinations.

Heading south and southeast from Raleigh puts you in golf country—North Carolina claims to be the birthplace of American golf. The sand hills that make for such good golf courses also are home to one of the world's largest military complexes, Fort Bragg, where the nearby Special Ops Museum is a must-see. The sand meets the sea in the coastal city of Wilmington and, a little farther to the south, charming Southport. Are you beginning to get my point about North Carolina being the variety vacationland?

Going west, young or not, takes you to the college town of Chapel Hill, to the Colonial town of Hillsborough, and to the Moravian village of Old Salem— with lots in between. For example, marvel at the world's largest Duncan Phyfe chair in Thomasville. It rises 18 feet above its base and has seated President Lyndon B. Johnson as well as several Miss Americas. Or stand beneath what was once the world's largest coffeepot. Erected by two Moravian tinsmiths in 1858 and measuring 16 feet in circumference and 12 feet in height, it's located on the north side of Old Salem.

All of this, however, is only a taste of what's ahead of you as you seat yourself behind the wheel to travel the scenic ribbons of road that traverse the Old North State. Remember always to enjoy the journey. It can be just as rewarding as the destination. And remember too to permit yourself to be detoured now and then. One of our own said it best. "You can travel the interstate highways and miss the whole country," said Wilmington-born Charles Kuralt. "I always choose the back roads whenever possible." It is there, passing through farmland and forests, towns and cities, that you will find what is best and true of our great state.

TRAVEL TIPS

Carry a Road Map

Don't leave home without one! Two, in fact. For your glove compartment, pick up the free State Transportation Map, published by the North Carolina Department of Transportation. Order one by calling (919) 733-7600 or pick up one at offices operated or concessioned by NCDOT, such as the Driver's License office. The second map that we wouldn't leave home without is the exotically named DeLorme North Carolina Atlas & Gazetteer. Retailing for $19.95 and available at bookstores and on-line, this eighty-eight-page reference will become well worn from use over the years.

Follow the Rules of the Road

It may seem to be common sense, but keep your eyes on the road. In 1999, the latest year for which figures were available, of the 218,277 crashes reported in the state, a third involved only a single vehicle. Apparently some of those drivers weren't paying attention.

Don't speed. It's the leading violation in fatal crashes.

Obey the law. In 82 percent of all crashes in North Carolina at least one driver was in violation of a traffic law.

Choose your travel times carefully. Fully 73 percent of all crashes occur between 7:00 A.M. and 7:00 P.M. Sunday is the lowest crash day, with only 10 percent of all crashes.

Don't drink. More than a quarter of highway fatalities are the result of alcohol violations.

The North Carolina Governor's Highway Safety Program provides information to help keep you safe behind the wheel. For more information call (919) 733-3083 or visit www.dot.state.nc.us/services ghsp/.

Watch Out for Wild Animals

Deer caused 5.6 percent of all reported North Carolina driving accidents in 1999, according to a University of North Carolina at Chapel Hill study. Eastern counties showed the highest rates overall. The state's Wildlife Resources Commission estimates North Carolina's deer population to stand at nearly one million animals. Keep your eye out not only for deer but also for bears (abundant in eastern North Carolina), raccoons, opossums, and livestock. North Carolina ranks as the ninth most dangerous state, by the way, for wildlife/automobile accident frequency, according to the Insurance Information Institute.

On the other hand, these are animals to look for, as opposed to look out for: the cardinal (state bird), the Channel Bass (state fish), the honeybee (state insect), the box turtle (state reptile), and the gray squirrel (state mammal). We even have a state dog, the Plott Hound.

Plan Accordingly

Our day trips are designed to be just that: trips that can be done well within one revolution of the clock, including travel to and from Raleigh-Durham. Should you want to linger, however, some trips will require an overnight. If you prefer a long weekend, look for day trips that can be combined. Combining trips also allows you, in many instances, to go and come by different roads so that you get to know our state even better.

Sleeping Away from Home

We've listed hotels and bed-and-breakfasts, should you decide to spend a little more time away from home. The North Carolina Division of Tourism, Film and Sports Development publishes *North Carolina: The Official Travel Guide* both in print and on-line. Call (800) VISIT–NC (in Raleigh, 733–8372) or visit www.visitnc.com.

North Carolina Bed & Breakfasts and Inns publishes a brochure listing more than 150 small lodging establishments across the state. Call (800) 849–5392 or log on to www.bbonline.com/nc/ncbbi/.

USING THIS TRAVEL GUIDE

Highway designations: Federal highways are designated US. State routes are indicated by NC for North Carolina.

Hours: Hours of operation have been included when possible but are subject to frequent changes. Addresses, phone numbers, and Web sites appear for obtaining up-to-date information.

Restaurants: Restaurant prices are designated as $$$ (expensive; $15 or more for an entree), $$ (moderate; $5 to $15), and $ (inexpensive; $5 and under).

Accommodations: Room rates are designated as $$$ (expensive; over $100 for a standard room), $$ (moderate; $50 to $100), and $ (inexpensive; under $50).

> *The prices and rates listed in this guidebook were confirmed at press time. We recommend, however, that you call establishments before traveling to obtain current information.*

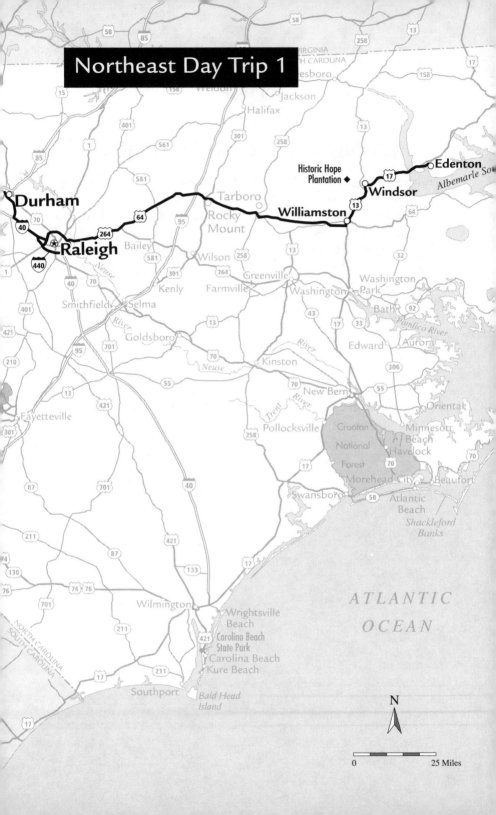

Northeast Day Trip 1

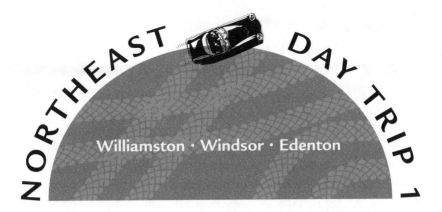

NORTHEAST DAY TRIP 1

Williamston · Windsor · Edenton

Travel back to the roots of North Carolina on this day trip, which takes you to three eighteenth-century towns, including North Carolina's first Colonial capital, Edenton. But before landing in Edenton, stop first in Williamston, on US 64 east of Raleigh. Founded just three years after the signing of the Declaration of Independence, Williamston has two National Register Historic Districts that highlight nineteenth- and early twentieth-century life. Along the town's tree-shaded streets, you'll walk past well-preserved nineteenth-century structures to get a feel for this charming town.

Pick up US 13/17 north for Windsor, the next stop on this trip, founded nearly a decade earlier than Williamston. Windsor has a scenic boardwalk that borders the waterfront of what was once a busy port. A customs house and a branch of the State Bank served West Indian and coastal water trade. Just outside town is Historic Hope Plantation, dating from the 1720s.

Continue north on US 13/17 to the old Colonial capital of Edenton. You'll have traveled 140 miles from Raleigh to the town that bills itself as the "Prettiest Town in the South," and upon arrival, you will likely agree that the drive was worth the trip. Edenton certainly is picturesque, but what makes this visit so special is the town's well-preserved and well-presented history. Established in 1712 and incorporated in 1722, Edenton was a political, cultural, and commercial center.

From Edenton, you could travel on to Elizabeth City, settled in the 1650s, and to the eastern edge of the state along the Outer Banks, doubling back through Manteo, home of the fabled "Lost Colony," and on to Raleigh.

1

WILLIAMSTON

William Williams migrated to North Carolina from Wales in the early 1700s. He settled on the south bank of the Roanoke River in the upper end of the county, and bought and operated large plantations in the northwestern part of the county. The first incorporated town in Martin County, Williamston was founded in 1779 as the county seat. The town was named in honor of Williams's son, Colonel William Williams II, who was a delegate to the Hillsborough and Halifax conventions in 1776 and was elected colonel of Martin County's militia when it was organized. He was elected as the county's first state senator in 1777.

The Civil War saw both Confederate and Union soldiers marching back and forth across Williamston and Martin County. Union soldiers occupied the 1810 Williams-Knight House after the capture of Williamston in July 1862. Across Main Street another home, the Hassell-King House, was used by Union soldiers to slaughter livestock.

Following Reconstruction, the railroad and tobacco plantings revitalized the town as a commercial market. With the bridging of the Roanoke River in 1922, Williamston became the hub of a system of major highways and roads, including US 17 ("the beach highway," as it is known locally), running north to south, and US 64, running east to west. The town is a featured site on the Historic Albemarle Tour Highway. For more information about this tour, see www.historicalbemarletour.com.

WHERE TO GO

Martin County Travel and Tourism and Visitor's Center. 100 East Church Street, Williamston 27892. The visitors center is in the circa 1831 Asa Biggs House. Located downtown behind Town Hall in a picturesque residential neighborhood, the house is owned by the Martin County Historical Society and is open for tours from 8:00 A.M. until 5:00 P.M. Monday through Friday. (800) 776–8566, www.visitmartincounty.com.

Commercial Historic District. Pick up a map at the visitors center for a self-guided tour through the business district, composed of parts of seven city blocks with Main Street as its primary thoroughfare. Get a hand-stirred vanilla Coke or orangeade at Clark's Drugstore on Main Street, or eat at the R&C (see "Where to Eat"). Be sure to pop into the post office to see the 1940 *Wright Brothers First Flight* mural.

Morningstar Nature Refuge. 1967 Meadow Branch Road, Williamston 27892. With nature tours conducted by a resident naturalist guide, Morningstar Nature Refuge is open by appointment after 2:00 P.M. daily. Eight short educational nature trails include observation areas, plant identification, feeding stations, and rest benches. The refuge is in a migratory flyway, and more than 250 species have been documented in the area. Free. (252) 792-7788.

Fort Branch. Fort Branch Road, off NC 125 North, Hamilton 27840. Twelve miles north of Williamston off NC 125, Fort Branch is the best-preserved earthwork Civil War site east of the Mississippi. Seven of the fort's original eleven cannons are on display here. The fort is open to the public 1:30 to 5:30 P.M. Saturday and Sunday from April through the first weekend in November, when an annual battle reenactment is held. (800) 776-8566, www.fortbranchcivilwarsite.com.

St. James Place. Located on the corner of Outerbridge Street and Business US 64 in Robersonville, 12 miles west of Williamston, this restored Primitive Baptist church serves as a museum of Southern folk art. Included are the original pews and pulpit, more than one hundred North Carolina quilts, and hundreds of pieces of North Carolina pottery. Open by appointment. (252) 795-4719.

WHERE TO EAT

Cobb's Corner. 101 East Boulevard, Williamston 27892. Located in the Holiday Inn, Cobb's Corner offers home-cooked chicken pastries, collards, corned backbone, and a variety of steaks and seafood, plus fifteen vegetables daily. Try "Mr. Dillon's Famous Banana Fritters." Open daily for breakfast, lunch, and dinner. $-$$. (252) 792-6493.

Cypress Grill. 1520 Stewart Street, Jamesville 27846. Ten miles from Williamston on US 64 east, Cypress Grill serves lunch and dinner seasonally, during the annual herring run on the river, usually mid-January to mid-April. The restaurant specializes in herring and seafood. $$. (252) 792-4175.

Deadwood's Smokehouse Grill. 2302 Ed's Grocery Road, Williamston 27892. The only late-night menu in town, this Western-style opry house features live music weekend nights. Menu includes appetizers, sandwiches, great steaks, and baby back ribs. There's also a miniature golf course and arcade, all in a Western-style setting near Bear Grass, about 5 miles southwest of Williamston. Open 6:00 P.M. until 2:00 A.M. Fridays and Saturday, and 1:00 until 9:00 P.M. Sunday. $$–$$$. (252) 792-8938, www.deadwoodnc.com.

R&C Restaurant. 211 Washington Street, Williamston 27892. Here's country cooking at its best, with the crispiest corn bread you've ever tasted. Weekly menu features collards on Mondays, Wednesdays, and Fridays. Eat in or take out for breakfast, lunch, or dinner. $–$$. (252) 792-3161.

Sunnyside Oyster Bar. 1102 Washington Street, Williamston 27892. Listed on the National Register of Historic Places, Sunnyside serves up shrimp and shucking oysters (with a bowl of hot melted butter) the way this popular restaurant has done it for sixty years. Dinner is served from 5:00 P.M. $$. (252) 792-3416, www.martincountync.com/mc/sunnyside.

WHERE TO STAY

Roanoke River Canoe Camping Trail. 25345 US 64 at Gardner's Creek between Williamston and Jamesville. A series of camping platforms situated just above the water in the tributaries of the Roanoke River allow you to wake up in the swamps of Devil's Gut, Three Sisters, or the Cashie River. Watch for bald eagles during the day, and listen for owls during the night. The Roanoke River Canoe Camping Trail meanders through what the Nature Conservancy calls "one of the last great places," part of the largest intact and least disturbed bottomland hardwood and cypress-tupelo forest ecosystem remaining in the Mid-Atlantic region. Call (252) 794-6501 to reserve a platform; www.roanokeriverpartners.org.

Big Mill Bed & Breakfast. 1607 Big Mill Road, Williamston 27892. Situated on 200 acres of woods, farmland, and landscaped gardens, Big Mill offers two rooms, continental breakfast, private entrances, and baths. The B&B overlooks a pond, a grape orchard, and eighty-year-old pecan trees that proffer the luscious pecans used in making breads for guests. $$. (252) 792–8787, www.bigmill.com.

WINDSOR

Created by the Colonial Assembly in 1768, New Windsor was established on the site known as Gray's Landing where William Gray offered one hundred acres for a town. Today, Windsor's National Register Historic District encompasses that same area.

WHERE TO GO

Freeman Hotel. 102 North York Street, Windsor 27983. Pick up maps here at the home of the Windsor Chamber of Commerce and the Windsor Visitor's Center for the self-guided walking tour through the historic district. Constructed in the 1840s as a hotel and renovated for offices in the 1980s, the Freeman Hotel is a Greek Revival building with double portico and fanlighted gables; two of its first-floor rooms have original tin walls and ceilings. It's listed on the National Register of Historic Places. (252) 794–4277, www.albemarle-nc.com/windsor/.

Historic Hope Plantation. 132 Hope House Road, Windsor 27983. Located in southern Bertie County on the edge of Roquist Pocosin, 4 miles west of Windsor, adjacent to NC 308, Hope Plantation was a grant in the 1720s from the lords proprietor of the Carolina colony to the Hobson family. Hope was a self-contained plantation, with a water-powered gristmill, a still, a sawmill, a blacksmith shop, a cooper's shop, and houses for spinning and weaving. Farmlands produced wheat, corn, oats, rye, flax, and cotton.

Built on an "aboveground" basement, the Hope mansion portrays basic Palladian design with some neoclassic elements. The five-bay facade has a pedimented double portico, and the hipped roof is topped by a widow's walk surrounded by a Chinese Chippendale balustrade. The floor plan is adapted from Abraham Swann's *The British Architect.*

The first-floor rooms are entered from the front hall. On the second floor are a large drawing room and a library, which housed 1,400 volumes. In addition to the main stair, a service stair runs from the basement to the attic.

Moved four miles from its original site, the 1763 King-Bazemore house is now one of only two gambrel-roofed houses in North Carolina with brick end walls. Evidence indicates that the house is similar to the eighteenth-century Hobson House that first stood at Hope.

The King-Bazemore house and the Hope mansion represent a continuing agrarian culture during the Colonial and Federal periods in northeastern North Carolina. Open January through December, Monday through Saturday 10:00 A.M. until 4:00 P.M., Sunday 2:00 to 5:00 P.M. Closed Thanksgiving Day and during the Christmas and New Year season. Admission is charged. (252) 794–3140, www.albemarle-nc.com/hope.

Roanoke River National Wildlife Refuge. 114 West Water Street, Windsor 27983. Established in 1989 to protect the natural habitat, the refuge is home to deer, otters, beavers, muskrats, black bears, and more than 191 species of migrating birds. Informal trail systems, including the newly opened Charles Kuralt Trail, are open to the public for hiking and bird-watching. Some of the trails are accessible by boat. Open daily during daylight hours. (252) 794–5326.

Cashie-Roanoke River Interpretive Center. 112 West Water Street, Windsor, 27983. Opened in the fall of 2000, the center focuses on the vast floodplain and bottomland swamp system of the lower Roanoke basin. Historic items on the property include an "in situ" brick vault, a 150-year-old grave marker, and an outbuilding from a historic home that houses various artifacts. (252) 794–2001, www.partnershipforthesounds.org.

WHERE TO EAT

Bunn's Barbecue. 127 North King Street, Windsor, 27983. Located in historic downtown Windsor, Bunn's serves home-style Northeast North Carolina barbecue made from the proprietor's "secret recipe." Daily specials. $–$$. (252) 794–2274.

Little Mint of Windsor. 103 West Granville Street, Windsor 27983. Mouthwatering chicken is served a variety of ways, either for take out or for dining in. $–$$. (252) 794–3468.

WHERE TO STAY

King Street Bed and Breakfast. 401 South King Street, Windsor 27983. Located in one of the oldest homes in Windsor (circa 1790), the King Street B&B is furnished with period antiques and reproductions. Each of the three spacious sleeping chambers has a private bath, cable TV, and fireplace. The common areas include the parlor, ballroom, and screened porch. A complimentary full breakfast is served. $$. (252) 794–2255, www.kingstbnb.com.

EDENTON

Alongside the north shore of the Albemarle Sound, Edenton was established in 1712 and incorporated in 1722. A leading center for political, social, educational, and industrial activity, the town served as the first Colonial capital until 1743. As the seat of the provincial and colonial governments, one of its citizens signed the Declaration of Independence, and another signed the U.S. Constitution.

Edenton was home to two early North Carolina governors, U.S. senators, and an associate justice of the U.S. Supreme Court. Artisans in Edenton and the surrounding Chowan and Roanoke River Basins were leaders in building and cabinetmaking. A prosperous port in the eighteenth and early nineteenth centuries, Edenton cleared more than 800 ships for trade with Europe and the West Indies between 1771 and 1776.

Edenton's prosperity as a shipping center, however, began to decline by the end of the eighteenth century. Roanoke Inlet was closed by a hurricane in 1795, and the construction of the Dismal Swamp Canal, completed in 1805, further diverted shipping to Norfolk, Virginia.

Having escaped destruction during the two major wars fought in this country since its founding, Edenton's fame for its history and architectural qualities derives primarily from its colonial past. Today, the town provides fine examples of Jacobean, Georgian,

Federal, Greek Revival, and Victorian architectural styles spanning a period of more than 250 years.

Edenton's historic district includes two structures designated National Historic Landmarks and numerous buildings listed on the National Register of Historic Places. The waterfront has been given over to parks, with vistas across Edenton Bay, and to transient slips for dockage. The heart of the community is a quaint and viable downtown lined with shops and businesses that cater to both residents and visitors.

WHERE TO GO

Historic Edenton Visitor Center. 108 North Broad Street, Edenton 27932. In addition to a fourteen-minute audiovisual program, exhibits, a gift shop, and visitor information/orientation, the visitor center offers well-conducted guided tours of the following five properties. A fee is charged for tours. (252) 482–2637.

At 100 West Church Street is **St. Paul's Episcopal Church,** the second oldest church building in North Carolina and the oldest in regular use. This handsome Flemish bond brick edifice is one of the most important Colonial period buildings in Edenton. The parish was organized in 1701 as the first parish in the colony under the provisions of the Vestry Act of 1701.

A National Historic Landmark, **The Cupola House,** at 408 South Broad Street, dates from 1758–59. The original first-story interior woodwork was removed in 1918 and was carefully reconstructed in the 1960s.

Built in 1782, **The Barker House** (505 South Broad Street) was the home of Thomas and Penelope Barker. On October 25, 1774, Penelope orchestrated the famed Edenton Tea Party: Fifty-one women met for a party but refused to drink tea. The group had penned a letter that expressed dissatisfaction with Parliament's Tea Act of 1773: "We the ladyes of Edenton do hereby solemnly engage not to conform to ye pernicious Custom of Drinking Tea or that we, the aforesaid Ladyes, will not promote ye wear of any manufacture from England, until such time that all Acts which tend to enslave this our Native Country shall be repealed."

In November 1712, the Colonial assembly passed an act "to promote the building of a courthouse to hold the assembly in, at the fork of Queen Anne's Creek," effectively establishing the town as the seat of the provincial government. By 1718, the first **Chowan County Courthouse** was completed; a second building was constructed on the same site on East King Street in 1724, and a new courthouse was built there in 1767. The 1767 Structure, the finest Georgian courthouse in the South, is one of the most important public buildings in Colonial America. As the oldest government building in North Carolina, it is a National Historic Landmark. It provided the setting for the roles of Joseph Hewes, Samuel Johnston, James Iredell, and others in their local, state, and national political actions during the 1770s and 1780s.

You can also tour the **Iredell House Historic Site** at 105 East Church Street. In 1778, silversmith Joseph Whedbee acquired four lots here for 160 pounds. Whedbee built a house and made considerable improvements on the two western lots, selling them for 800 pounds to James Iredell Sr., a justice on the first United States Supreme Court. Covered with beaded weatherboard, the one-bay by three-bay house had a single exterior chimney. The side-hall interior, and the fact that the house may have been an expansion of an older residence, might explain the gable's atypical orientation to the street.

Archaeologists who worked underneath the house thought there had been a wing west of Whedbee's original dwelling, which was later replaced with the Iredell wing. This earlier wing may well have been a house that was erected around 1756. The entrance to Whedbee's house is on the west elevation; the configuration of the original porch is unknown.

Providence Burial Ground. West Albemarle Street, Edenton 27932. As the burial ground of prominent African-American, free blacks, and military people from the late eighteenth and nineteenth centuries, notables buried here include Thomas Barnswell, free black and noted builder; Molly Horniblow, grandmother of Harriet Jacobs, a slave who escaped from Edenton by boat, traveling eventually to New York, where she went to work as a nursemaid for the family of abolitionists; and Jonathon Overton, private of the Continental Line of Captain Jones's Company, tenth regiment. (252) 482–2637.

The Historic Edenton Trolley Tour. 108 North Broad Street, Edenton 27932. This forty-five-minute trolley tour through the historic district acquaints the visitor with the rich history and outstanding architecture of Edenton. (252) 482-2637.

WHERE TO EAT

Water Street. 112 West Water Street, Edenton 27932. Located within the historic district, this fine-dining experience offers lunch, dinner, and Sunday brunch. $$$. (252) 482-3411.

Creekside Restaurant and Bar. 406 West Queen Street, Edenton 27932. Creekside offers signature entrees and seasonal menus for lunch and dinner. $$. (252) 482-0118.

Kramer's Garage–Bistro by the Bay. 113 West Water Street, Edenton 27932. This restaurant, which combines a deli with a French café, serves sandwiches on fresh baked breads, signature salads, soups, light dinner entrees, Mediterranean-inspired appetizers, and specialty coffee. Open for lunch and dinner. $. (252) 482-9977.

Lane's Family Barbecue. 421 East Church Street, Edenton 27932. Great beef and pork barbecue is accompanied by homemade side dishes made from locally grown vegetables. $. (252) 482-4008.

The Lovin' Oven Bakery. 302 South Broad Street, Edenton 27932. Enjoy gingerbread, cookies, snaps, cakes, and fresh pastry with a variety of delicious coffees. $. (252) 482-7465.

Mario's. South Broad Street at Gaslight Square, Edenton 27932. Mario's serves New York–style pizzas, pastas, wings, and subs. $. (252) 482-7656.

Snooker's. South Broad Street, Edenton 27932. Snooker's offers a full-service breakfast and daily lunch specials of homemade soups and fresh salads. $. (252) 482-7517.

Waterman's Grill. 427 South Broad Street, Edenton 27932. This casual seafood restaurant located one block from the waterfront has daily lunch and dinner specials. Try the warm pecan pie with ice cream for a mouthwatering dessert. $$. (252) 482-7733.

WHERE TO STAY

The Lords Proprietors' Inn. 300 North Broad Street, Edenton 27932. This lovely inn has sixteen rooms and two suites. A gourmet breakfast is served daily, as well as gourmet dinners Tuesday through Saturday. Inn guests may include the four-course dinner for an additional charge of $35 plus tax per person. Gratuities are included in guest dinner rates. $$$. (252) 482-3641 or (888) 394-6622, www.lordspropedenton.com.

Granville Queen Themed Inn. 108 South Granville Street, Edenton 27932. The nine guest rooms provide themed accommodations. The Egyptian Queen guest room, for example, invites guests to "experience the everlasting romance of Antony and Cleopatra." Appropriately, the room is adorned with Sphinx-flanked thrones, leopard-skin bed, tomb mural garden tub, and a bust of Queen Nefertiti. A five-course "plantation breakfast" is served on the porch; wine tastings are held on the weekends. $$-$$$. (252) 482-5296.

Albemarle House. 204 West Queen Street, Edenton 27932. This circa 1900 home is two blocks from the sound and downtown. $$. (252) 482-8204, www.bbonline.com/nc/albemarle/.

Trestle House Inn at Willow Tree Farm. 632 Soundside Road, Edenton 27932. Built in 1972 as a retreat, the five-room inn, surrounded on three sides by water on a wildlife refuge, offers a gourmet breakfast. $$. (252) 482-2282 or (800) 645-8466, www.edenton.com/trestlehouse.

Captain's Quarters Inn. 202 West Queen Street, Edenton 27932. Located in Edenton's historic district, this comfortable and elegant circa 1907 inn has eight guest rooms. Guests may choose from either a continental breakfast delivered to their door or a three-course breakfast served in the Harbor Room. Mystery weekends and sailing and golf packages are offered. $$. (252) 482-8945 or (800) 482-8945, www.captainsquartersinn.com.

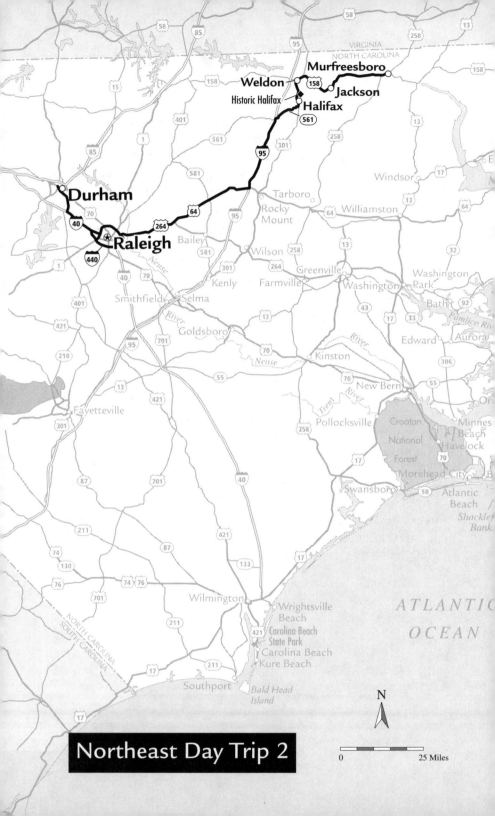

Northeast Day Trip 2

Colonists who found the valley's fertile bottomlands ideal for large-scale farming settled the Roanoke River Valley of northeastern North Carolina in the early 1700s. By the late eighteenth century, the growth of that plantation system had created a society of merchants, craftsmen, wealthy planters, small farmers, freedmen, and slaves.

On this day trip, you'll travel US 64 east to I-95 north to visit Historic Halifax, a North Carolina historic site that bills itself as the "birthplace of independence."

From Halifax, US 158 wends its way east through a couple of small towns worth craning your neck for, if not stopping to stretch your legs. The first is **Weldon,** where the Wilmington to Weldon Railroad terminated (the rail line, the longest in the world at the time, was the lifeline of the Confederacy). The other is **Jackson,** where the courthouse, built in 1858, is one of the state's few surviving examples of a Greek Revival public building.

The trip terminates in Murfreesboro, a small town with an interesting history and accommodations in this otherwise desolate part of the state. From here, you could head back toward Windsor, 40 miles south (see Northeast Day Trip 1), for an extended weekend.

Should you want to beeline it home, head back on US 158 toward I-95 south, but don't hit the interstate before treating yourself to **Ralph's Barbecue,** 2 blocks east of the interstate at exit 173.

HALIFAX

The town of Halifax was founded on the south bank of the Roanoke River in 1760 and quickly became a focal point for the entire valley. Halifax was a river port, county seat, crossroads, and social center. A farmers market operated here, and inns and taverns did a brisk business. By 1769 Halifax could boast of nearly sixty houses and public buildings.

During the American Revolution, the town was the scene of important political events: North Carolina's Fourth Provincial Congress met in Halifax in the spring of 1776, and on April 12, unanimously adopted a document later called the Halifax Resolves, which was the first official action by an entire colony recommending independence from England.

The Fifth Provincial Congress assembled in the town late in the fall of that year, drafting and approving North Carolina's first state constitution and appointing Richard Caswell the first governor. Cornwallis briefly occupied the town in May 1781 on his northward march toward Virginia and eventual surrender at Yorktown.

After the Revolution, Halifax and the Roanoke River Valley entered a golden age. Wealth, power, and influence were concentrated here. The society was among the most cultured in the state; planters and merchants built fine homes. Halifax remained prosperous until the late 1830s, when its political power was diminished and when the new railroad bypassed the town. The first eighty-five years of the town's life are highlighted in the preservation of Historic Halifax.

WHERE TO GO

Historic Halifax State Historic Site. St. David and Dobbs Streets, Halifax 27839. The home of the Halifax Resolves, the first official action for independence by any colony, Historic Halifax offers an audiovisual presentation, exhibits, guided tours, and displays depicting the history of the town. A guided walking tour takes you into several authentically restored and furnished buildings.

The Owens House, with its gambrel roof, is the oldest building, dating from about 1760. It is furnished as the home of a prosperous Halifax merchant. Two other buildings within the historic district also are thought to have been built during the eighteenth century: **Eagle Tavern,** which was moved and converted into a residence during the 1840s, and the **Tap Room,** a smaller tavern built sometime between 1760 and 1810. Both are newly opened for visitors.

The prosperity of the Roanoke River Valley is reflected in the many Federal-style plantation dwellings constructed here between the 1790s and the 1820s. The **Sally-Billy House** is an elegant example of such a dwelling; the tripartite house was constructed about 1808. The **Burgess Law Office** probably dates from the same period, although the roofline and other features of the structure follow the older Georgian style. Thomas Burgess owned the building in the early 1800s, and it is furnished as his law office and town house.

The same contractor built the two public buildings within the historic district. Both are fashioned of brick and are fireproof. **The Clerk's Office,** built in 1832–33, served as a location for storing valuable court records. One of its rooms is furnished as a court official's office and one as a printer's office, complete with a working press. **The jail** was built in 1838; two earlier jails at the same location were burned to the ground by escaping prisoners.

Other sites reflect everyday life in Halifax: **Magazine Spring,** long a source of water for townspeople; the **cemetery; Market Square,** which served as the town park, pasture, and marketplace; and **the river outlook,** near the site of an early ferry landing.

In addition to the historic structures, the **Montfort Archaeological Exhibit,** constructed over the excavation of Joseph Montfort's house, is open for public viewing. Through exhibits and walkways over foundations exposed by the scholar's spade and trowel, the building depicts the lifestyle of this wealthy resident of early Halifax.

Guided tours originate at the Historic Halifax Visitor Center, open April 1 through October 31, Monday through Saturday 9:00 A.M. until 5:00 P.M., Sunday 1:00 to 5:00 P.M. From November 1 through March 31, open Tuesday through Saturday 10:00 A.M. until 4:00 P.M., Sunday 1:00 to 4:00 P.M. Free. (800) 522–4282, www.visithalifax.com.

WHERE TO SHOP

Independence Station. 18 King Street, Halifax 27839. Independence Station is a co-op of crafters and artisans. The gallery displays hand-fashioned articles such as porcelain, tinware, baskets, paintings, Native American pottery, quilts, forged iron, wood carvings, and more. During a visit to the gallery, you will see artisans caning chairs, quilting, and making baskets. Open Tuesday through Saturday 10:00 A.M. to 4:00 P.M. (252) 583-2278.

MURFREESBORO

As the northernmost point of navigation on the Meherrin River, Murfreesboro as far as a seagoing vessel on the Albemarle Sound could penetrate into the large and productive farming area of southern Virginia and northeastern North Carolina.

Congress designated Murfreesboro in 1790 as an official port of entry, and customs records indicate a profitable three-cornered trade with New England and the West Indies. The vessels and their cargoes were mostly owned by captains from New England, many of whom put down roots here and impressed their outlook on the new town in ways that remain evident.

WHERE TO GO

Murfreesboro Historic District. 116 East Main Street, Murfreesboro 27855. A twelve-block historic district, listed on the National Register of Historic Places, its guided tour headquarters are at **Roberts-Vaughan Village Center** (circa 1790). The folks at the Murfreesboro Historic District offices say they are happy to open any of the following sites for those who call in advance. All of the sites are within walking distance of one another. (252) 398-5922, www.murfreesboronc.com.

Originally constructed in 1810 as a store by William Hardy Murfree and his partner George Gordon, the **Wheeler House** was sold in 1814 to John Wheeler, a native of New Jersey who came south around 1790. Wheeler converted the building to a residence, as it appears today. John Hill Wheeler, his son, became famous as a legislator, treasurer of the mint in Charlotte, the nation's first minister of Nicaragua, and the first native historian on North Carolina. The house is authentically furnished with period pieces, some original to the Wheeler family. For visitors interested in the decorative arts, an outstanding and rare example of neoclassic wall coverings is found here.

Built in the late 1870s, the **Winborne Law Office/Country Store** was used as a law office by several generations of the Winborne family, including B. B. Winborne, whose famous *History of Hertford County* still serves as a primary reference concerning the area and the early families who lived here. Originally located on the town's Main Street, the building was moved to the historic district in 1976. The first floor is furnished as a "country store," with hundreds of items such as may have been found in a store of this vintage.

William Rea of Boston was the first of five brothers to make his home in the Murfreesboro area. Arriving here in the 1790s, he became a successful merchant ship owner and, with his brother Joseph, operated a store in the redbrick building that now serves as the **Rea Museum.** The only surviving eighteenth-century brick commercial structure in North Carolina, the museum presents exhibits on local Native American tribes, agriculture, and river transportation. A room interior moved from the Gatling Plantation to the museum houses a large collection of Gatling family memorabilia and an authentic Gatling gun.

At the **Blacksmith Shop** you can see hand-hammered ironware wrought on a full-scale forge typical of those throughout the country in the nineteenth century. The smithy and his tools were an indispensable part of the village life, keeping wagons and buggies repaired, shoeing horses, and producing implements for household and farm use.

Built in the early 1800s by William Hardy Murfree, son of Murfreesboro's founder, the **Murfree-Smith Law Office** was later used by W. N. H. Smith, the first North Carolinian to become chief justice of the Supreme Court. Tradition has it that the building has served variously as a theater, jail, school, and post office. It currently houses the Murfreesboro Historical Association's gift shop.

The **Agricultural Exhibit** has early examples of wheeled vehicles of all kinds, along with a wide range of horse-drawn farming implements. Be sure to see the surry with "the fringe on top" as well as a rare early peanut picker and swing cart.

Brady C. Jefcoat Museum of Americana. High Street, Murfreesboro 27855. Located in the Old Murfreesboro High School, the world's largest collection of washing machines, flatirons, and dairy equipment contains thousands of artifacts and Americana items. Open Saturday 11:00 A.M. until 4:00 P.M. and Sunday 2:00 to 5:00 P.M. (252) 398-5922, www.murfreesboronc.com.

WHERE TO EAT

Walter's Grill. 317 East Main Street, Murfreesboro 27855. Famous for its hot dogs, Walter's Grill offers plate lunches daily, as well as chili and homemade soups. $. (252) 398-4006.

WHERE TO STAY

Piper House Bed and Breakfast, 809 East High Street, Murfreesboro 27855. A restored 1900s home on High Street in Murfreesboro offers two bedrooms for guests. The inn has a wonderful hostess and serves a delicious breakfast. $$. (252) 398-3531.

Woodson Manor. 301 Holly Hill Road, Murfreesboro 27855. Stay overnight in the home of a local artist, designer, gardener, and cook. Woodson Manor offers two rooms in an attractive setting. $$. (252) 398-4142, www.bbonline.com/nc/woodson.

Winborne House Bed and Breakfast. 333 Jay Trail, Murfreesboro 27855. This restored 1850s home offers two bedrooms. $$. (252) 398-5224.

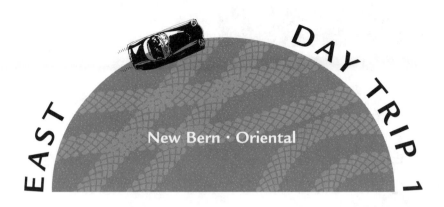

From Raleigh, New Bern is 113 miles east, an easy day's drive there and back, with sufficient time for touring the sites and for soaking up the charm of this historic river town. Traveling US 70 east, the drive is pleasant across the Neuse River Basin, as the road makes its way past tin-roofed farmhouses under broad leafy oaks sitting in expansive green fields. The highway continues through small towns where folks still shop for groceries at the local Piggly Wiggly.

In New Bern, you'll visit historic Tryon Palace, stroll the pleasant downtown, and drive along the picturesque waterfront, where you will find fine Southern homes with broad wraparound porches that look out on the Neuse and Trent Rivers. Along the riverfront, be sure to look for the historical marker depicting the birthplace of Bayard Wooten, one of the South's first professional female photographers.

As with many North Carolina towns, New Bern's city center fell into decline in the 1970s, when the sprawl of shopping malls and suburban housing drew citizens away from the business district. But in 1979, a nonprofit corporation of civic leaders was charged with breathing new life into the downtown, and their efforts have been successful in attracting art galleries, specialty shops, antique stores, restaurants, and other businesses. Still, don't expect New Bern to be bustling. It is a quiet town where the slow-paced lifestyle invites leisurely strolls down the charming streets of this friendly river town.

A thirty-minute drive east of New Bern, Oriental is a charming village that, largely because of its proximity to the Intercoastal Waterway and Pamlico Sound, has earned its place as the sailing capital of North Carolina.

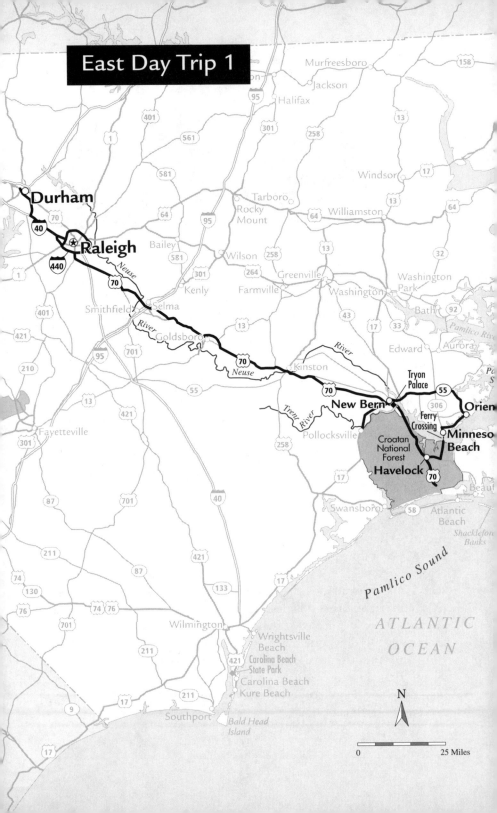

East Day Trip 1

On your way back to New Bern (or Raleigh), drive along the Pamlico Sound to Minnesott Beach, where the ferry takes you across to Havelock and US 70.

NEW BERN

As North Carolina's second oldest town, New Bern claims many firsts: home of the state's first four-faced clock; originator of the state's first celebration of both Independence Day and George Washington's birthday; and home to the first steamboat in North Carolina.

Other claims have grander historical significance: New Bern is home to the first state capital, the first meeting of the state legislature, the first incorporated public school in the state, the first public school for African-Americans in North Carolina, the first printing press in the state and the first newspaper published, the first torpedo put into practical use, the first motion picture theater built in the state, and the first postal service in the Carolina colony. The first Pepsi was poured here. Clearly, this is a town worth getting to know.

A Swiss baron settled New Bern in 1710. With German Protestant and Swiss colonists, Christophe von Graffenried pitched camp on a triangle of land at the confluence of the Neuse and Trent Rivers. He named the settlement for Bern, his home in Switzerland. Like the Swiss capital, New Bern's symbol, the black bear, is ubiquitous throughout the town. Another reminder of the town's Swiss heritage is the 1910 redbrick clock tower above City Hall.

The Swiss baron eventually returned to Switzerland, and the British were next to assert their dominion over New Bern. By the middle of the eighteenth century, the port city had grown in size and importance. The Colonial assembly often met here. The colony's first printing press was established in 1749 and two years later, the printer, James Davis, published the first newspaper, pamphlet, and book.

British Royal Governor William Tryon saw the need for a permanent capital in the growing colony and selected New Bern as the site. Tryon Palace was completed in 1770, but the governor left the lovely

Georgian-style palace a little more than a year later, after being reassigned to the New York colony.

In March of 1862, 13,000 Union forces captured the town and occupied it until the end of the war. Because of Union occupation, New Bern survived with less damage to its homes and buildings than many other small Southern towns. Thus, in addition to finding more than 150 homes and buildings listed on the National Register of Historic Places, you will find a fair number that date back to the 1700s.

WHERE TO GO

Craven County Convention and Visitor's Bureau, 314 South Front Street, New Bern 28563. The visitor's center is convenient to historic downtown, so you'll want to begin your visit here; there's free parking across the street. Pick up brochures or ask questions of the staff, who will point you in the right direction for walking tours. Before shuffling your peds out the door, spend a moment to look over the large display board listing Craven County firsts. (800) 437–5767, www.visitnewbern.com.

Historic Downtown District. For a dose of history and charm, walk the downtown district, then board the New Bern Tours trolley, across from Tryon Palace Visitors Center, for a ninety-minute narrated tour. From the comfortable open-air (but covered) trolley, you will see such sites as the Coor-Gaston House, a Georgian-style home built around 1770. Its most famous resident was Judge William Gaston, the first chief justice of the North Carolina Supreme Court and composer of the state song, "The Old North State." Purchase tickets on the trolley ($12.00 per adult, $6.00 for children 12 and under). Departure times vary with season but are typically at 11:00 A.M. and 2:00 P.M. (252) 637–7316 or (800) 849–7316, www.newberntours.com.

Tryon Palace Historic Sites and Gardens. 610 Pollock Street, New Bern 28563. Completed in 1770, then burned to the ground in 1798, Tryon Palace was rebuilt in the 1950s. That's right, the Tryon Palace you see today is a replica of the original palace. The twenty-seven-room brick Georgian-style mansion and its furnishings were painstakingly reproduced from meticulous records kept by British Royal Governor Tryon.

In addition to serving two royal governors the palace was used by four state governors before the capital was moved from New Bern to Raleigh in 1794. Guides in period dress conduct an informative forty-five-minute palace tour (daily except Thanksgiving, Christmas holidays, and New Year's Day). You'll learn, among other things, that George Washington not only slept but also danced here.

After you've done the digs, tour the eighteenth-century-style English gardens surrounding the palace on your own. You could easily spend a day at Tryon Palace and its gardens, but two hours will suffice. Admission for adults is $15.00 ($6.00 for students through grades 12) to tour the palace, buildings, and fourteen-acre grounds. (252) 514–4900 or (800) 767–1560, www.tryonpalace.org.

John Wright Stanly House. Included with admission to Tryon Palace, this Georgian-style home was built in the early 1780s. On his Southern tour in 1791, President George Washington slept here— twice, as New Bernians are eager to point out. Washington described his overnight accommodation as "exceeding good lodgings." The Stanly House remains one of the finest examples of Georgian architecture in the South.

Robert Hay House. Also part of Tryon Palace, this unimposing house features character interpreters, who greet and respond to you as if it were the year 1835. Nothing can shake them out of this delusion. I know. I've tried. Ask questions of the staff to learn about what life was like for the early colonists.

New Bern Academy Museum. Nearby, and also part of the Tryon Palace complex, New Bern Academy was the first established school in North Carolina. During the Civil War, the building was converted to a military hospital to treat the victims of spinal meningitis, smallpox, and yellow fever epidemics, as well as casualties of war. Now operated as a museum, the building has four rooms that chronicle the history of New Bern: its founding and early history, architecture, Civil War and Reconstruction, and education.

The Firemen's Museum. 408 Hancock Street, New Bern 28560. The museum displays century-old hose wagons, an 1884 Button steamer, and an assortment of eighteenth- and nineteenth-century firemen's hats, leather fire buckets, and hand-drawn reels. Don't miss the mounted, stuffed (and somewhat macabre) head of Fire Horse Fred, who pulled the Atlantic hose wagon for seventeen years and died answering a false alarm. Open Monday through Saturday 10:00 A.M. to

4:30 P.M., Sunday 1:00 to 5:00 P.M. except January 1 through April 1. Admission: $2.00, $1.00 for children. (252) 636–4087.

Croatan National Forest, 141 East Fisher Avenue, New Bern 28560. Hike, swim, boat, hunt, fish, camp, and picnic at the 157,000-acre Croatan National Forest, 9 miles south of New Bern just off US 70 east. Look for the rare Venus's flytrap, black bears, and alligators. (252) 638–5628.

The Isaac Taylor House. 228 Craven Street, New Bern 28562. Born in Scotland, the wealthy merchant shipowner Isaac Taylor was a gentleman planter, whose Glenburnie plantation, named for the town of his origin, was 3 miles north on the Neuse River. Taylor built his Federal-style town house in 1792. Isaac, by the way, is the great-great-great-grandfather of North Carolina–born folksinger James Taylor.

Isaac Taylor's granddaughters, Phoebe and Catherine, were living in the house when Union troops took the town in 1862. The two women, both in their eighties, refused to abandon their home, so they withdrew to the third and fourth floors and remained there for the duration of the war. The spinsters used a bracket-and-pulley system to transport food and supplies to their upper-storied refuge. You can still see the device on the south side of the building. The Isaac Taylor House is now home to the Gallery Cafe. See the separate listing in Where to Eat. (252) 633–6407.

WHERE TO SHOP

Antique Shops. New Bern has a slew of them, all located in the compact town center. Just point yourself in any direction downtown and walk. You'll indubitably land at the threshold of an antique shop.

Birthplace of Pepsi-Cola. 256 Middle Street, New Bern 28560. The restored Caleb Bradham's Pharmacy marks the spot where Pepsi-Cola was invented in 1898. Be sure to see the thirty-five-minute video about the history of Pepsi, narrated by Walter Cronkite. Also offered is a twenty-minute video that chronicles the history of Pepsi through commercials. The store sells fountain Pepsi in a cup (for 60 cents) and Pepsi collectibles. The most popular items: T-shirts, drinking glasses, coffee mugs, key chains, and men's caps. Open Monday through Saturday 10:00 A.M. to 6:00 P.M. (252) 636–5898, www.pepsistore.com.

Mitchell Hardware. 215 Craven Street, New Bern 28560. A hardware store since 1898, this jam-packed, turn-of-the-twentieth-century establishment is as much a museum as it is a store. Inside, you could spend a good hour browsing the mix of hardware, garden tools, and yard equipment. You might even want to take home one of the store's country hams. An honest-to-goodness hardware store where the locals shop, Mitchell Hardware opens at 6:30 A.M. Monday through Saturday. (252) 638–4261.

Tryon Palace Museum Store/Craft and Garden Shop. 610 Pollock Street, New Bern 28563. Tryon Palace Museum Store carries New Bern and Colonial memorabilia. The Craft and Garden Shop carries just what the name implies: heirloom plants, crafts, gardening books, and more. Both shops are open daily. Museum Store, (252) 514–4932; Garden Shop, (252) 514–4927.

WHERE TO EAT

The Gallery Cafe. 228 Craven Street, New Bern 28562. The cafe is on the lower floor of the Isaac Taylor House (see previous mention). Try "The Duffy," a combination of Brie, turkey, cranberry-mango chutney, lettuce, tomato, and mayonnaise served on a buttered croissant with terra chips and fruit. Open for lunch and dinner. $$. (252) 633–6407.

Captain Ratty's Oyster and Piano Bar. 202 Middle Street, New Bern 28563. Here you'll find the only palpable nightlife in downtown New Bern, which is not to say a lot, as New Bern is a small town. The best thing hopping is the Imperial pint of Newcastle that you can get here. Captain Ratty's specializes in seafood, serving lunch and dinner. $$–$$$. (252) 633–2088.

The Chelsea. 335 Middle Street, New Bern 28563. It's modeled after an English-style pub, thus the friendly bartender at the Chelsea will serve you a Guinness Stout or Bass Ale. The Chelsea's excellent food is fusion cuisine. For an appetizer that won't leave you hungry for dinner, try the Blue Chip Dip, a blend of blue, cheddar, and cream cheeses, bacon, and scallions and served hot with homemade chips for dipping ($4.95). Pepsi inventor Caleb Bradham used this building as his second drugstore. $$–$$$. (252) 637–5469, www.thechelsea.com.

New Bern Roasting Company. 215 Middle Street, New Bern 28563. Stop here for your daily caffeine fix. (252) 634–1952.

Trent River Coffee Co. 208 Craven Street, New Bern 28560. The locals gather here for coffee and, on occasional weekend nights when it's offered, live entertainment. (252) 514–2030.

WHERE TO STAY

The Aerie. 509 Pollock Street, New Bern 28562. This two-story 1880 Victorian house has seven guest rooms with private baths, a cozy parlor with player piano, and a library with an extensive Civil War collection. A full breakfast with a choice of three hot entrees is served. Herbal flower gardens cover 1,500-square-feet. $$. (800) 849–5553 or (252) 636–5553, www.aerieinn.com.

Harmony House Inn. 215 Pollock Street, New Bern 28560. Purchased by Benjamin Ellis in 1850, Harmony House began as a four-room, two-story Greek Revival home. During the Civil War the Harmony House was occupied by Company K of the 45th Massachusetts Volunteer Militia. The house has seven guest rooms and three suites. Breakfasts include such specialty entrees as orange French toast, egg and bacon casserole, or the inn's unique stuffed French toast. All are served with home-baked coffee cake and breads, fresh fruit, coffee, tea, and juice. $$. (252) 636–3810 or (800) 636–3113.

Hanna House Bed and Breakfast. 218 Pollock Street, New Bern 28560. Listed in the National Register of Historic Places and designated a historic home, Hanna House is furnished in fine antiques and Oriental carpets. $$. (252) 635–3209 or (866) 830–4371, www2.coastalnet.com/~hannahouse/index.htm.

Meadows Inn. 212 Pollock Street, New Bern 28560. Formerly the King's Arms Bed and Breakfast, the Meadows Inn is located in the heart of the historic district. John Alexander Meadows built the home in 1847, four years after a fire destroyed most of the structures on Pollock Street. It was a private residence until 1980, when it became New Bern's first bed-and-breakfast. Each of the eight spacious guest rooms has a nonworking fireplace, private bath, TV/VCR, and phone. $$. (252) 634–1776 or (877) 551–1776, www.meadowsinn-nc.com.

New Berne House. 709 Broad Street, New Bern 28560. This Colonial-style bed-and-breakfast hosts Mystery Weekends several times throughout the year. Guests solve these fun, scavenger-hunt whodunits by collecting clues from downtown businesses and attractions. Seven guest rooms are available. $$. (252) 636-2250 or (800) 842-7688.

Sheraton Grand New Bern. 1 Bicentennial Park, New Bern 28563. Billed as both a hotel and an inn, the Sheraton faces the scenic Trent River waterfront. The hotel's one hundred guest rooms afford views of the river. The adjacent inn, connected by a breeze-way, has seventy-one guest rooms, suites, and mini suites. $$-$$$. (252) 638-3585 or (800) 325-3535, www.newbernsheraton.com.

ORIENTAL

A quaint sailing and fishing village thirty minutes east of New Bern on NC 55, Oriental is the place to hoist your sails. If you've no time for that, you'll still enjoy breathing in the salt air of this yachting town. After a few hours (or a few days) here, you can return by way of Minnesott Beach, where the year-round ferry will take you to Cherry Branch and US 70. Head west to return to New Bern or Raleigh.

WHERE TO GO

Whittaker Creek Yacht Harbor. 200 Whittaker Point Road, Oriental 28571. If you yearn to get out on the water, here is the place to do it. With nine boats in its fleet, Whittaker Creek Yacht Harbor's bareboat charters begin at $697 for three days (minimum) on a 28-foot sailboat. (252) 249-1020, www.whittakercreek.com.

WHERE TO EAT

M&Ms Café. 205 South Water Street, Oriental 28571. M&Ms is not only a fine restaurant where you can dine alfresco but also the local watering hole. Open daily except Tuesday. $$-$$$. (252) 249-2000.

Oriental Marina Restaurant. Hodges Street, Oriental 28571. The moderately upscale menu includes fresh fried seafood and specialty items, including pasta and ribs. Try the delicious crab cake dinner: two five-ounce crab cakes (no filler) with baked sweet potato, salad, and vegetable. Afterward, head up to the Topside Lounge, open nightly from 5:00 P.M., or outside to the Tiki Bar, open seasonally Wednesday through Sunday. $$. (252) 249-2204, www.orientalmarina.com.

WHERE TO STAY

The Inn at Oriental. 508 Church Street, Oriental 28571. The inn's twelve guest rooms are tastefully decorated and feature private baths and cable TV. A full American breakfast of homemade favorites is served in the dining room. $$. (252) 249-1078 or (800) 485-7174, www.innatoriental.com.

The Cartwright House. 301 Freemason Street, Oriental 28571. Located on a quiet tree-lined street in the heart of Oriental, this AAA three-diamond inn offers a view of the river and is a short walk from the art and craft galleries, shops, restaurants, and the harbor. Begin your day with morning coffee at your door, followed by a generous English breakfast served by the English hosts in the dining room. $$$. (252) 249-1337 or (888) 726-9389, www.cartwrighthouse.com.

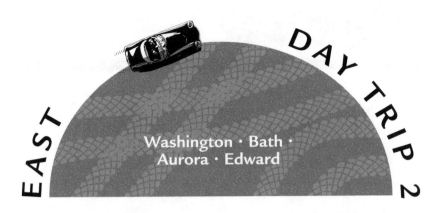

Washington · Bath · Aurora · Edward

Head east on US 264 to the wide Pamlico River for this day trip to North Carolina's oldest town. Here you'll get a glimpse into the state's past at North Carolina's first church and the three historic homes that comprise the historic site at "North Carolina's First Town."

But before plunging into Bath, linger a little in Washington—the original Washington, as the local residents are fond to point out. As you stroll along on the Historic Washington Walking Tour, you'll learn more about this quaint Southern town, such as the fact that prolific film producer Cecil B. DeMille spent time here as a boy. Washington is a good place to overnight if you're extending your trip.

On the way to Bath, take a short detour through the incorporated district of Washington Park. CBS newsman Charles Kuralt lived here during his kindergarten years. Your detour will reward you with the sight of beautiful homes facing the Pamlico River, where cypress trees expose their knotty knees along the river's bank.

Travel downriver to Bath on NC 92 east to immerse yourself in North Carolina's earliest history, then proceed to the ferry terminal for a thirty-minute journey across the Pamlico River. On the other side, you'll make for tiny Aurora, population 652, where you'll have to do some digging at the Fossil Museum to find evidence of a history that predates even Bath. Some of the artifacts that you'll discover at the museum date back 22 million years.

From Aurora, it's a short drive to Edward, where you'll visit a winery before driving the flat coastal plain back to Washington on NC 33 north. Of course, you could detour toward New Bern, the state's second oldest town, for an extended day trip. Combining

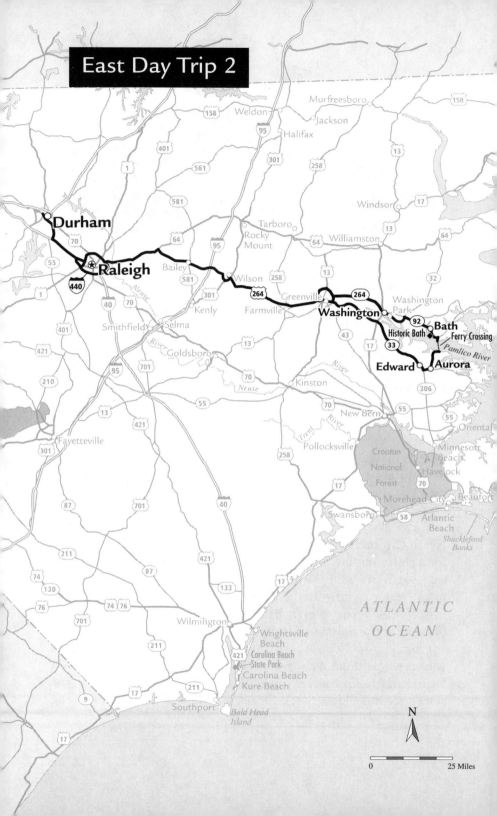

East Day Trip 2

Bath with East Day Trip 1 to New Bern provides you with a double dose of history.

WASHINGTON

English explorers came here as early as 1585, but the first settlement did not appear until more than a century later. In the 1770s, a farmer started a town on his property, flanked by Pamlico and Tar Rivers. He called the town Forks of the Tar, but in 1776 it was renamed, becoming the first town in the nation to be named after General George Washington.

Washington became a major supply port during the War for Independence, when Savannah, Charleston, and Wilmington were under siege. During the Civil War, Federal troops devastated Washington by setting fire to the naval stores they left behind upon vacating the port town. The fire destroyed most of Washington's buildings. Residents rebuilt the town only to watch it burn again in 1900, when a faulty stove flue sparked flames that spread to other buildings in the business district. Downtown today consists of late Victorian commercial architecture.

Movie producer **Cecil B. DeMille** spent most of his boyhood in Washington with his grandmother and aunt, who lived on the corner of Bridge and Second Streets. A historical marker indicates the spot where the house once stood.

WHERE TO GO

Washington Visitors Center. 102 Stewart Parkway, Washington 27889. Begin your visit here by picking up maps for your walking tour of the historic district. (800) 999–3857, www.washingtonnctourism.com.

Historic Washington Walking Tour. After picking up a map at the visitor center, begin the 1.9-mile self-guided Historic Washington Walking Tour at the old Atlantic Coast Line Railroad Depot on the corner of Main and Gladden Streets. Most of the private homes and buildings are closed to the public, but the walk is pleasant in this quaint downtown. The tour takes about an hour to complete.

Old Beaufort County Courthouse. 158 North Market Street, Washington 27889. Dating from about 1786, this is the second oldest courthouse standing in North Carolina and one of only a handful of surviving federal courthouses in the state. Listed on the National Register of Historic Places, the courthouse is now home to the Beaufort-Hyde-Martin Regional Library, open to the public Monday through Friday 9:00 A.M. to 5:00 P.M. The original courtroom may be viewed on the second floor by request at the lending desk. The courtroom contains a portrait of Henry, Duke of Beaufort, the lord proprietor for whom the county was named. The library also houses paintings and sketches of historic buildings in Washington, some of which are no longer standing. (252) 946–0011.

North Carolina Estuarium. 223 Water Street, Washington 27889. Adjacent to the visitors center, the state's only estuarium presents 200 displays and a thirteen-minute film that focuses on the scenic beauty of North Carolina's coastal rivers and sounds. The Pamlico/Tar River Estuary, by the way, is the second largest in the nation behind Chesapeake Bay. Admission is $3.00 for adults, $2.00 for children through grade 12, and no charge for children 4 and under. Open 10:00 A.M. to 4:00 P.M. Monday through Saturday during the summer months, Tuesday through Saturday the rest of the year. Allow forty-five minutes to one hour. (252) 948–0000.

St. Peter's Episcopal Church. 101 North Bonner Street, Washington 27889. Washington has one church for every fifty residents. Imagine what it must sound like to be within earshot of all the clanging bells on a Sunday morning. One of the more interesting houses of worship is St. Peter's Episcopal Church, where Cecil B. DeMille's family is buried. (252) 946–8151.

Catch the Wind Sailing School. 11 West Main Street, Washington, 27889. A wide range of sailing and navigation instruction is provided for enthusiasts of all levels. Located on historic Haven's Wharf, the school offers bareboat charters and two-day sailing instruction. (252) 940–7245, www.catch-the-wind.com.

Sailing Carolina Cruises. McCotter's Marina, South Dock Entrance, Washington 27889. Cruise on a 42-foot trimaran, from two and a half to five hours. Private, customized charters are also available for individuals or groups of up to six. (252) 944–9876, www.sailingcarolinacruises.com.

Washington Park. Now here's a tip that you won't find in any other guidebook. Leaving Washington on NC 32 east, turn right on Edgewater Street, then left on Riverside Drive. The drive through Washington Park would still be a pleasant diversion, even if you didn't know that one of America's most beloved journalists once lived here. CBS newsman Charles Kuralt lived here when he was five years old. Green Court Apartments are long gone, but not the banks of the river, where Kuralt played with the neighborhood boys. Turn left on Walnut Street to return to NC 32, then head east on NC 92 to Bath.

WHERE TO EAT

Curiosity Shop Cafe and Bar. 201 West Main Street, Washington 27889. The Curiosity Shop specializes in fresh seafood but also serves prime cuts of beef and some game. Try the delicious jumbo lump crab cakes (the most popular item on the menu). Peruse the extensive wine list, and don't miss dessert, prepared daily by the owner's mom. Open for dinner Tuesday through Sunday. $$$. (252) 975-1397.

P.J.'s on Main Street. 107 West Main, Washington 27889. The menu includes lots of sandwiches to choose from for lunch. For dinner, try P.J.'s Steak Oscar, a Black Angus tenderloin filet served with lump crabmeat, fresh asparagus, and P.J.'s special Dijon Parmesan sauce. Open for lunch and dinner. $$-$$$. (252) 946-9483.

The Rumor Mill Cafe. 156 West Main Street, Washington 27889. This is a great choice for deli sandwiches, burgers, and salads for lunch. For dinner, try a fresh seafood dish. $$-$$$. (252) 948-0921.

A Slice of Heaven. 210 West Main, Washington 27899. At this gourmet dessert and coffee bar, try my favorite: Louisiana Blackout, a dark chocolate cake made with dark cocoa. (252) 948-2300.

WHERE TO STAY

Pamlico House Bed and Breakfast, 400 East Main Street, Washington 27889. This AAA three-diamond inn is in the center of historic Washington. Built in 1906 as the rectory for St. Peter's Episcopal Church, this Colonial-Revival home features a broad wraparound porch and is within walking distance of downtown. The classic Victorian parlor is decorated with period antiques, many of them family pieces. Upstairs are four spacious guest rooms. A full gourmet breakfast is served in the dining room. $$. (252) 946–7184 or (800) 948–8507, www.pamlicohouse.com.

The Moss House. 129 Van Norden Street, Washington 27889. This four-guest-room 1902 Victorian home, located only a block away from the waterfront, belonged to the owner's great-grandfather. The Moss House serves a full breakfast highlighted by traditional Southern favorites and creative turns on classics from across the country. These hearty entrees, accented by fresh juices, freshly ground coffee, seasonal fresh or baked fruit, and an assortment of muffins and breads baked in-house, will prepare you for a full day. $$–$$$. (888) 975–3393, www.themosshouse.com.

Carolina House Bed and Breakfast. 227 East Second Street, Washington 27889. Located only two blocks from the waterfront, this three-guest-room home, built in 1880 and listed on the National Register of Historic Places, puts you within walking distance of downtown and the estuarium. $$. (252) 975–1382, www.carolinahousebnb.com.

BATH

With easy access to the Pamlico River and to the rest of the world via the Atlantic Ocean—50 miles downriver at Ocracoke Inlet—French Protestants from Virginia decided in 1705 to make Bath their permanent home. Only three years after becoming North Carolina's first town, Bath could boast fifty people and twelve houses.

As the first port of entry into the colony, Bath's sea trade consisted of naval stores, furs, and tobacco. Ferries plied the Pamlico River, linking Bath to New Bern and Edenton via post roads. The colony's first shipyard and gristmill were established here, as was the first public library. The 1,050 books and pamphlets from England that had been entrusted to a plantation owner found a home in St. Thomas Church, built in 1734, the oldest existing church in the state.

Bath's importance began to fade as violent rebellions, drought, and an outbreak of yellow fever sent people packing to Washington, 15 miles upriver. Today, Bath is a quaint historical village, occupying only a few blocks. Still, allow at least a couple of hours to see the town.

Bath was also the haunt of Edward Teach, better known as Blackbeard. He is said to have married a local girl and briefly settled in the little harbor town about 1716.

WHERE TO GO

Historic Bath Visitor Center. 207 Carteret Street, Bath 27808. Begin your exploration by viewing the free video, *Bath: The First Town,* shown every fifteen minutes. (You can get a jump on this by viewing the video on-line at the Bath Historic Site Web site, www.ah.dcr.state.nc.us/sections/hs/bath/bath.htm.) Take the guided tours of two historic homes, Van Der Veer House (1790) and the Bonner House (1830). You can do either or both (the cost is $1.00 per home for adults, 50 cents for students). The free self-guided tour of the Palmer–Marsh House (1751) includes an exhibit detailing the history of Bath. You can easily walk from the visitor center to the historic sites. (252) 923-3971.

St. Thomas Episcopal Church. Craven and Main Streets, Bath 27808. Inside the state's oldest church, built in 1734, you will find Queen Anne's Bell. Cast in 1750, it is eighteen years older than the Liberty Bell. Also of significance but not on display: a large silver chalice presented by the Bishop of London in 1838, and a silver candelabra reputed to have been given by King George II in 1740. (252) 923-9141.

WHERE TO EAT

The Old Schoolhouse. 101 North Main Street, Bath 27808. Sit down by the waterfront or take out. Deli sandwiches and salads are served for lunch, and dinner entrees after 4:00 P.M. Try the house specialty, New York strip topped with caramelized onions and melted Swiss cheese, or enjoy the seafood and pasta entrees. $-$$. (252) 923-0339.

Old Town Grill. 436 Carteret Street, Bath 27808. Open for breakfast, lunch, and dinner, the Old Town Grill features country cooking with daily specials. Try the seafood and steak combo. $-$$. (252) 923-1840.

WHERE TO STAY

Pirate's Den Bed and Breakfast. 116 South Main Street, Bath 27808. This four-room inn offers Southern charm across the street from the water. $$. (252) 923–9571, www.bbonline.com/nc/piratesden.

    Bath Harbor Marina and Motel. 101 Carteret Street, Bath 27808. You have a choice of four waterfront efficiency units. If you stay here, ask for the $10 guest discount on canoe, kayak, powerboat, and sailboat rentals. $$. (252) 923–5711, www.bathharbor.com.

AURORA

From Bath, head to the ferry landing at Bayview, 15 miles east on NC 92. Just follow the signs to the Aurora-Bayview ferry, which departs regularly year-round (call 800–BY–FERRY for schedules or visit www.ncferry.org). There's no charge for the thirty-minute crossing. At the ferry landing, follow NC 306 to Aurora.

WHERE TO GO

Aurora Fossil Museum. 400 Main Street, Aurora 27806. An eighteen-minute video describes the great geologic forces that created the Coastal Plain over millions of years. Explore two rooms of fossilized bones, teeth, shells, and coral on display. Find your own fossils (some dating back 22 million years) or shark teeth by sifting through tons of fossil bed diggings delivered to the site. Be sure to bring your own tools to dig. (252) 322–4238, www.pamlico.com/aurora/fossils.

WHERE TO EAT

Wayside Restaurant. NC 33, Aurora 27806. Serving breakfast and lunch, the Wayside has daily specials, meat with choice of vegetables, plus rolls and hush puppies. (252) 322–7299.

WHERE TO STAY

Creekside Cottage Waterfront. 457 Muddy Creek Road, Aurora 27806. Short-term completely furnished housing in a rural setting (one-week minimum stay) is perfect for those enrolled in weeklong sailing schools in the region. $. (252) 322–4473.

EDWARD

Named for Josephus Edwards, who built a mill on nearby Durham Creek in 1868, this small town is 22 miles from Washington and 3 miles off the route between the Aurora and the Minnesott ferries.

WHERE TO GO

Bennett Vineyards. 6832 Old Sandhill Road, Edward 27821. Bennett Vineyards is the largest muscadine and scuppernong vineyard in the Carolinas. It lies on a 138-acre parcel of Colonial grant land in North Carolina east of US 17 between the Neuse and the Pamlico Rivers. The wine barreled in a converted tobacco barn derives from recipes and techniques that emulate those of the earliest colonists. The winery offers tours and tastings. (877) 762–9463, www.ncwines.com.

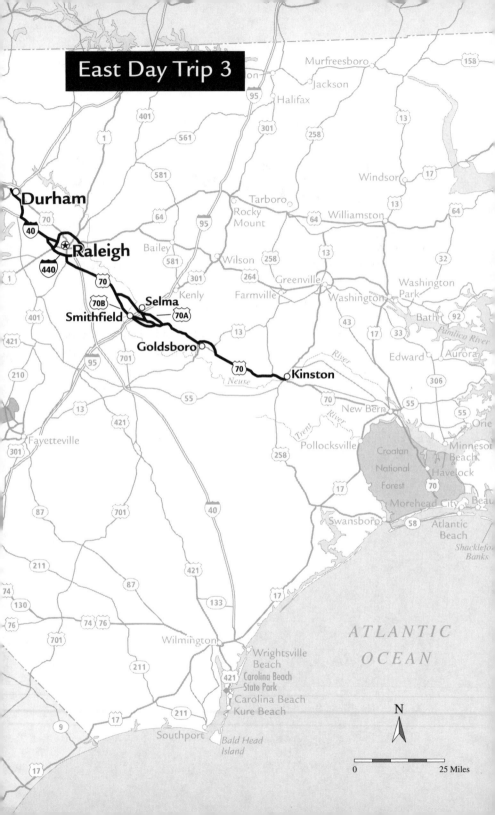

East Day Trip 3

Durham

Raleigh

Selma

Smithfield

Goldsboro

Kinston

Fayetteville

Wilmington

Murfreesboro

Jackson

Halifax

Tarboro

Rocky Mount

Williamston

Windsor

Wilson

Bailey

Kenly

Farmville

Greenville

Washington

Washington Park

Bath

Edward

Aurora

Pamlico River

New Bern

Pollocksville

Croatan National Forest

Havelock

Morehead City

Beau

Minneso Beach

One

Swansboro

Atlantic Beach

Shacklefo Banks

Wrightsville Beach

Carolina Beach State Park

Carolina Beach

Kure Beach

Southport

Bald Head Island

ATLANTIC OCEAN

N

0   25 Miles

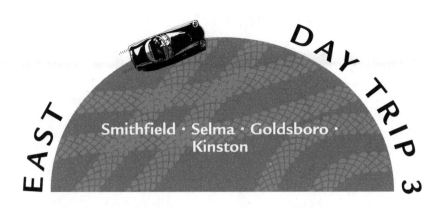

Smithfield · Selma · Goldsboro · Kinston

The road from Raleigh to Morehead City should be called the Barbecue Highway. That's because the towns that dot US 70 east boast some of the best barbecue in the state. Along this corridor from the capital to the coast, you'll not only visit noteworthy attractions but also sample Eastern North Carolina–style barbecue, distinct from the Western North Carolina–style barbecue found west of Raleigh. There is a difference between the two variations.

Few topics have inspired such intense debate as North Carolina barbecue. The *New Yorker*'s Calvin Trillin wrote in his book *Alice, Let's Eat* of being "subjected to stern geographical probings" when he mentioned to North Carolina residents that he had sampled barbecue in their home state.

The debate was perhaps best characterized by the feuding between Jerry Bledsoe, who was a columnist for the *Greensboro Daily News* at the time, and Dennis Rogers of the *News and Observer*. Bledsoe wrote: "In the East, you get all these little things in your mouth and wonder what the hell they are. They're ground up pork skin. That's the only way they have to give the meat any flavor."

Rogers replied in his column: "When I am hankering for a big piece of dead hog meat, I like to follow the advice of my good friend Jerry Bledsoe and head west, where you find lots of it. For some reason, Jerry calls that barbecue."

The difference between the two is more in the sauce than in the skin. While both varieties use a vinegar base, Western (or, as it is sometimes called, Lexington, North Carolina) barbecue adds tomato sauce. Beyond that, restaurants have their own recipes for augmenting their house sauces and their own time-tested methods for roasting the pig. Wash down your pig with a Pepsi, which has been bottled in this region longer than anywhere else.

In Smithfield the locals gather, as they have for nearly five decades, at White Swan Barbecue. In addition to sampling Smithfield's mouthwatering barbecue, you'll have the chance to visit the Ava Gardner Museum. Cast in many popular and memorable roles, Gardner was born just 7 miles east of Smithfield. She is buried at Smithfield's Sunset Memorial Gardens on US 70.

While you're in the area, take a short detour north of Selma to Atkinson's Mill, where cornmeal is ground to make the hush puppy mix used at some of the barbecue restaurants you'll visit. On the way back to US 70, stop by the American Music Jubilee Theatre to appreciate the music that goes along with good barbecue.

Continue east on US 70 to Goldsboro, home to Wilber's Barbecue, where two U.S. presidents have eaten. Also popular is McCall's Barbecue and Seafood Restaurant, which started as a home-based take-out service. Farther east still, in Kinston, stop at King's Restaurant, home of the "pig in a pup."

Should you lose your way, roll down your car window and follow your nose.

SMITHFIELD

Only 28 miles east of Raleigh, Smithfield was established on the banks of the Neuse River in 1777, making it one of the ten oldest towns in the state. A classic Southern town, Smithfield's downtown is the heart of this community of 11,000 residents.

WHERE TO GO

Ava Gardner Museum. 325 East Market Street, Smithfield 27577. An incredible collection of items includes childhood memorabilia, film clips, costumes, domestic and foreign posters, black-and-white stills, film scripts, magazine covers, and scrapbooks. Stored and forgotten in a London attic, Gardner's childhood and career keepsakes were shipped to the museum in 2002. Among the items were teenage Ava's scrapbook with dance cards, cotillion invitations, and telegraphs from a boyfriend, as well as three scrapbooks completed by Ava's sister that chronicle the actress's career up to 1953. Gardner, who was born near Smithfield, is buried in Sunset Memorial Gardens, 3 miles from the museum. Museum and gift shop open Monday through Saturday 9:00 A.M. until 5:00 P.M., Sunday 2:00 to 5:00 P.M. Admission for adults, $4.00; teens up to age 16 and seniors, $3.00; children ages 3 through 12, $2.00; children under age 3, free. (919) 934–5830, www.avagardner.org.

WHERE TO SHOP

Carolina Outlet Center. 1025 Industrial Park Drive #905, Smithfield 27577. The more than eighty factory-direct stores include Liz Claiborne, Nike, The Gap, Rack Room Shoes, Carolina Pottery, Polo, Ralph Lauren Factory Outlet, Tommy Hilfiger, Reebok, and Fossil Company Store. Open Monday through Saturday 10:00 A.M. until 9:00 P.M., Sunday 1:00 to 6:00 P.M. (800) SHOP-USA, www.carolinaoutletcenter.com.

WHERE TO EAT

White Swan Barbecue. 3198 Highway 301 South, Smithfield 27577. The White Swan, which has been serving barbecue since 1959, also serves ribs, fried seafood, Brunswick stew, hush puppies, slaw, potatoes, and desserts. Open Monday through Wednesday 10:00 A.M. until 7:00 P.M., Thursday through Saturday 10:00 A.M. until 8:30 P.M., and Sunday from 10:00 A.M. until 5:00 P.M. Join the crowd of locals on Thursday nights from 4:00 to 9:00 P.M., when barbecue sandwiches are just 99 cents each (regularly $2.25). $$. (919) 934–8913.

SELMA

Billing itself at the "antique mecca of the South," tiny Selma offers more than twenty shops and malls covering 90,000 square feet, all within walking distance in a 1950s small-town setting. Selma also boasts the very best fine-ground cornmeal around, ground by millstones at the more-than-two-century-old Atkinson Milling Company.

WHERE TO GO

Atkinson Milling Co. 95 Atkinson Mill Road, Selma 27576. This old gristmill was built in 1757, while North Carolina was still a colony. The mill has been in continuous operation for more than 240 years. Today, Atkinson's Mill is the only water-powered gristmill operating in the area. A wide variety of cornmeal products, including a selection of hush puppy mixes, is available at the gift shop. (919) 965–3547, www.atkinsonmilling.com.

American Music Jubilee Theatre. 300 North Raiford Street, Selma 27576. Offering a touch of Branson and Myrtle Beach in eastern North Carolina, the theater presents evenings of Southern hospitality, American music, and sidesplitting comedy to delight audiences every weekend. The Branson-style variety show entertains visitors with music from '50s rock 'n' roll to classic and contemporary country and gospel. Admission rates vary by season, but begin at $14.50 per adult. (877) 843–7839, www.amjubilee.com.

Selma Union Station. Railroad Street, Selma 27576. Built in the 1920s, the new station serves as a working depot for passengers boarding Amtrak's *Carolinian* from Selma to Charlotte and Jacksonville to New York. Be sure to see the interpretive exhibits from the days when Selma was a major hub in the state. Opens October 2002.

GOLDSBORO

Goldsboro's marketing moniker, "Where Legends Begin," plays on this area's rich history. Among the enduring legends: Sherman invaded Goldsboro during the War Between the States, and Andy Griffith was a high-school teacher here before going on to become Sheriff Taylor in Mayberry. Local legend also has it that barbecue was born here.

WHERE TO GO

Old Waynesborough Historic Village. 801 South US 117, Goldsboro 27530. Visit a nineteenth-century family home, a medical office, a one-room school, a law office, and a Quaker meeting-house. Listen to the blacksmith beating upon his iron. Walk down to the Neuse River. Enjoy your day in this tranquil setting and learn more about the demise of this faded town, now a living history museum. Open Monday through Saturday 10:00 A.M. until 4:00 P.M., Sunday 1:00 to 4:00 P.M. Free admission. (919) 731–1653, www.wcpl.org/waynesborough.htm.

Waynesborough State Park. 801 South US 117, Goldsboro 27530. Located adjacent to Old Waynesborough Historic Village. Take advantage of two hiking trails through what was once a bustling colonial area. Open daily 9:00 A.M. until 5:00 P.M. Closed on all state holidays from October through April. Free admission. (919) 778–6234, ils.unc.edu/parkproject/ncparks.html.

Wayne County Museum. 116 North William Street, Goldsboro 27530. Located in a stately Jeffersonian-style building in downtown Goldsboro's historic district, the museum has a permanent War Between the States exhibit. Free admission. (919) 734–5023, www.historicalwaynenc.com.

Cherry Hospital Museum. 201 Stevens Mill Road, Goldsboro 27530. Opened by the state in 1880 for black citizens with mental illness, Cherry Hospital was named in 1959 for R. Gregg Cherry, governor from 1945 to 1949. It has been open to all races since 1965. Patients worked about 3,500 acres of farmland until the 1970s. The museum depicts more than a century of history with photographs, logbooks, and a variety of medical and farming equipment once used at the hospital. Open weekdays 8:00 A.M. until noon and 1:00 to 5 P.M. Free admission. (919) 731–3483.

Willow Dale Cemetery. 306 East Elm Street, Goldsboro 27530. Visit the Confederate monument, erected in 1883, that marks the site of a mass grave where 800 Civil War soldiers, both Union and Confederate, are buried.

WHERE TO EAT

McCall's Barbecue and Seafood Restaurant. 139 Millers Chapel Road, Goldsboro 27534. This popular Goldsboro restaurant began as a home-based operation. Owner Randy McCall roasted pigs at his house on Thursday nights and sold take-out barbecue from his home on Fridays. In 1989, McCall quit his day job and opened his restaurant, which specializes in barbecue, chicken, and seafood. The secret to McCall's succulent pork is that it is cooked on a rotisserie through the night, then roasted over wood coals in the morning. Traveling with the family? Try the "Family Special," which easily feeds four. For takeout only, it includes a pound of barbecue, one whole chicken, boiled potatoes, slaw, and a dozen hush puppies, all for $13.99. Dining in? Try the lunch specials. Open 11:00 A.M. until 9:00 P.M. daily except Christmas Eve and Christmas Day. $$. (919) 751–0072.

Wilber's Barbecue. 4172 US 70 East, Goldsboro 27534. Only a short distance up the road from McCall's, Wilber's claimed *Our State* magazine's Award of Excellence for best barbecue in the state, and *Southern Living* recognized Wilber's as best barbecue in the South. Since 1962, Wilber's has roasted its chopped barbecue over oak coals. Presidents Bill Clinton and George Bush Sr. have eaten here. Open daily 6:00 A.M. until 9:00 P.M. $$. (919) 778–5218.

KINSTON

At the museums and nature park in Kinston, you'll have plenty of opportunity to burn off the extra calories that you'll ingest at King's Restaurant. Then point your car west on NC 70 to head back to Raleigh, or east for the thirty-minute drive to New Bern for an extended day trip (See East Day Trip 1).

WHERE TO GO

Caswell Center Museum and Visitor Center. 2415 West Vernon Avenue, Kinston 28504. Built in the 1800s, the Stroud House became home in 1914 to the first residents of Caswell Center, the first facility serving people with mental retardation in the state. The museum, which includes a videotape presentation, describes early life at Caswell Center. Free admission. Open Monday through Friday 8:00 A.M. until 5:00 P.M. (252) 208–3779.

CSS *Neuse* State Historic Site and Governor Richard Caswell Memorial. 2612 West Vernon Avenue, Kinston 28504. The CSS *Neuse* was one of three Civil War ironclads. Although the visitor center here was severely damaged by floodwaters from Hurricane Floyd, limited exhibits on the *Neuse* and Governor Richard Caswell, as well as a video detailing the history of the CSS *Neuse*, can be seen in the Caswell Memorial. The memorial is a self-guided museum depicting the life and career of North Carolina's first elected governor. Free admission. Open April through October, Monday through Saturday 9:00 A.M. until 5:00 P.M. and Sunday 1:00 to 5:00 P.M.; November through March, Tuesday through Saturday 10:00 A.M. until 4:00 P.M. and Sunday 1:00 to 4:00 P.M. Closed Monday. (252) 522–2091, www.ah.dcr.state.nc.us/sections/hs/neuse/neuse.htm

Harmony Hall. 109 East King Street, Kinston 28501. One of the oldest homes in Lenoir County, Harmony Hall has been tastefully restored with authentic eighteenth-century furnishings. Built in 1772, it was once the home of Governor Richard Caswell. Free admission. Open Monday, Wednesday, and Friday 10:00 A.M. until 1:00 P.M. or by appointment. (252) 522–0421.

Caswell No. 1 Fire Station Museum. 118 South Queen Street, Kinston 28501. Enter the world of the late-1800s fire fighter. The Caswell No. 1 Fire Station was built in 1895 after a disastrous fire destroyed much of the downtown Kinston area. A 1922 LaFrance Pumper is the focus of the museum, along with a collection of helmets, nozzles, ladders, fire extinguishers, and other memorabilia that span a period of one hundred years. Free admission. Open Tuesday, Thursday, and Saturday 10:00 A.M. until 4:00 P.M. (252) 527–1566.

Neuseway Nature Park and Campground and the **Exchange Nature Center.** 401 West Caswell Street, Kinston 28501. Located on fifty-five acres along the Neuse River, this nature-based park's nature center has more than forty types of native and exotic animals, including snakes, ferrets, caimans, and geckos. Also on the site: three 550-gallon aquariums, two developed fishponds stocked with catfish every year, and a saltwater touch tank. The park features nature trails, primitive camping, fishing, picnicking, and canoeing. Free admission. Open November through May, Tuesday through Saturday 9:30 A.M. until 5:00 P.M.; June through October, Tuesday through Saturday 9:30 A.M. until 6:00 P.M.; Sunday year-round from 1:00 to 5:00 P.M. Closed Monday. (252) 939–3367.

WHERE TO EAT

King's Restaurant. US 70 East, Kinston 28501. King's acclaimed barbecue uses a vinegar and red pepper–based sauce. It's also hand chopped so that the sauce will be properly absorbed. Should you stop at King's, abandon all aspirations to count calories, and order the "pig in a pup," an oversize hush puppy stuffed with barbecue that goes for $2.50. Top it off with King's famous banana pudding or pecan pie. No time to dine at King's? Order your pork barbecue to be shipped overnight by FedEx (no kidding—call 800–332–OINK or visit www.kingsbbq.com). $–$$. (800) 332–6465.

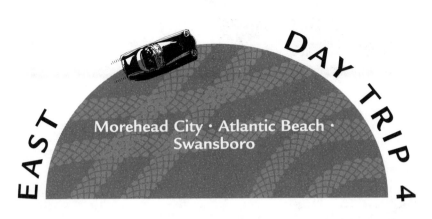

Morehead City · Atlantic Beach · Swansboro

Okay, so the drive to the "Crystal Coast" may be a stretch for a guidebook that purports to highlight destinations within two hours of Raleigh-Durham. Sure, it will take you an additional half hour to make the Atlantic coast, 147 miles from Raleigh, a straight shot on US 70 east, but for the extra effort, you'll be rewarded with a quaint downtown, beautiful beaches, and coastal charm.

The four-lane US 70 becomes Arendell Street as you enter the peninsula that claims Morehead City. You'll pass the Crystal Coast Visitor Center on the way in; stop here for maps and detailed information about the area. Farther on is the bridge to Atlantic Beach, but you'll want to explore Morehead City before crossing.

Beachgoers have been coming to Atlantic Beach since 1887, when a small one-story pavilion was all that was here—well, that and the beach itself. Back then, visitors stayed in Morehead City and traveled by sailboat to the beach.

Today, you cross a high-rise bridge then pitch camp in one of the many fine properties along the coast. You'll be joining the 3,000 residents who live here year-round and the 35,000 visitors who come here during the summer months. For the kids—or the young at heart—the town center has amusement park rides.

Head back to Raleigh through Swansboro, a quaint fishing village 23 miles south of Morehead City via NC 24, or take the scenic drive down Emerald Isle. Either way, the trip back to Raleigh from Swansboro is 135 miles.

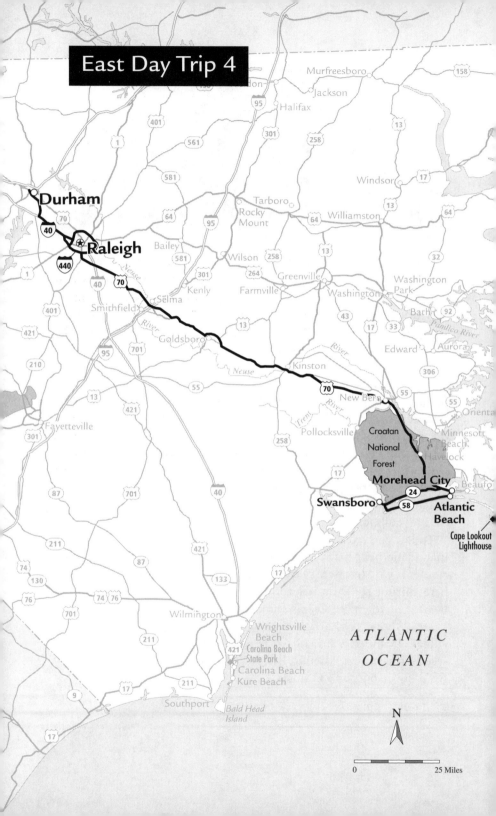

East Day Trip 4

MOREHEAD CITY

Incorporated in 1861 and named for Governor John Motley Morehead, the site formerly known as Shepherd's Point is located on a peninsula flanked by Bogue Sound and the Newport River. A summer resort, Morehead City is also the state's only deepwater port north of Wilmington.

East of the bridge to Atlantic Beach, from 25th to 3rd Street, the oldest part of Morehead City is found skirting both sides of Arendell Street. The noticeable divider along the way is the railroad track that bisects the main street. The train brought passengers from the Triangle a century before there was a Triangle. Now it serves the North Carolina State Port at Morehead City with state exports like wood chips and tobacco.

The two or three streets parallel to the Bogue Sound waterfront make up the more well-to-do residential area of past years. On both sides of Arendell, the renovation of houses and summer cottages has created neighborhoods with lots of architectural character.

One block south on Evans Street between 10th and 4th Streets is the downtown Morehead City waterfront, where the peninsula narrows into single-digit street numbers. Here you'll see that seafood rules in Morehead City. The Gulf Stream fishing charter boat fleet is harbored here next to combination seafood market/restaurants where commercial fishing boats dock.

The smell of hush puppies is in the air by eleven in the morning. Memorials to captains and fishermen invite you to linger on a walk along the waterfront. The captains' memorial is located beside Capt. Bill's Seafood Restaurant at Seventh Street, and the statue of the *Core Sounder* in Jaycee Park on the waterfront between Ninth and Tenth streets remembers the strength required of commercial fishermen.

A walk along the Morehead City waterfront introduces you to the character of this town that has always flaunted its greatest assets: fishing and feeding tourists. At the Sanitary Seafood Market and Restaurant, stop to browse the memorabilia before you exit. The restaurant is filled with comments of visitors since 1938, along with photographs of beauty queens and politicians.

WHERE TO GO

Crystal Coast Visitor Center. 3409 Arendell Street (US 70 east), Morehead City 28557. Designed after lighthouses of the eighteenth century, the Crystal Coast Visitor Center is a harbor of information. Find out how to get around the Crystal Coast, and learn about attractions, lodgings, and dining. The adjacent rest area is well kept, and a picnicking area is under cool live oak trees by Bogue Sound. A North Carolina Wildlife launch ramp is available for trailerable boats, but parking is limited on busy weekends. (800) 786–6962, www.sunnync.com.

Downtown Waterfront. Tenth to Fourth Street on Evans, Morehead City 28557. Seafood, sportfishing, and art galleries come together along this beautiful waterfront area where the smell of hush puppies is mixed with the excitement of Gulf Stream sportfishing. The lifestyle, scenery, and heritage of commercial fishing in this Cape Lookout region of the North Carolina Outer Banks are reflected in the art galleries of downtown Morehead City. (252) 808–0440, www.downtownmoreheadcity.com.

The History Place. 1008 Arendell Street, Morehead City 28557. Newly opened in late 2001, the History Place is home of the Carteret County Historical Society and Museum of History and Art. The museum collection includes artifacts of Native American inhabitants of this coastal region, costumes of the eighteenth and nineteenth centuries, furnishings, medical displays, and Civil War artifacts. The research library contains a notable genealogy collection, publications, archival manuscript material, and an extensive photography file. Tours are offered Monday through Saturday, 10:00 A.M. to 4:00 P.M. Free admission. (252) 247–7533, www.rootsweb.com/~nccchs/.

Cape Lookout Lighthouse. In 1804 Congress authorized construction of a lighthouse on Cape Lookout, the southernmost tip of the Outer Banks barrier islands. Completed in 1812, the Cape Lookout light was reconstructed in 1859 to its height of 163 feet, and it is still an acting aid to navigation. It was painted with its distinctive black-and-white diamond pattern in 1873. A new keeper's quarters, constructed at the same time, is accessible to visitors on a seasonal basis. There is no access by road to the undeveloped islands of the Cape Lookout National Seashore. The island's only permanent inhabitants are loggerhead sea turtles—which waddle to shore to bury their eggs—and 7,200 species of birds, including piping plovers, peregrine falcons, and Arctic birds migrating south.

At the point of Cape Lookout, the chilly Labrador Current meets the warm Gulf Stream with such force that it sends plumes of sea mist soaring skyward. These powerful currents wreak havoc on the ocean floor, shifting sand and shoals so that sailors and sea captains can scarcely navigate. For good reason, this region is known as the Graveyard of the Atlantic. More than 600 ships wrecked along this treacherous stretch of coast from the sixteenth century.

From Morehead City, Cape Lookout ferry services operate seasonally, generally Easter through October. Contact the Crystal Coast Visitor Center for more information: (800) 786–6962, www.sunnync.com.

WHERE TO SHOP

Dee Gee's Gifts and Books. 508 Evans Street, Morehead City 28557. A landmark on the Morehead City waterfront where, in addition to best-sellers, greeting cards, and specialty gifts, you will find the complete collection of local nautical charts and every book that has ever been written about the Crystal Coast area. Dee Gee's schedules frequent book signings with state and local writers. Open daily year-round. (252) 726–3314.

Morehead City has a number of fine art galleries that show the works of local and regional artists. Among my favorites:

Carolina Artist's Studio Gallery. 800 Evans Street, Morehead City 28557. A cooperative representing thirty or more regional and local artists, the sunny gallery rooms display original paintings, pottery, batiks, photography, and other art forms. Open Tuesday through Saturday year-round. (252) 726–7550.

Carteret Contemporary Art. 1106 Arendell Street, Morehead City 28557. Thematically, the North Carolina and Southeastern artists featured in the special exhibits share an appreciation of the coast. Open daily year-round. (252) 726–4071.

Windward Gallery. 508 Evans Street, Morehead City 28557. Alexander Kaszas's works in oils, watercolors, and pastels combine the painting style of an impressionist and the love of a Down East

native for the dynamics and natural beauty of the barrier islands.
(252) 728-6393.

WHERE TO EAT

Bistro by the Sea. 4031 Arendell Street, Morehead City 28557.
Located beside the Hampton Inn, Bistro is a favorite with a faithful
local clientele for dinner choices, presentation, and service. You
won't go wrong with the mahimahi or the beef filet. For an appetizer, try the sushi tray. Open Tuesday through Thursday 5:00 to
9:30 P.M., Friday and Saturday until 10:00 P.M. Closed Sunday,
Monday, and January. $$-$$$. (252) 247-2777.

Amos Mosquitos. 509 Evans Street, Morehead City 28557.
Waiters and waitresses are dressed as garage mechanics at this
waterfront restaurant that serves lunch sandwiches and salads as
well as crab cakes. Outside dining is available, but limited, on the
deck. A children's menu is available. Open daily for lunch and
dinner. $$. (252) 247-6222.

The Sanitary Fish Market and Restaurant. 501 Evans Street,
Morehead City 28557. The saying goes that if you haven't been to
the Sanitary, you haven't been to Morehead City. After sixty-three
years of serving seafood, the Sanitary continues to be a destination
as well as a restaurant. The hush puppies are on the table before the
chairs are completely pulled in, and all dishes are served with
coleslaw and french fries. Lunch and dinner, generally fried or
broiled, are served daily. Closed from Thanksgiving through
January. $$. (252) 247-3111.

Calypso Cafe, 506 Arendell Street, Morehead City 28557. This
dinner-only restaurant has a following that keeps the tables full. A
tiny place that is almost more Caribbean than the Caribbean,
Calypso is a great escape for extraordinary seafood. Dinner daily
during the summer; closed Monday the rest of the year. $$-$$$.
(252) 240-3380.

WHERE TO STAY

Hampton Inn. 4035 Arendell Street, Morehead City 28557. Morehead City's only waterfront hotel, the Hampton Inn offers comfortable rooms, a complimentary continental breakfast with morning

newspaper, and an inviting outside pool. It is adjacent to Bistro by the Sea, one of the town's more popular restaurants. $$. (252) 240-2300 or (800) 467-9375.

Comfort Inn. 3212 Arendell Street, Morehead City 28557. The reliable comforts of this national chain are within close proximity to the Atlantic Beach Bridge. The economy of staying on the mainland and driving over the bridge to the beach is often an inviting alternative for overnighting day-trippers. A complimentary continental breakfast and outdoor pool are available to guests. $$. (252) 247-3434 or (800) 422-5404.

Best Western Buccaneer. 2806 Arendell Street, Morehead City 28557. The Best Western offers the standard motel accommodations along with a complimentary full breakfast at the on-site Old Anchor Inn Restaurant. $$. (252) 726-3115 or (800) 682-4982.

Econo Lodge. 3410 Bridges Street, Morehead City 28557. The Econo Lodge has comfortable rooms, low mainland rates, an outdoor pool, and complimentary continental breakfast, but no view. $$. (252) 247-2940 or (800) 533-7556.

Holiday Inn Express and Suites. Intersection of NC 24 and US 70, Morehead City 28557. This new property offers reasonable rates, outdoor pool, sauna, exercise room, meeting room, laundry, and complimentary breakfast. $$. (252) 247-5001 or (800) 465-4329.

ATLANTIC BEACH

The bridge to Atlantic Beach is in Morehead City at 24th and Arendell Streets. From the top of the high-rise bridge, the view that stretches ahead of you is a densely developed beach resort town that meets the blue Atlantic.

At the bottom of the bridge, the road intersects with Fort Macon Road (NC 58). Ahead is Atlantic Beach Circle, a commercial and amusement area. The circle is the chosen destination of many day visitors to the beach because of lifeguard services and nearby beach food, especially hot dogs and beer.

Those who prefer less boardwalk ambience choose Fort Macon State Park as their destination, 1.5 miles east on Fort Macon Road.

Flanking the circle east and west are parallel streets of beach cottages with all the architectural flourish of eastern Carolina farmers' postharvest fishing retreats of the 1950s. Makeovers are adding some Caribbean color to these densely built blocks of clapboard rental cottages. Many permanent residences are now among the vacation rentals.

East of the circle toward Fort Macon State Park is a mix of condominium developments and small motels with fishing piers. One delightful development of vacation cottages is Sea Dreams, a string of three-storied Caribbean-colored structures that seem to tumble over the dunes from Fort Macon Road to the beach. Sea Dreams is a head-turning happy sight by the ocean.

WHERE TO GO

Fort Macon State Park. Located on the east end of the island at milepost 0 on NC 58, Fort Macon is a popular destination for the variety of activities available. The Civil War fort is an interesting site hiding in the dunes to protect Beaufort Inlet. From the fort walls, you can see the wreck site of Blackbeard's flagship, *Queen Anne's Revenge*, which lies in 20 feet of water just off Beaufort Inlet. The trailhead of a one-mile nature walk from the fort leads to frequently good bird-watching. At the mouth of Beaufort Inlet, the rock jetty is a reliable destination for lucky surf fishing. A museum and bookstore are on-site. Open year-round with interpretive programs offered daily. There are picnicking facilities, a bathhouse (user fees are $3.00 per adult, $2.00 per child), and lifeguard services. Surf fish from the rock jetty at Beaufort Inlet or take a nature walk on Coues Trail, which starts near the fort parking lots. (252) 726-3775, www.clis.com/friends/.

Roosevelt Natural Area. At milepost 7 on NC 58, this rare and undisturbed ancient maritime forest surrounds the North Carolina Aquarium. There are two trails to explore here: The Theodore Roosevelt Trail is an interpreted loop trail that takes about thirty minutes to walk. Of interest is the natural vegetation—especially the live oaks—and freshwater lakes. The trailhead is on the south side of the Aquarium parking lot. The Alice Hoffman Trail is accessible from inside the Aquarium. This trail is interpreted along a salt marsh habitat that includes viewing stations for fiddler crabs and shorebirds. A reptile exhibit includes live animals that are at home in a salt marsh habitat and a maritime forest. (252) 726-3775.

North Carolina Aquarium. Roosevelt Drive at milepost 7, NC 58. The aquarium is perfectly set in the Theodore Roosevelt Natural Area, an area preserved by the children of the twenty-sixth U.S. president who inherited the part of the island that is now Pine Knoll Shores. An interpreted trail through an ancient maritime forest begins at the aquarium parking lot. Another trail along a saltwater marsh begins inside the aquarium. Tank exhibits include the marine life and reptiles that call this area home. Some programs require preregistration, so consult the aquarium's calendar. Contact the aquarium for a current schedule of events and to register for a kayaking trip, a surf fishing workshop, a seafood cooking class, and any number of arts and crafts classes involving marine plant and animal life. Open daily 9:00 A.M. until 5:00 P.M. Admission for adults, $3.00; children ages 6 through 17, $1.00. (252) 247-4003, www.aquariums.state.nc.us/pks/.

Fun 'n' Wheels. 100 Atlantic Boulevard, Atlantic Beach 28512. View the ocean from the Ferris wheel, go round on the go-cart track, or bang along on bumper boats. Open from February through November (open weekends only from February through April and September through November). Free admission, but tickets are required for individual amusements. (252) 247-0050.

Jungleland. 2800 West Fort Macon Road, Atlantic Beach 28512. Enjoy two eighteen-hole miniature golf courses (Jungle Golf and Gorilla Golf), bumper boats, a high-tech arcade, and a concession stand. Get your cotton candy here, as well as snow cones, hot dogs, french fries, and more. Duffers, watch out for the Japanese Imperial carp in the fishpond on the Jungle Golf Course. Free admission; tickets are required for individual amusements. Open weekends between Easter and Memorial Day, daily from Memorial Day to Labor Day, then weekends until October. Purchase the Magic Armband, $14.50, for carte blanche on all rides and attractions. (252) 247-2148.

WHERE TO SHOP

Something Fishy. Crow's Nest Shopping Center, Atlantic Beach Causeway, Atlantic Beach 28512. Here's the cure for home decor needing a touch of sea fever. Objets d'art *a la mer* are everywhere, and changing with a frequency that pleases even a daily shopper. This is a gift shop that is too much fun to miss, especially if your taste is fishy. Open Monday through Saturday year-round. (252) 247–4228.

Atlantic Station Shopping Center. West Fort Macon Road, Atlantic Beach 28512. With convenient park-and-walk shopping in Atlantic Beach, shops include **Trillium,** a bright and colorful stop for home accessories and women's sportswear, (252) 247–7210; and **Outer Banks Outfitters,** with marine equipment and accessories from tools and outboards to hooks, line, and sinkers, (252) 240–0055.

WHERE TO EAT

Island Grille. 401 Money Island Drive, Atlantic Beach 28512. This cozy beach restaurant is located at the parking lot of Sportsman's Pier. There's no view, but the food is spectacular and the regulars are regular. Two-for-one specials are offered on Monday and Tuesday nights. One popular dish: filet stuffed with feta and served with garlic mashed potatoes. Choices always include a fish fillet (such as mahimahi), and a shellfish and pasta dish. Make reservations if you want to be seated on Monday or Tuesday night, even in January. Open daily. $$–$$$. (252) 240–0000.

Crab's Claw Restaurant and Oyster Bar. 201 West Atlantic Boulevard, Atlantic Beach 28512. On the beach, this restaurant is a popular lunch destination. Have a burger on the second-story deck, or try the salads and hot sauces, but the biggest treat may just be the steamed oysters. Open for lunch and dinner. $$–$$$. (252) 726–8222, www.crabsclaw.com.

Watermark. 1010 West Fort Macon Road, Atlantic Beach 28512. Located in the Atlantic Station Shopping Center, this restaurant specializes in grilled steaks and seafood and is popular for its prime rib. No view to lure you, but the inside atmosphere is brightly tropical. Open daily. $$–$$$. (252) 240–2811.

WHERE TO STAY

Atlantis Lodge. Milepost 5 on NC 58. One of the oldest lodging properties on the Crystal Coast, this forty-two-room oceanfront lodge saw very little natural vegetation removed during building.

Thus natural barriers, wildlife, and vegetation remain very much a priority. It's difficult to get a reservation here unless you've been a regular guest, but don't let that stop you from trying. The private pool arguably is the island's most invitingly cool place, the definition of "having it made in the shade." All rooms are efficiencies. $$-$$$. (252) 726-5168 or (800) 682-7057, www.atlantislodge.com.

Sheraton Atlantic Beach Oceanfront Hotel. 2717 West Fort Macon Road (milepost 4.5 on NC 58). A full-service oceanfront retreat, the Sheraton is great for families, particularly as the theme park Jungleland is across the street. There are ocean views from all guest rooms, an on-site restaurant, poolside and oceanfront food services, indoor pool, private pier, lifeguard services—everything for comfortable family getaways by the ocean. Just park, check in, and vacation. $$$. (252) 240-1155 or (800) 624-8875, www.sheratonatlanticbeach.com.

AmeriSuites. Milepost 4.5 on NC 58. This all-suite lodging property neighbors the Bogue Banks Country Club's golf course to the east, Jungleland theme park to the west, and overlooks the ocean beach. This is the island's newest lodging property; its accommodations, rates, and location make it a perfect choice for families. Each suite accommodates four. Refrigerators and microwaves make lunch plans easy, and breakfast is complimentary. AmeriSuites has an outdoor pool and a private path to the beach. $$-$$$. (252) 247-5118, www.amerisuites.com/hotels/ajpj.shtml.

Sea Dreams. A development of multistory beach houses of tropical pastel colors near the rolling sand dunes at milepost 3 on East Fort Macon Road (NC 58), some of these distinctive houses are available as vacation rentals. The Crystal Coast Tourism Authority can offer details at (252) 726-8148, www.sunnync.com.

SWANSBORO

Traveling west on either NC 24 inland or NC 58 down Emerald Isle will take you to Swansboro. The town's history began around 1730, when the first permanent settlement was established on the former site of an Algonquian Indian village at the mouth of the White Oak River. In 1783, the colonial port town of Swannsborough was incorporated in honor of Samuel Swann, former speaker of the North Carolina House of Commons.

The bustling port thrived, and shipbuilding became its major industry. The town's most famous shipbuilder was Captain Otway Burns, builder of the *Prometheus,* the first steamboat constructed in North Carolina. Captain Burns's earlier exploits as the commander of the privateer vessel the *Snapdragon,* had already brought much honor to the town. The port continued to prosper until the end of the Civil War.

The decline of the shipping industry initiated considerable growth of lumber and naval stores, which succumbed to the Great Depression in the 1920s. The townspeople then turned to another natural resource, the sea, and the development of the commercial fishing industry.

Swansboro has managed to retain the quaint charm and quiet character of a picturesque colonial port. From the unique waterfront shops, boutiques, and dining to boating, water sports, and fishing, this waterfront town on the White Oak River is well worth the visit. Shop along the river on Front Street and its adjoining side streets, take some time to walk along the White Oak River, enjoy lunch at one of the restaurants, and relax in Bicentennial Park.

WHERE TO SHOP

Russell's Olde Tyme Shoppe. 116 Front Street, Swansboro 28584. Stop at Russell's to browse the country crafts, jewelry, handcrafted clothing, pottery, furniture, baskets, and silk and dried flowers, along with kitchen and cooking utensils. Open daily. (910) 326–3790.

Through the Looking Glass. 101 Church Street, Swansboro 28584. A broad selection of home and garden accessories, fragrances, jewelry, tableware, candles, wines, and children's gifts are sold here. Be sure to take a peek at the Christmas Wonderland department. Open daily, but call ahead in winter to verify. (910) 326–3128 or (800) 891–8447.

Sunshine and Silks. 129 Front Street, Swansboro 28584. This quaint shop sells gifts and collectibles, including writing papers, tapestry throws, long-lasting candles, scented home sprays, beautiful Italian and American pottery, bell pulls, an extensive selection of Victorian greeting cards and holiday ornaments, and silk floral designs custom made exclusively for Sunshine and Silks. Open daily. (910) 326-5735.

Phil Shivar and Sarah Lawrence Gallery of Art. 105 East Church Street, Swansboro 28584. Here you'll find limited-edition and original art by North Carolina resident Phil Shivar, who produces prints of lighthouses and local scenes. Co-owner and Naples, Florida, resident Sarah Lawrence displays her mixed-media impressionism. Ayers Antiques shares the same shop space and offers art glass, porcelain, and furniture. Open Monday through Saturday year-round, Sunday seasonally. (910) 326-3600.

WHERE TO EAT

Capt. Charlie's Restaurant. NC 24 at Front Street, Swansboro 28584. Specializing in fresh seafood, prime rib, and steaks, the menu offers fried seafood as well as stuffed flounder or broiled shrimp and scallops. Open evenings for dinner. $$-$$$. (910) 326-4303.

Gourmet Café. 99 Church Street, Swansboro 28584. A selection of salads and sandwiches are offered for lunch, including an a la carte sandwich. Dinners are served with homemade breads and salad. The menu offers seafood prepared Alfredo or Florentine style, stir-fries, and house specialty preparations of seafood, beef, and veal. Desserts include a selection of cheesecakes made by the chef's mom. Open year-round except Monday. $$-$$$. (910) 326-7114.

White Oak River Bistro. 206 West Corbett Street, Swansboro 28584. Located near the bridge to Emerald Isle in an attractive white building with porches, White Oak Bistro offers European cuisine for lunch and dinner. Service is in the brightly varnished dining room or on the porch overlooking a lawn that spreads under willow trees to the river. For lunch, select from pastas and sauces or specialty Italian sandwiches. Dinner choices include pastas with veal, chicken, and seafood. Open year-round. Reservations are recommended. $$-$$$. (910) 326-1696.

Yana's Ye Olde Drugstore Restaurant. 109 Front Street, Swansboro 28584. Yana's serves breakfast and lunch. If you're extra hungry, try the Bradburger, a hamburger with egg, cheese, bacon, lettuce, and tomato. Milk shakes are made with real ice cream and milk. Open daily. $-$$. (910) 326-5501.

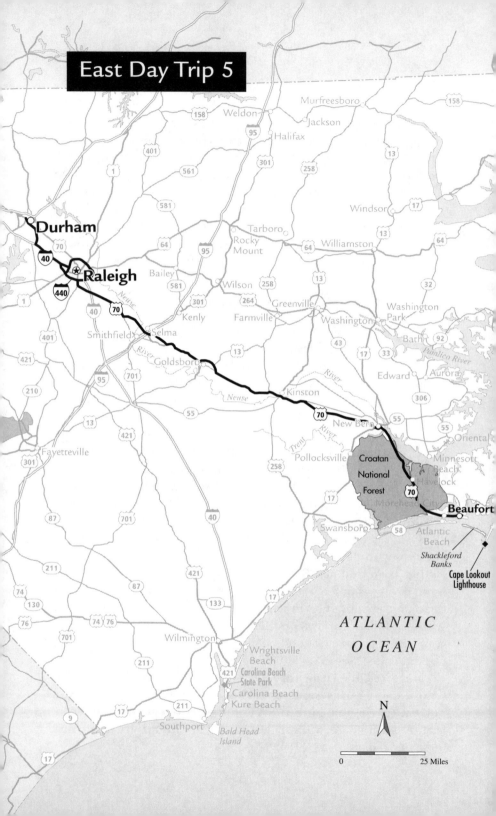

East Day Trip 5

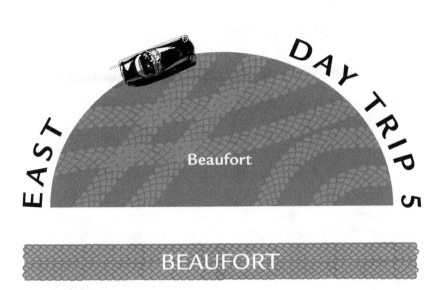

EAST

DAY TRIP 5

Beaufort

BEAUFORT

Travel US 70 east past Morehead City to Beaufort, the "crown jewel of the Crystal Coast." With homes dating back to the 1700s, Beaufort has lots of charm and history. It used to be little more than a small commercial fishing village, but a couple of decades back, the town began an urban renewal program to heighten its appeal to visitors. Transient sailors were welcomed, the waterfront was restored, and today Beaufort is a wonderful walk-around small town with a rich maritime history. Begin on the town's shop-lined main thoroughfare, Front Street, and proceed on Anglican-named back streets—Queen, Ann, Orange—where restored Colonial homes date back to the early 1700s.

The third oldest town in North Carolina, Beaufort was named for Englishman Henry Somerset, the Duke of Beaufort. The town was surveyed in 1713, nearly twenty years before George Washington's birth, and was incorporated in 1722.

Blackbeard's ship, *Queen Anne's Revenge,* was found a few years ago at the mouth of Beaufort Inlet, in 24 feet of water that the locals had sailed and fished over for years. Recent hurricanes shifted the sands, exposing pieces of the 289-year-old vessel. Following the loss of *Queen Anne's Revenge,* Blackbeard made his way to Bath, North Carolina's oldest town. There, in 1718, he received the king's pardon from North Carolina's Governor Charles Eden. The pirate, however, was eventually tracked down and killed by volunteers from the Royal Navy.

A number of operators offer sailing tours from the Beaufort waterfront to Shackleford Banks and Carrot Island for horse sightings (more than one hundred wild ponies roam freely on the island, let loose when a Spanish galleon ran aground here in the seventeenth century), as well as bird-watching, shelling, and self-guided tours along the Rachel Carson National Estuarine Research Reserve.

Following NC 70 east from Raleigh, I pulled into Beaufort late one night and parked myself at the Front Street Grill, right on the waterfront, where I straddled a bar stool between two yachters who had made landfall here. From where I sat, Bermuda, 600 miles to the east, is almost as close as the state's western border, and that proximity to the sea has served Beaufort well.

Sailors have long considered this tiny town a good jumping-off spot. Some leave here for Bermuda or the Bahamas, some stop here on their way up or down the Atlantic coast. Thus, what you'll find here is a true sailing town and all of the charm that being so implies. If ever there was a place for you to drop anchor—or hoist your sails—Beaufort is it.

WHERE TO GO

North Carolina Maritime Museum. 315 Front Street, Beaufort 28516. The sea's influence on Beaufort—and on the entire Outer Banks region—is captured in the cozy, wood-paneled confines of the Maritime Museum, which contains centuries-old small boats, nautical tools, maps, and flags. At the museum's Watercraft Center, visitors can watch from a balcony as the museum's boatbuilder restores old sailing vessels. From the craft of Native Americans to varnished Sunday runabouts, boats tell a story of transportation, industry, life by the sea, and rescue from the sea. The newest additions to the collection are artifacts of Blackbeard the pirate's flagship, *Queen Anne's Revenge*. This shipwreck is one of the most significant marine archaeological finds in history, and its remains lie in 20 feet of water just off Beaufort Inlet. The museum offers a range of interpretive field programs that take visitors out to the marshes and natural reserves or for bike rides along the waterfront. Admission is free. Open daily except New Year's, Thanksgiving, and the Christmas holidays. (252) 728-7317, www.ah.dcr.state.nc.us/sections/maritime/default.htm.

Beaufort Historic Site and Double Decker Bus Tour. 100 block of Turner Street, Beaufort 28516. Preservation efforts have kept Beaufort much as it was when the state's third oldest town was incorporated in 1723. At the Beaufort Historic Site, you can tour ten restored homes and public buildings of the eighteenth and nineteenth centuries, including the Carteret County Courthouse of 1796. The oldest home in Beaufort is Hammock House, built in 1709 and reputed to have been the headquarters of the notorious pirate Blackbeard. Tour the historic district on a double-decker English bus (starting at $6.00 per person) and listen to costumed guides wax poetic about the past, when Beaufort's visitors included pirates, sea captains, star-crossed lovers, and Confederate spies. Visit the old jail, the courthouse, and the apothecary shop, or join a tour of the Old Burying Ground. The Old Beaufort Museum gift shop offers a selection of books on local history, decoys by local carvers, fresh herbs, rugs woven by hand at the historic site, and other gifts. Open Monday through Saturday. (252) 728–5225 or (800) 575–7483, www.historicbeaufort.com.

Shackleford Banks is visible from the third level of most any building in Beaufort or from the sandy beach of Fort Macon State Park. It is one of three barrier islands that comprise the Cape Lookout National Seashore. Shackleford Banks is distinguished by its indigenous herds of wild horses that are traceable to the Spanish mustangs of the earliest New World explorers. These horses and their spring foals are a beautiful sight on the dunes of the island, which stretches 7 miles to the Cape Lookout lighthouse. Other than two park service docks and one toilet facility, there are no comforts on Shackleford Banks; if you go, take your own and bring back any trash. Take a bag for shells too, and prepare to enjoy a fabulous beach where you may be the only person in sight. Access is fastest from the Beaufort downtown waterfront, where passenger ferry services operate year-round for $12 per person round-trip. The 2002 Rand McNally Atlas picked Shackleford Banks as one of the Best of the Road destinations for its beaches and wild horses. (252) 728–2250, www.nps.gov/calo.

Rachel Carson Estuarine Reserve is the island that you will see directly across from the Beaufort downtown waterfront. Named for the author of *Silent Spring*, a book that forecast the devastation of the chemical DDT on the natural environment and stopped its use as an insecticide, this state reserve is an easy destination by rowboat or ferry service ($8.00 round-trip). It's a fast island getaway and a great place to rake clams and take home some steamers. The horses here are released domestic horses that have lived wild on the island since the 1920s, and about 160 species of birds make the Rachel Carson Reserve their home. (252) 728–2170, www.ncnerr.org/cerf.

WHERE TO SHOP

With the transiting yachts at the dock, boating activity in Taylor's Creek, and the wild horses of the Rachel Carson Reserve on the island that parallels Front Street, shopping along Beaufort's downtown waterfront is a pleasure. A few favorite retail stops along the four-block waterfront shopping area:

Down East Gallery. 519 Front Street, Beaufort 28516. Here you'll find the beautifully detailed paintings and prints of artist Alan Cheek, whose favorite subject is the beauty of the Crystal Coast. Open daily, except Monday during winter. (252) 728–4410.

The Jarrett Bay Boat House. 507 Front Street, Beaufort 28516. A broad selection of yacht-themed gifts is offered. Open daily. (252) 728–6363.

Bird Shoal Peddler and The Red Door. 222 Front Street, Beaufort 28516. I enjoyed the humor, color, and Down East saltiness of this gift shop's proprietors, as well as the selection of silver jewelry, sarongs, and coastal and tropical housewares. Open daily. (252) 728–5361.

Tierra Fina. 117 Turner Street, Beaufort 28516. Featuring Spanish pottery and glassware, this shop offers a frequently changing variety of pottery. Open daily. (252) 504–2789.

WHERE TO EAT

Clawson's 1905. 429 Front Street, Beaufort 28516. The varied atmospheres of this restaurant include an espresso bar, a traditional bar, a dining room with private booths, and private dining in several locations. It's a great restaurant choice for a burger or the house specialty, a stuffed baked potato called a Dirigible. Entrees are varied, and seafood specials are announced each night. Lunch favorites always include the seafood bisque in warm months and chili when it's cold. $$–$$$. (252) 728–2133, www.clawsonsrestaurant.com.

The Net House Steam Restaurant and Oyster Bar. 133 Turner Street, Beaufort 28516. Across the street from the Beaufort Historic Site, this restaurant specializes in local seafood. It's the restaurant choice for a cool night in oyster season, and it's the only restaurant in the area where steamers include clams and crabs. $$–$$$. (252) 728–2002.

The Sandbar at Town Creek Marina. 232 West Beaufort Road, Beaufort 28557. A perfect destination on an outdoor day when dining on the deck is essential. Away from the downtown hubbub, the Sandbar is distinctive among Beaufort restaurants for actually having a rather peaceful atmosphere. It's upstairs, with porches surrounding it on three sides. Views and breezes are constant. The lunch and dinner menus are food wise, may be a bit trendy, but reliably delicious and not overpriced. $$–$$$. (252) 504–7263.

Beaufort Grocery Company. 117 Queen Street, Beaufort 28557. Fabulous dishes come from a professional kitchen and inspired menus in a setting with brick walls, wood floors, and close tables, which makes it a noisy choice if you want to visit with your dining partners. Really great take-out lunches include specialty salads and breads. Pick one up and enjoy it outside in the Rachel Carson Reserve on the other side of Taylor's Creek from the downtown waterfront area. $$. (252) 728–3899.

Loughry's Landing. 502 Front Street, Beaufort 28516. Located on the Beaufort boardwalk, Loughry's Landing specializes in seafood, steaks, ribs, and pastas. Enjoy your meal with a view of the harbor and wild horses on Carrot Island. Open for lunch and dinner. $$. (252) 728–7541, www.loughryslanding.com.

WHERE TO STAY

Langdon House. 135 Craven Street, Beaufort 28557. This bed-and-breakfast, the oldest in Beaufort, is a mere 265 years old. Hand-forged nails and hand-wrought timbers testify to the authentic charm of this old home. Owners Jimm and Lizzet Prest will help you wind down so that you can quickly adapt to the town's tranquillity. Rockers on their broad porches help achieve that state of mind, as does the absence of televisions in guest rooms. "We're out on the edge of the continent without all the day-to-day distractions," Jimm says. "It can be very refreshing, but it can also take some getting used to. I had a guest from New York tell me that he had to turn on his bathroom fan. It was too quiet for him. He couldn't get to sleep." Great breakfasts, genuine hospitality, and the delightful upper-floor porch turn guests into old friends. $$. (252) 728–5499, www.langdonhouse.com.

Beaufort Inn. 101 Ann Street, Beaufort 28516. The AAA three-diamond Beaufort Inn has forty-four guest rooms, a dining room, an exercise room, and a large outdoor hot tub spa. Within walking distance of all attractions, its rooms have private balconies with rockers, and a complimentary breakfast is served in the dining room. $$-$$$. (252) 728–2600 or (800) 726–0321, www.beaufort-inn.com.

Inlet Inn. 601 Front Street, Beaufort 28516. Well located, the inn offers some rooms with views to the Cape Lookout Lighthouse, Beaufort Inlet, and Shackleford Banks; others offer balconies, fireplaces, or window seats. All have a perfect location and cozy comforts on Beaufort's downtown waterfront. $$. (252) 728–3600 or (800) 554–5466.

Pecan Tree Inn. 116 Queen Street, Beaufort 28557. This inn offers rooms or suites with Jacuzzis, Victorian architecture, English gardens, surrounding porches, and a half-block walk to the waterfront. (252) 728–6733.

The Cedars Inn. 305 Front Street, Beaufort 28516. Located in the heart of Beaufort's historic district, this charming inn (circa 1768) has eleven rooms and suites, all with private baths and cable television. Sitting rooms, fireplaces, and old-fashioned claw-footed tubs complete the romantic setting. The Cedars is known for its sumptuous full American breakfasts. Wine bar and free bicycles are available for guests' convenience. $$. (252) 728–7036, www.cedarsinn.com.

Harborside Suites. Located over the street-level shops at 507 Front Street, Beaufort 28516. With efficiency rooms and two- and three-bedroom suites on the downtown waterfront of Beaufort, all units open to a private deck on top of the building with an upper deck that offers a fabulous view of Shackleford Banks, Beaufort Inlet, and the Cape Lookout Lighthouse. Distinguishing this property, other than its location and views, are the retro furnishings and tile work in each unit. One two-bedroom unit allows pets. Rentals are offered by Beaufort Realty Company, (252) 728–5462, www.beaufortrlty.com/rentals/rental008.html.

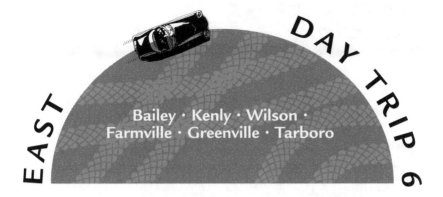

For this day trip, head east on US 64 toward Rocky Mount, taking the exit for US 264 east in the direction of Wilson, forty-five minutes from Raleigh. On the way, stop off in Bailey to visit the Country Doctor Museum, then detour on NC 581 south for a dot of a town known as Kenly. After crossing I-95, look for the signs pointing the way to the Tobacco Farm Life Museum.

Hopefully, you've timed your visit so that you will arrive in Wilson, north on US 301, for lunch at Dick's Hot Dogs, celebrating more than eighty years in business. Spend the afternoon in Wilson before kicking up the trail dust to make way for Farmville, where you can stretch your legs and learn a bit more about farm life.

With your car still pointed east on US 264, head for Greenville, a college town that bills itself as the "Gateway to Eastern North Carolina." If you have a long weekend, you could combine this day trip with Washington (East Day Trip 2) and New Bern (East Day Trip 1), making an extended loop back to Raleigh-Durham. If you do this, make sure you see East Day Trip 3 to learn about "Barbecue Highway," which follows US 70, the main artery between New Bern and Raleigh.

Otherwise, leave Greenville by way of NC 43 north, which passes B's Barbecue. (There's more about B's on the pages that follow.) Follow the signs to Tarboro, where you'll make a quick stop before heading west on US 64 back to Raleigh-Durham.

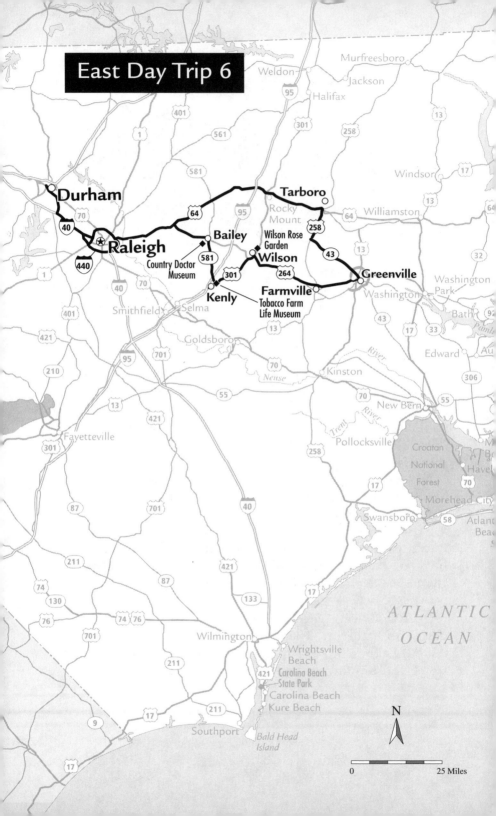

East Day Trip 6

Durham

Tarboro

Raleigh

Bailey

Wilson Rose
Garden

Wilson

Country Doctor
Museum

Kenly

Farmville

Tobacco Farm
Life Museum

Greenville

N

0   25 Miles

BAILEY

Just thirty minutes east of the capital city, Bailey (population 670) is farm country. The town was settled in about 1860, incorporated in 1907, and named for Joe Bailey, an early settler.

WHERE TO GO

Country Doctor Museum. 6642 Peele Road, Bailey 27807. The Country Doctor Museum is the only medical museum in the nation dedicated to rural physicians who practiced medicine in North Carolina and the South during the nineteenth and early twentieth centuries. A composite restoration of two doctors' offices includes the Dr. Howard Franklin Freeman Office, built in 1857, which comprises the Apothecary Area, and the Dr. Cornelius Henry Brantley Office, circa 1887, which portrays the early doctor's office, with instruments and equipment of the day. In three century-old and two modern buildings, the Country Doctor Museum collects and preserves the medical instruments and tools of pharmacy used by country doctors, and the diaries, papers, and medical books of these rural physicians. Open Tuesday through Saturday 10:00 A.M. until 4:00 P.M., Sunday 2:00 to 5:00 P.M. (252) 235-4165, www.ncmsalliance.org/doctorsmuseum.htm.

WHERE TO SHOP

Finch Pottery and Nursery. 5714 Finch Nursery Lane, Bailey 27807. Browse through acclaimed potter Dan Finch's stoneware, porcelain, wood-fired, salt-glazed, and raku pottery selection. Along with pots, you'll also find handcrafted bluebird homes and blueberry plants at the nursery. (252) 235-4664, www.danfinch.com.

KENLY

More than double the population of Bailey, Kenly is located in the heart of tobacco country. The town, settled in about 1875, was named for an executive of the Atlantic Coast Line Railroad.

WHERE TO GO

Tobacco Farm Life Museum. 709 Church Street (US 301 North), Kenly 27893. This exceptional museum bills itself as a "living time capsule, offering a window back in time through which visitors experience a way of life that has all but disappeared." That way of life was tobacco farming. Flue-cured tobacco became the first major cash-producing agricultural commodity for the region during the late 1800s. A 6,000-square-foot exhibit hall displays artifacts from all aspects of farm life, along with a hands-on children's exhibit. Household goods, musical instruments, clothing, and agricultural tools are displayed. A restored farmstead with main house, detached kitchen, and smokehouse depicts rural life as it was during the Great Depression. Open Monday through Saturday 9:30 A.M. until 5:00 P.M., Sunday 2:00 to 5:00 P.M. Adults, $3.00; children K–12 and seniors age 65 and over, $2.00. (800) 441-7829, www.tobmuseum.bbnp.com.

WHERE TO EAT

Patrick's Cafeteria. US 301, Kenly 27542. Pull up a chair at Patrick's for down-home Southern-style cooking: fatback, grits, homemade sweet potato biscuits, collard greens, fried chicken, meat loaf, pecan pie, and more. $–$$. Open Monday through Saturday 5:00 A.M. until 8:30 P.M., Sunday 10:30 A.M. until 3:00 P.M. (800) 948-4184, www.southernstylecooking.com.

WILSON

The Tuscaroras were the first to settle in Wilson, but European settlers soon moved into the native tribe's domain, forcing them out. The new settlers carved out family farms from the wilderness, and the town of Wilson, incorporated in 1849 as a farm market, could boast three grocery stores and two physicians a few years later.

During the Civil War, Wilson was strategically important to the Confederacy, although no battles were fought here. The Wilmington to Weldon Railroad, connecting Robert E. Lee's Army of Northern Virginia to its primary source of supplies at Wilmington, traveled through Wilson, which also served as the site of a military hospital.

Following the war, falling cotton prices prompted farmers in the region to adopt a new cash crop: tobacco. The first bright leaf tobacco was planted in the 1870s. From that time until the end of the last century, farmers, auctioneers, and buyers kept Wilson's tobacco warehouses humming.

WHERE TO GO

Historic Walking Tour of Downtown Wilson. 124 East Nash Street, Wilson 27893. More than twenty-five historic buildings, churches, and homes are listed on the National Register of Historic Places. Enjoy the tree-lined streets of downtown Wilson on foot or by car. (800) 497-7398.

Tobacco warehouses. Wilson is home to America's largest tobacco market. From July to November, the tobacco markets are open for tours. Listen to auctioneers selling tobacco at 500 words per minute! The best time to observe a sale is around 10:00 A.M. Free tours are available Monday through Thursday 9:30 to 11:00 A.M. (252) 243-8440.

Wilson Rose Garden. 1800 Herring Avenue, Wilson 27893. More than 1,000 rose plants consisting of 155 different varieties, ranging from old garden to modern hybrids, include old garden roses, English roses (David Austin roses), hybrid teas, floribundas, grandifloras, climbing roses, miniatures, and shrub roses. Art statuary is incorporated into the garden, the centerpiece of the collection being a 10-foot-tall Georgia marble fountain sculpture by internationally known sculptor Horace Farlowe. The garden is open to the public daily from dawn until dark. Admission is free. (252) 399-2266.

Imagination Station. 224 East Nash Street, Wilson 27893. Located in downtown Wilson, Imagination Station presents adventure for children and adults. There are more than 200 hands-on exhibits, with live science shows daily. Open Monday through Saturday 9:00 A.M. to 5:00 P.M. Admission is $3.00 for adults, $2.50 for children under 17. (252) 291-5113.

Vollis Simpson's Whirligigs. 7219 Oscar Loop, Lucama 27851. This is one of the most unique sights you will ever see. Eight miles south of Wilson, Vollis Simpson has created large, living sculptures in the form of windmills. To add to the effect, many pieces have reflective parts. Drive by in the day to see the giant colorful creations, then again at night when the wind is kicking up. Some of Simpson's works have been exhibited in museums from Boston to Atlanta, as well as at the 1996 Olympics. www.sci.mus.mn.us/sln/vollis/.

WHERE TO SHOP

Boone's Antiques. 2014 US Highway 301 South, Wilson 27893. With more than thirty antique shops, Wilson claims to be one of the largest antique markets in the eastern United States. Boone's is a good place to begin your shopping extravaganza. Open Monday through Saturday 10:00 A.M. until 5:00 P.M. (252) 237–1508.

WHERE TO EAT

Bill's Barbecue and Chicken Restaurant. 3007 Downing Street, Wilson 27893. A favorite among the locals, Bill's serves barbecue, chicken, and seafood. Open daily from 9:00 A.M. until 9:00 P.M. $–$$. (252) 237–4372.

  Dick's Hot Dog Stand. 1500 West Nash Street, Wilson 27893. Founded in 1921 by Socrates "Dick" Gliarmis, a native of Samos, Greece, Dick's Hot Dog Stand is still going strong. Dick is long gone, but his son Lee "Socrates" carries on the tradition. Ever optimistic about his business's continuing longevity, in 2001 he published a brochure, *Dick's Hot Dog Stand: The First 80 Years,* which thanks customers for their patronage. "We served Dick's Hot Dogs through the roaring 20s and both world wars and never missed a beat. Even through the Great Depression, we found the support to continue without ever having to close our doors." Local girl Ava Gardner, who hailed from just down the road in Smithfield, dined here. Make sure to order your dog with chili, which Gliarmis makes from a secret family recipe. Open Tuesday through Thursday 10:00 A.M. until 3:00 P.M., Friday and Sunday 10:00 A.M. until 8:30 P.M., Saturday 7:30 A.M. until 3:30 P.M. $–$$. (252) 243–6313.

WHERE TO STAY

Miss Betty's Bed & Breakfast Inn and Executive Suites. 600 West Nash Street, Wilson 27893. Located in the gracious setting of downtown Wilson's historic district, Miss Betty's is a recipient of AAA's three-diamond rating. Quiet Victorian charm abounds in an atmosphere of modern-day conveniences. Miss Betty's is a complex of four buildings, all historic homes that together provide fourteen lovely overnight accommodations, ten of which are in the B&B inn. Guests have their choice of three king suites, two queen guest rooms, four double guest rooms, and one twin guest room. A full country breakfast is included. $$. (800) 258–2058. www.missbettysbnb.com.

FARMVILLE

Settled in about 1850 and known as New Town before it was incorporated in 1872, Farmville is a pretty, small town with a central main street lined with shops. As you may surmise, the town was named for the fact that it was in the center of rich farming land.

WHERE TO GO

The May Museum and Park. 213 South Main Street, Farmville 27828. The museum, located in the Farmville Historic District, chronicles the cultural and commercial heritage of Farmville and western Pitt County from colonial times to the present. The museum is housed in an 1870s-era home and interprets the area's history through both permanent exhibits and special programs that are offered periodically throughout the year. The museum is home to an extensive collection of nineteenth- and early twentieth-century quilts, one of the oldest collections in the state, which are displayed on a rotating basis. Open 10:00 A.M. until 5:00 P.M. Wednesday through Saturday or by appointment. Free. (252) 753–5814, www.farmville-nc.com.

GREENVILLE

Founded in the mid-1700s, Greenville was originally known as Martinsborough in honor of Josiah Martin, who served from 1771 to 1775 as the last royal governor of North Carolina. The county seat of Pitt County changed its name in 1786 to honor Revolutionary War hero Nathanael Greene.

Home to East Carolina University, established in 1908, the city is the cultural, commercial, educational, and medical hub for Pitt County's 126,000 residents. Be sure to drive or walk through the College View Historical District, placed on the National Register of Historic Places in 1992, on the north side of Fifth Street.

Greenville presents national-quality performing arts, including Sunday in the Park during the summer and Freeboot Fridays, a series of outdoor "Alive at Five"-style Friday night concerts preceding ECU Pirates home football games.

WHERE TO GO

Wellington B. Gray Gallery. East Carolina University School of Art, Fifth Street, Greenville 27858. Located on the East Carolina University campus, the gallery features exhibits of nationally and internationally known contemporary artists in fine arts, crafts, graphics, video, and installation art, as well as student and faculty exhibitions. Open Monday through Saturday 10:00 A.M. to 5:00 P.M., Thursday until 8:00 P.M. (252) 328-6336, www.ecu.edu/graygallery/.

Greenville Museum of Art. 802 South Evans Street, Greenville 27834. One of the state's oldest museums, founded in 1939, the Greenville Museum of Art presents changing exhibits from its permanent collection of nineteenth- and twentieth-century American art, as well as traveling regional and national exhibits. The museum also owns one of the largest public collections of North Carolina Jugtown pottery. Open Tuesday through Friday 10:00 A.M. until 4:30 P.M., Saturday and Sunday 1:00 to 4:00 P.M. Admission is free. (252) 758-1946.

Ledonia Wright African-American Cultural Center. Bloxton House on East Carolina University Campus, Greenville 27858. The cultural center houses East Carolina University's 150-piece art collection made by the Kuba of Zaire. Open Monday through Thursday 8:00 A.M. until 8:00 P.M., Friday until 5:00 P.M. (252) 328-1680, www.ecu.edu/lwcc/.

WHERE TO SHOP

Artisans Market. 2500 South Charles Boulevard, Greenville 27858. More than sixty shops sell decorative accessories and fine gifts. (252) 355-5536.

New River Pottery. 3750 Sterling Point Drive, Winterville (6 miles south of Greenville's city center). Offering selections of flowers, glassware, pottery, and linens, New River is open Monday through Saturday 9:00 A.M. until 9:00 P.M., Sunday 11:00 A.M. until 6:00 P.M. (252) 756–1776.

WHERE TO EAT

B's Barbecue. Corner of NC 43 and B's Barbecue Road, Greenville 27858. Don't be put off by the appearance. It's been said that "B's Barbecue is . . . a joint so exclusive, elusive and way cool that it doesn't even have a phone or published address." $–$$.

TARBORO

Incorporated in 1760, Tarboro is a beautiful small town with a forty-five-block residential historic district. Stroll the tree-lined streets and restored neighborhoods of this town located on the Tar River. A thriving riverport throughout the eighteenth and nineteenth centuries, Tarboro was once a candidate to become North Carolina's capital city.

WHERE TO GO

Blount-Bridgers House. 130 Bridgers Street, Tarboro 27886. This Federal-style plantation house was built around 1808 by Thomas Blount, a prominent Edgecombe County businessman and United States Congressman. "The Grove," as it was known then, occupied a 296-acre tract of land purchased in 1795. Today the home serves as a museum and art gallery. The first floor displays a collection of nineteenth-century furniture, furnishings, and Edgecombe County memorabilia. The second floor houses the Hobson Pittman Memorial Gallery and a living museum to Pittman (1899–1972), Edgecombe County's premier artist. Open April through November, Monday through Friday 10:00 A.M. until 4:00 P.M., Saturday and Sunday 2:00 to 4:00 P.M. Admission is $2.00. (252) 823–4159, www.albemarle-nc.com/tarboro.

WHERE TO STAY

Lady Ann of Tarboro Bed and Breakfast Inn. 1205 Main Street North, Tarboro 27886. This elegant Italianate-style Victorian home is just around the corner from the historic Blount-Bridgers House. Call after 5:00 P.M. for reservations or more information. $$. (252) 641–1438.

Little Warren Bed and Breakfast. 304 East Park Avenue, Tarboro 27886. This large and gracious family home, renovated and modernized with spacious rooms, is located in a quiet neighborhood of the historic district. Originally built in 1913, the home has a deeply set wraparound front porch that overlooks the Town Common, which is one of only two originally chartered commons remaining in the United States. Full English, American Southern, and expanded continental breakfasts are elegantly served. Patsy and Tom Miller purchased the home in 1984 after twenty-four years of living in Africa, the Orient, England, and several parts of the United States. Fresh flowers, fluffy towels, terry cloth robes, and electric blankets are among the guest room amenities. $$. (800) 309–1314, www.bbonline.com/nc/littlewarren/.

SOUTHEAST DAY TRIP 1

Wilmington · Wrightsville Beach · Carolina Beach · Kure Beach

This day trip, a straight shot from Raleigh-Durham on I–40 east, mixes history, Hollywood, beaches, amusements, and great food. The area offers riverboat tours, plantation visits, and beaches only minutes away.

The core of this trip is Wilmington, which has the charm of Charleston, South Carolina, but without the crowds. Wilmington appeals to visitors, who can begin with a carriage ride, then visit the many historic homes downtown, dine by the Cape Fear River, and browse the eclectic shops.

Only fifteen minutes away from downtown is Wrightsville Beach. Located on an island, the small town still retains much of its turn-of-the-century charm. A little farther is Carolina Beach, which offers several interesting nature excursions, including guided kayak ecotours of the coastal marshlands. Carolina Beach State Park provides visitors a chance to see the rare Venus-flytrap.

Down the road, at Kure Beach, is historic Fort Fisher, a Civil War earthen fortress that was lost to Union troops. A few minutes from the historic site is the new aquarium, which boasts a 200,000-gallon ocean aquarium. From here you could head back to Wilmington or take the ferry to charming Southport (see Southeast Day Trip 2) before looping back to Raleigh.

WILMINGTON

Although the town of Brunswick was founded on the west bank of the Cape Fear River in 1726, a new settlement farther upriver began

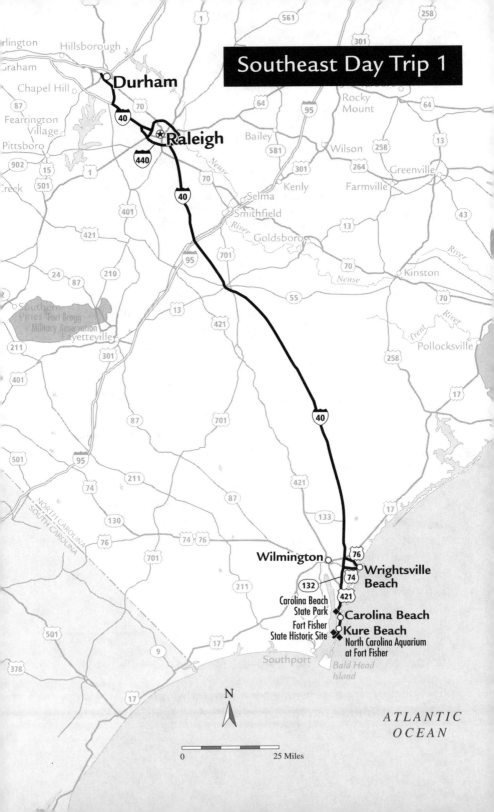

Southeast Day Trip 1

Durham

Raleigh

Wilmington

Wrightsville Beach

Carolina Beach State Park

Carolina Beach

Fort Fisher State Historic Site

Kure Beach

North Carolina Aquarium at Fort Fisher

ATLANTIC OCEAN

N

0   25 Miles

to take root in 1729. The new settlement, a trading post, was referred to as Dram Tree, and later called New Liverpool, New Carthage, New Town, and Newton. When Colonial Governor Gabriel Johnston took office, he incorporated the City of Wilmington in 1740, naming it after Spencer Compton, Earl of Wilmington.

British forces captured the city in 1781. General Cornwallis occupied the **Burgwin-Wright House,** which you will visit on this day trip, but he withdrew to Yorktown later that year only to watch his army collapse. Following the Revolutionary War, Wilmington flourished. Estates and plantations were established on the outskirts, and fine homes were built downtown. Although nearly 30 miles along the Cape Fear River from the Atlantic Ocean, Wilmington flourished as a major port and shipbuilding center. The city became the site of the world's largest cotton exchange.

To get cotton and other exports to the port, the world's longest rail line, the Wilmington & Weldon Railroad, was completed in 1840 and helped to make Wilmington the largest city in the state that year. With its railroad and access to the Atlantic, Wilmington became the Confederacy's most important port. Nearby **Fort Fisher** was built in 1861 to protect the port city.

At the turn of the twentieth century, the Wilmington & Weldon and several other railroads merged to become the Atlantic Coast Line Railroad. The company headquarters were established in Wilmington, but by 1910 the city had lost its claim as the state's largest as inland cities grew fat on the tobacco and textile industries. During World War I, shipbuilding and cotton exports thrived in Wilmington, but the Great Depression brought production in both industries to a halt. World War II saw a resurgence in shipbuilding, and the port city sent to sea 243 ships.

In 1960, the Atlantic Coast Line moved its headquarters, along with 1,000 employees and their families, to Jacksonville, Florida, representing the largest single move of employees ever staged by a Southeastern industry. The move dealt a severe blow to Wilmington's economy. City leaders, however, undertook a major initiative to bring new industry to the area, and by 1966, Wilmington, showing signs of recovery, was designated an "All American City" by the National Civic League.

During the 1970s, downtown developers began a strong revitalization effort while preservationists sought protection for the historic downtown homes and buildings. Their combined efforts resulted in a revitalized downtown that attracts visitors today.

In the 1980s, a major film studio came to Wilmington. Often referred to as "Hollywood East" or "Wilmywood," Wilmington has consistently ranked among the nation's top locations for film production. Several stars call Wilmington home.

A carriage tour is the best way to get an overview of the city's history. The historic district is compact enough that you can walk to the many buildings and sites open to visitors.

WHERE TO GO

Cape Fear Coast Convention and Visitors Bureau. 24 North Third Street, Wilmington 28401. Look for the tall redbrick building with the clock. The CVB also operates a kiosk on the river at the foot of Market Street. (800) 222–4757, www.cape-fear-nc.us.

Cape Fear Museum. 814 Market Street, Wilmington 28401. Established in 1898 as a Confederate museum, this is the state's oldest history museum. Explore regional history in the exhibition *Waves & Currents: The Lower Cape Fear Story*, featuring a model of 1860 Wilmington and a diorama of the historic battle of Fort Fisher. Discover regional ecology in the Michael Jordan Discovery Gallery. (The basketball star was born nearby.) Open Tuesday through Saturday 9:00 A.M. until 5:00 P.M., Sunday 2:00 to 5:00 P.M. Also open Monday from Memorial Day through Labor Day. Admission: Adults, $6.00; children ages 3 through 12, $3.00. (910) 341–4350.

Wilmington Railroad Museum. 501 Nutt Street, Wilmington 28401. Displays include artifacts and memorabilia from the Wilmington & Weldon Railroad, which ran on 161 miles of track, making it the longest rail line in the world in 1840. For more than a century, railroading was Wilmington's chief industry. Explore extensive displays of model trains, photographs, and artifacts, ranging from a 150-ton locomotive to a conductor's four-ounce timepiece. A steam locomotive (be sure to clang the working bell) and caboose may be boarded, and there's a hands-on children's corner. Open Monday through Saturday 10:00 A.M. until 5:00 P.M. and Sunday 1:00 to 5:00 P.M. March 15 through October 14; Monday through Saturday 10:00 A.M. until 4:00 P.M. October 15 through March 14. Adults, $3.00; seniors/ military, $2.00; children ages 3 to 12, $1.50. (910) 763–2634.

Jungle Rapids Family Fun Park. 5320 Oleander Drive, Wilmington 28403. Cool off in the one million-gallon wavepool. This waterpark and entertainment facility features water slides, go-cart tracks, jungle golf, laser tag, more than one hundred arcade games, kids' indoor playground, cafe, and pizzeria. Open year-round; waterpark open seasonally. (910) 791–0666, www.junglerapids.com.

Poplar Grove Plantation. US 17 North, Wilmington 28411. Poplar Grove was the homestead of a successful farming family. The home, outbuildings, and crafts are typical of an 1800s-era working community. The 628-acre plantation produced peas, corn, and beans, and held some sixty-four slaves. Open Monday through Saturday 9:00 A.M. until 5:00 P.M., Sunday noon until 5:00 P.M. Closed Easter Sunday and Thanksgiving Day. Admission, which includes home tour, is $7.00 for adults, $6.00 for seniors, and $3.00 for ages 6 to 15. (910) 686–9518, www.poplargrove.com.

Henrietta III **Riverboat.** Boards at Dock and Water Streets. Captain Carl Marshburn narrates the history of the Cape Fear River as North Carolina's largest riverboat makes its way downstream and back. Narrated sightseeing tours, some with lunch, are offered several times daily from April through October. Dinner cruises are offered through December. (800) 676–0162.

River Taxi. Travels between the foot of Market Street and the battleship *North Carolina* during June, July, and August. The taxi can be boarded at either Market Street or the battleship. (800) 676–0162.

Ghost Walk of Old Wilmington. Explore Wilmington's haunted alleyways and cemeteries. Under the shadows of moss-draped live oaks, discover acts of murder, mayhem, betrayal, and other unfortunate circumstances. Offered April 1 through October 31, 8:30 P.M. nightly; November 1 through March 31, Friday and Saturday at 6:30 P.M. Admission is $12 for adults, $10 for seniors and children, under 7 free. For location and reservations (required) call (910) 602–6055.

Historic Downtown Wilmington. Protected as North Carolina's largest historic district, within these 230 blocks are beautiful homes dating from the late 1700s that are open for touring, and more than 200 specialty shops. In the core downtown are twenty-nine restaurants within five blocks, plus twenty-six inns and bed-and-breakfasts. Actor Dennis Hopper owns property downtown.

Springbrook Farms Inc. Water and Market Streets, Wilmington 28402. Owners John and Janet Pucci offer seven separate carriage and horse-drawn-trolley tours through historic downtown Wilmington. Costumed drivers narrate the journey through past and present downtown. It's a great way to get acquainted with the rich history of this port city. Adults, $9.00; children under 12, $4.00. Carriage tours are offered year-round, but call ahead for schedules in January and February. (910) 251-8889, www.horsedrawntours.com.

Bellamy Mansion. 503 Market Street, Wilmington 28402. Built as the city residence of prominent planter and doctor John D. Bellamy, this home is one of the state's most spectacular examples of antebellum architecture. Wrapped by stalwart Corinthian columns, the restored twenty-two-room home features white marble mantels, ornate cornice moldings, and elaborate brass chandeliers. Open Wednesday through Saturday 10:00 A.M. to 5:00 P.M., Sunday 1:00 to 5:00 P.M. Admission is $6.00 for adults, $3.00 for children ages 5 to 12. (910) 251-3700, www.bellamymansionmuseum.org.

Latimer House. 126 South Third Street, Wilmington 28401. Prosperous local businessman Zebulon Latimer chose the popular Victorian Italianate style for his new home in 1852. Designed to be symmetrical, the fourteen-room home displays more than 600 historic objects, including furniture, jewelry, ephemera, tableware, tools, and more. Open Monday through Friday 10:00 A.M. until 4:00 P.M., Saturday and Sunday noon until 5:00 P.M. Admission is $6.00. (910) 762-0492, www.latimer.wilmington.org.

Burgwin-Wright House. 224 Market Street, Wilmington 28401. Using an old jail as its foundation, the Burgwin-Wright House was built in 1770 by John Burgwin, planter, merchant, and treasurer of the colony of Carolina. In 1781, Lord Cornwallis occupied "the most considerable house in town" shortly before his defeat and surrender at Yorktown, Virginia. Purchased by Joshua Grainger Wright in 1799 for 3,500 Spanish milled dollars, the home was occupied as a residence until 1937, when the National Society of the Colonial Dames of America bought it. Beautifully restored, the Burgwin-Wright House is the oldest museum house in Southeastern North Carolina. See fine details of Georgian-style architecture. A formal or parterre garden, a terraced garden, and an orchard grace the house. Open Tuesday through Saturday 10:00 A.M. until 4:00 P.M. Guided tours are available. (910) 762-0570, www.geocities.com/picketfence/garden/4354/.

Tour Tip: Tickets for all three house museums in Wilmington—the Latimer House, the Bellamy Mansion, and the Burgwin-Wright House—are available for $14.50 from any of the museums.

Airlie Gardens. 300 Airlie Road, Wilmington 28403. Designed in the early 1900s, Airlie Gardens encompasses sixty-seven acres of post-Victorian European-style gardens with ten acres of freshwater lakes. Offered is a one-mile walking tour amid azaleas, camellias, statuary, and the historic Airlie Oak. Open May through October, Friday and Saturday from 9:00 A.M. until 5:00 P.M. and Sunday 1:00 to 5:00 P.M. Admission is $8.00 for adults, $7.00 for seniors, $2.00 for children. (910) 256–6160, airliegardens.wilmington.org.

Thalian Hall. 102 North Third and 310 Chestnut Street, Wilmington 28401. Built in 1855 for combined government and theater use and restored in 1909, this classic nineteenth-century opera house hosted such famous performers as Buffalo Bill Cody, Lillian Russell, John Philip Sousa, and Oscar Wilde. Today, Thalian Hall hosts a variety of performing arts. Call for event listings. (800) 523–2820.

Louise Wells Cameron Art Museum. 3201 South 17th Street, Wilmington 28401. Formerly St. John's Museum, the new 42,000-square-foot museum highlights two centuries of such North Carolina artists as Minnie Evans, Claude Howell, Mary Cassatt, Jugtown potters, and more. Open Tuesday through Thursday 10:00 A.M. to 5:00 P.M., Friday 10:00 A.M. to 8:00 P.M., Saturday 10:00 A.M. to 5:00 P.M., and Sunday 10:30 A.M. to 4:00 P.M. Admission is $8.00 for families, $5.00 for adults, $2.00 for children ages 5 to 12. (910) 395–5999, www.cameronartmuseum.com.

Battleship North Carolina. US 17, Wilmington 28402. Moored across the river from downtown Wilmington, this 1941 vessel played a part in every major naval offensive in the Pacific during World War II. Open daily from 8:00 A.M. until 8:00 P.M. mid-May through mid-September, until 5:00 P.M. the rest of the year. Admission: adults, $8.00; seniors and active military duty, $7.00; children ages 6 to 11, $4.00; 5 and under, free. (910) 251–5797, www.battleshipnc.com.

Wilmington Trolley Company. Duck and Water Streets, Wilmington 28401. This 8-mile narrated sightseeing tour lasts forty-five minutes. Tours are conducted Tuesday through Sunday from April through October, (910) 763–4483.

Tote-Em-In Zoo and Gift Shop. 5811 Carolina Beach Road, Wilmington 28401. The largest zoo in southeastern North Carolina houses more than one hundred animals. Besides the menagerie-type zoo, there are two museums and a gift shop. (910) 791-0472.

The Children's Museum. 1020 Market Street, Wilmington 28401. the Children's Museum has hands-on exhibits and play areas for kids. Open Tuesday through Saturday 10:00 A.M. until 4:00 P.M. Open Mondays in June, July, and August. Open most holidays, and the first Sunday of every month, when admission is free from 1:00 to 4:00 P.M. Children, $3.50; adults, $1.50. (910) 254-3534.

WHERE TO SHOP

Historic Downtown Wilmington. You'll find several shopping areas all within walking distance of one another: Wilmington City Market, Jacobi Warehouse, and the Coast Line Center, as well as Chandler's Wharf, an original ship's chandler that provided supplies for seagoing vessels, and the Cotton Exchange, once home to the largest cotton exporting company in the world, comprising eight buildings that date from the nineteenth century.

Lumina Station. 1900 Eastwood Road, Wilmington 28403. For several decades near the turn of the twentieth century, Lumina was the social center of this region. People came to dance to the sounds of such greats as Cab Calloway, Benny Goodman, Guy Lombardo, and "Satchmo." Today's Lumina Station remains true to the original landmark's style and spirit. Fine dining and shopping are to be found in the twenty-seven shops. (910) 236-0900, www.luminastation.com.

WHERE TO EAT

The Pilot House. 2 Ann Street, Wilmington 28401. Providing Southern cuisine overlooking the Cape Fear River, the Pilot House offers indoor and outdoor dining in a quaint 1865 home moved here during the 1970s. River views can be enjoyed from the covered "uptown porch." Entrees include pasta, beef, lamb, pork, and seafood. Open daily for lunch and dinner. $$–$$$. (910) 343-0200.

Water Street Restaurant. 5 South Water Street, Wilmington 28401. This sidewalk cafe, housed in what used to be a peanut warehouse, offers full views of the river. The menu includes "something for everyone," ranging from vegetarian dishes to beef, seafood, and chicken. Indoor seating is available, and live entertainment makes this restaurant an inviting nightspot. Open Sunday through Thursday 11:30 A.M. until 10:00 P.M. for lunch and dinner, until midnight Friday and Saturday. $$-$$$. (910) 343-0042.

Trails End Steaks Etc. 613 Trails End Road, Wilmington 28401. Overlooking the Intracoastal Waterway near Whiskey Creek, Trails End prepares not only steaks and seafood but also a hospitality table, a local favorite that includes spicy meatballs, clam strips, cheeses, olives, and much more. Open for dinner Monday through Saturday year-round, and nightly during the summer season. $$-$$$. (910) 791-2034.

Eddie Romanelli's. 5400 Oleander Drive, Wilmington 28401. Voted best restaurant by *Encore* magazine, Eddie Romanelli's serves regional dishes with an Italian flair. Try the crab dip for starters, and follow it with a homemade 12-inch pizza. Open every day. $$-$$$. (910) 799-7000.

WHERE TO STAY

The Verandas. 202 Nun Street, Wilmington 28401. This elegant 8,500-square-foot Victorian Italianate Mansion in the historic district is only two blocks from the Cape Fear River and the River-walk. Originally built in 1853 by Benjamin Beery, the structure suffered extensive fire and water damage in 1992. Boarded up and decaying, the mansion was restored to provide a comfortable weekend retreat for tourists. All eight guest rooms are large corner rooms. Guests may choose from a selection of king, queen, or twin beds. Luxurious private baths have marble floors and oversize oval tubs. $$$. (910) 251-2212, www.verandas.com.

The Wilmingtonian. 101 South Second Street, Wilmington 28401. Located in historic downtown Wilmington, surrounded by beautifully restored nineteenth-century homes and tree-lined neighborhoods, the meticulously renovated Wilmingtonian offers forty luxury suites. It provides the privacy of an intimate inn, but has a diversity of services and accommodations. Extensive gardens and ponds with courtyards and balconies surround the buildings, dating from 1841 to 1994. The famed de Rosset House, built in 1841, provides sweeping views of the Cape Fear River. Its six luxurious suites are historically decorated yet equipped with modern conveniences, such as gas log fireplaces, large whirlpool tubs, and separate showers. The signature suite, the Cupola, offers views of the city and breathtaking sunsets. Amenities for all suites include kitchen or wet bar, refrigerator, coffeemaker, microwave, toaster, and VCR. $$$. (910) 343-1800 or (800) 525-0909, www.thewilmingtonian.com.

Graystone Inn. 100 South Third Street, Wilmington 28401. Luxurious rooms await you in this AAA four-diamond property. Originally "The Bridgers Mansion," the Graystone Inn was built in 1905–1906 by Elizabeth Haywood Bridgers, widow of Preston L. Bridgers, a local merchant and son of Robert Rufus Bridgers, who was past president of the Atlantic Coast Line Railway, founder of the Wilmington/Weldon Railroad, and two-time representative to the Confederate Congress. A historic landmark and one of the most elegant structures in Wilmington, the inn has been completely remodeled and returned to its original "turn of the century grandeur." The Graystone Inn was chosen by American Historic Inns, Inc. as one of the "Top 10 Most Romantic Inns in the U.S." $$$. (910) 763-2000, www.graystoneinn.com.

Wilmington Hilton. 301 North Water Street, Wilmington 28401. Located on the downtown waterfront, the Hilton has 274 guest rooms, with half overlooking the river. The Hilton's Poolside and Cabana Bar, adorned with ceiling fans and palm trees, is a great place for a sunset cocktail, and on Friday evenings in the summer the pool deck is the scene of the Sunset Celebration, a popular live-music party. $$$. (800) 445-8667.

WRIGHTSVILLE BEACH

Settled in 1889 and incorporated in 1899, the summer resort of Wrightsville Beach is a small island community that still retains its village charm. A variety of accommodations and restaurants can be found at Wrightsville. Downtown Wilmington is only a fifteen-minute drive.

WHERE TO GO

Wrightsville Beach Museum of History. 303 West Salisbury, Wrightsville Beach 28480. The beach cottage museum houses various exhibits on Wrightsville Beach history, as well as depicting the lifestyle at Wrightsville Beach circa 1900. One of the oldest cottages on the island, the house was built by the Tidewater Power Company in 1907 as part of a plan to encourage residential development. Open daily except Monday, from noon until 6:00 P.M. Admission, $3.00; under 12, free. (910) 256-2569, www.wilmington.org/wbmuseum.

WHERE TO EAT

The Oceanic. 703 South Lumina Avenue, Wrightsville Beach 28480. On the oceanfront, this restaurant offers indoor and outdoor seating. Go for a basket of fresh fish and chips on the old Crystal pier that serves as the patio, but make sure you begin with the hot crab dip for two, a favorite among the regulars. The appetizer is made from local crabmeat broiled with fresh cream, cheese, a secret blend of seasonings, and garlic bread for dipping. Entrees include seafood, chicken, and beef dishes. Leave room for the Key lime pie. $$-$$$. (910) 256-5551.

Bluewater, An American Grill. 4 Marina Street, Wrightsville Beach 28480. Overlooking the Intercoastal Waterway, the two-story Bluewater provides panoramas and great food. Try the hot crab dip for an appetizer. For entrees, the coconut shrimp plate and the seafood lasagna are excellent choices, or my favorite, the lump crab cake entree. Sit indoors, on a waterside patio downstairs, or on an intimate covered terrace upstairs. The restaurant offers live entertainment on Sunday afternoons during the summer. Open daily for lunch and dinner year-round. $$. (910) 256-8500.

Vito's Pizzeria. 8 West Lumina Avenue, Wrightsville Beach 28480. Vito's is a refreshing change of pace should you overdose on seafood during your visit. Offering delivery or dine in, the specialties are pizza, pasta, and subs. Open daily for dinner and for lunch during the summer. $-$$. (910) 256-5858.

The Bridge Tender. 1414 Airlie Road, Wrightsville Beach 28490. Overlooking the Intercoastal Waterway, the Bridge Tender has enjoyed a reputation for its prime rib and seafood since opening in 1976. Open Monday through Friday 11:30 A.M. until 2:00 P.M. for lunch, nightly for dinner from 5:00 P.M. $$-$$$. (910) 256-4519.

WHERE TO STAY

Blockade Runner Beach Resort. 275 Waynick Boulevard, Wrightsville Beach 28480. Built in the 1970s, this 150-room beachfront property has been thoroughly renovated over the years. Beautifully landscaped with tropical plants, the hotel's grass lawn and gardens serve as a buffer between the beach and the hotel. Truly a paradise. Kids' programs are offered during summer months. $$–$$$. (800) 541–1161, www.blockade-runner.com.

Holiday Inn SunSpree Resort Wrightsville Beach. 1706 North Lumina Avenue, Wrightsville Beach 28480. This new beachfront hotel offers such resort amenities as indoor and outdoor pools, two oceanfront whirlpools, a poolside bar and grill, and guest rooms that face either the ocean or the marsh. On-site Kidspree Vacation Club is a complimentary supervised children's program and activity room, and there's a beach playground for kids. $$$. (877) 330–5050, www.wrightsville-sunspree.com.

CAROLINA BEACH

The site of an engagement between Union and Confederate forces following the capitulation of Fort Fisher on January 15, 1865, this region was once known as the community of Sugar Loaf.

Carolina Beach was incorporated in 1925 and became known throughout the state for its boardwalk. The boardwalk fell into demise over recent years, but Carolina Beach is slowly recovering. One sure sign: A new Marriott is scheduled to be built, which will complement an assortment of accommodations that include family cottages, comfortable motels, and luxurious rental condominiums.

Carolina Beach State Park is home to a variety of natural areas that make it one of the most biologically diverse parks in North Carolina. This area is part of a small region of the world where the Venus-flytrap grows naturally.

WHERE TO GO

Kayak Carolina. 514 Dow Road, Carolina Beach 28428. Join Angela and John Pagenstecher for a two-hour guided ecotour of the coastal marshlands on extremely stable and comfortable touring kayaks, great for the uninitiated, plus day trips and skill-building for experienced kayakers. Kids Kayak Camp is offered during the summer. Rates for two-hour tours: $35 for adults, $17.50 for children 11 and under. (910) 458-9111, www.kayakcarolina.com.

Carolina Beach State Park. Dow Road, Carolina Beach 28428. This state park offers fishing, camping, and miles of hiking trails that traverse a variety of distinct habitats, including the Venus flytrap trail, a half-mile loop through pocosin, longleaf pine and turkey oak, and savanna communities. Open daily. (910) 458-8206, www.ils.unc.edu/parkproject/visit/cabe/home.html.

WHERE TO EAT

The Cottage Restaurant. 1 North Lake Park Boulevard, Carolina Beach 28428. Offering coastal cuisine, this seafood grill, housed in a 1916 bungalow, ranks among my favorite restaurants in the state. Popular appetizers include the Cottage's coastal crab cakes, served with two delectable sauces, the Abbey Sauce, made with cream of coconut, lime, cilantro, and other seasonings. For the main course, try the low-country shrimp and grits, made up of cheese grit cake, tasso (Cajun-cured) ham sauce, and, of course, shrimp. Desserts include Key lime pie and Mermaid's Delight, flourless chocolate at its finest. Indoor and outdoor dining. Open year-round Monday through Saturday for lunch and dinner. $$-$$$. (910) 458-4383.

KURE BEACH

Named for the Kure family who first came here in 1867, Kure Beach today is a small family-oriented beach located at the southern extreme of US 421. Kure Beach features large uncrowded beaches, good seafood, and historic Fort Fisher, where you can tour the museum or take a hike around the Civil War earthworks.

Less than 2 miles away is the North Carolina Aquarium, where you can view live marine life and participate in special aquatic programs. In thirty minutes you can be in historic downtown Wilmington or take the ferry to Southport (see Southeast Day Trip 2).

WHERE TO GO

Fort Fisher State Historic Site. US 421, Kure Beach 28449. Billed as "the last major stronghold of the Confederacy," the historic site includes interpretive exhibits and audiovisual presentations depicting two major battles fought here. Union forces overran the earthen fort and, in subsequent days, Wilmington. Open April through October, Monday through Saturday 9:00 A.M. until 5:00 P.M., Sunday 1:00 to 5:00 P.M.; November through March, Tuesday through Saturday 10:00 A.M. until 4:00 P.M., Sunday 1:00 to 4:00 P.M. Free. (910) 458–5538, www.ah.dcr.state.nc.us/sections/hs/fisher/fisher.htm.

North Carolina Aquarium at Fort Fisher. 2201 South Fort Fisher Boulevard, Kure Beach 28409. Newly expanded, the aquarium's centerpiece is a 200,000-gallon ocean aquarium that includes a two-story multilevel viewing of large sharks, groupers, barracudas, and loggerhead turtles swimming around re-created Cape Fear rock ledges. Admission is charged. (910) 458-7468, www.ncaquariums.com.

Southport · Bald Head Island

Follow I-40 east from Raleigh for the 158-mile drive to Southport. Yes, it will take you a bit more than two hours to make the trip, even pushing along at 70 miles per hour on I-40, but the end of the line (in Wilmington, pick up US 17 south and follow it to either NC 87 or NC 133 south) will deposit you in one of the most charming seaside villages in the state.

Situated amid graceful live oaks, Southport garnered praise from Rand McNally as one of the best places to retire. For visitors, Southport oozes coastal charm and boasts a rich maritime history. While walking the historic downtown, listen for the "Seneca Drums," mysterious, low-pitched offshore booms that locals attribute to chunks of the continental shelf dropping off cliffs in the Atlantic Ocean. Truth is, no one knows what causes the low rumbles.

A short ferry trip from Southport takes you to Bald Head Island. Once a preferred destination of pirates such as Blackbeard and Stede Bonnet, Bald Head Island is now a refuge for those who enjoy the true meaning of "getting away from it all."

To preserve Bald Head Island's unspoiled beaches and maritime forests, gasoline engines are prohibited. Hop on a bike, slide into an electric golf cart, or shuffle your peds to explore this resort.

If you opt to travel NC 133 south from Wilmington, you may want to take time to visit **Brunswick Town** and **Fort Anderson State Historic Site.** Brunswick Town, a Colonial site dating from 1726–1776, served as a Cape Fear river port that was the major export of Naval stores and the location of the Stamp Act Rebellion. Fort Anderson, a Confederate fortification, was part of the Cape

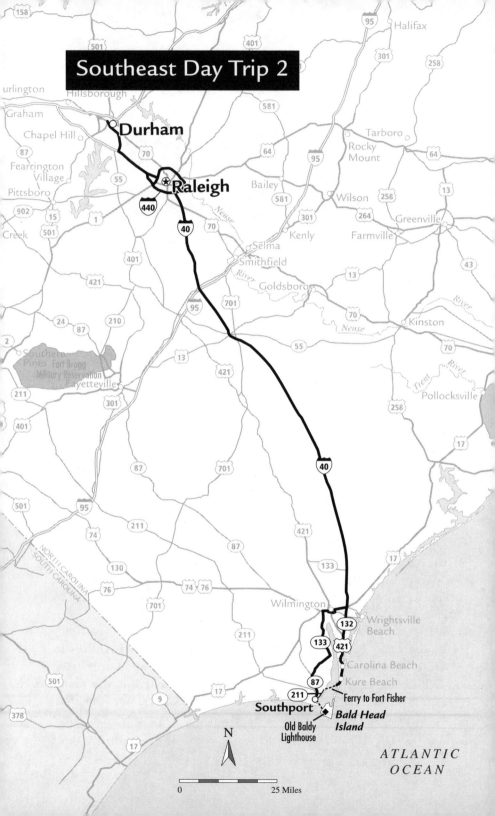

Southeast Day Trip 2

Halifax
Hillsborough
Durham
Raleigh
Tarboro
Rocky Mount
Chapel Hill
Fearrington Village
Pittsboro
Bailey
Wilson
Greenville
Farmville
Selma
Smithfield
Goldsboro
Kinston
Kenly
Pollocksville
Southern Pines Fort Bragg Military Reservation
Fayetteville
Wilmington
Wrightsville Beach
Carolina Beach
Kure Beach
Ferry to Fort Fisher
Southport
Bald Head Island
Old Baldy Lighthouse

NORTH CAROLINA
SOUTH CAROLINA

N

ATLANTIC OCEAN

0   25 Miles

Fear defense system until the Civil War engagement of February 1865. Admission is free. Call (910) 371–6613.

On your return trip, consider traveling by ferry from Southport to Fort Fisher, then driving to Wilmington (see Southeast Day Trip 1).

SOUTHPORT

Founded in 1792 as the town of Smithville, named for North Carolina's Colonial Governor Benjamin Smith, Southport became the town's adopted name in 1887, when town fathers sought to attract a state port to the region. Although the port was later located up the Cape Fear River in Wilmington, the river still plays a major part in Southport's economy. Much as they did some 200 years ago, river pilots still race to meet transoceanic vessels and skill-fully guide them up river. These large vessels tower over Southport's waterfront as they pass within 100 feet of Waterfront Park.

Southport is located at the mouth of the Cape Fear River, the Intracoastal Waterway, and the Atlantic Ocean. Filmmakers have used Southport as the backdrop for the films *Summer Catch* and *I Know What You Did Last Summer*, and for the TV series *Dawson's Creek*.

The town's protected harbor makes for popular water activities, such as boating, sailing, and fishing. The town was built in a live oak forest; the wide-crowned evergreen trees were cultivated as shade trees here and in other coastal regions of the southern United States. If you've ever been to Charleston, South Carolina, you have seen the live oak, but Southport's live oaks differ from their cousins in Charleston, where the branches are often covered with Spanish moss. In Southport, the branches are covered with resurrection ferns, remarkable plants with fronds that curl up and appear dead in prolonged dry weather. They unfurl and spring back to life in wet weather.

Southport's century-old homes sit among the huge sprawling oak trees that reach out over winding streets and sidewalks. Self-guided or guided tours of the town are the best ways to appreciate the character of this charming community. Don't miss the North Carolina Maritime Museum at Southport, with exhibits detailing the vast nautical history of the area.

WHERE TO GO

Southport Visitor Center. 113 West Moore Street, Southport 28461. Begin the mile-long self-guided walking tour here. Devised by the Southport Historical Society, this relaxed walk takes you through charming Historic Southport. Pick up a free pamphlet with tour highlights numbered and explained. Grab a copy of *The Pelican Post,* a handy reference for the town. Your first stop, the Indian Trail Tree, is adjacent to the center. Cape Fear Indians bent the live oak sapling to point the way to tribal fishing grounds. That was 800 years ago. Today, in the spring and the fall, you can see clusters of fishing boats on a line on either side of the tree. The Indian Trail Tree still points the way to the best spot to hook dinner. Open Monday through Saturday 10:00 A.M. until 5:00 P.M. and Sunday 1:00 to 4:00 P.M. (910) 457-7927, www.cityofsouthport.com.

Southport–Oak Island Area Chamber of Commerce Welcome Center. 4841 Long Beach Road Southeast, Southport 28461. Stop here for information on Oak Island, Bald Head Island, or Southport. Open Monday through Friday 8:30 A.M. until 5:00 P.M. and Saturday (March through November) 9:00 A.M. until 4:00 P.M. (800) 457-6964, www.southport-oakisland.com.

Carolina Power and Light Visitors Center. 8520 River Road, Southport 28461. Hands-on and visual presentations of more than thirty energy-related exhibits cover the production of electricity, electrical safety, alternative energy sources, and energy conservation. Open year-round, Tuesday through Thursday 9:00 A.M. until 4:00 P.M. Free. (910) 457-6041.

Franklin Square Art Gallery. 130 East West Street, Southport 28461. This association of local artisans showcases their works in varying media, including painting and pottery, all displayed in a beautiful historic building. Open Monday through Saturday 10:00 A.M. until 5:00 P.M. and, during June, July, and August, Sunday 1:00 to 4:00 P.M. Free. (910) 457-5450.

North Carolina Maritime Museum at Southport. 116 North Howe Street, Southport 28461. This collection of memorabilia pertains to the vast nautical history of Southport, the Lower Cape Fear, and southeastern North Carolina. The museum's twelve-station self-guided tour begins with a 2,000-year-old fragment of a canoe used by the Cape Fear Indians. In addition to an on-site research library, films and programs are offered year-round. Admission: adults (16 years and older), $2.00; seniors, $1.00; and children, free. Open Tuesday through Saturday 9:00 A.M. until 5:00 P.M. (910) 457-0003, www.ah.dcr.state.nc.us/sections/maritime/default.htm.

Fort Johnston. West Bay Street, Southport 28461. Commissioned by the British in 1745, Fort Johnston is the smallest working military installation in the United States. About all that remains is Garrison House, which serves as the residence of the commander and other officers at Sunny Point, a naval depot a few miles north. (The fact that the fort serves as a U.S. Navy barracks qualifies Fort Johnston as a working installation.)

Adkins-Ruark House. 119 North Lord Street, Southport 28461. Built in 1890, the Adkins-Ruark house is where Robert Ruark spent many of his childhood summers in his grandfather's home. His book *The Old Man and the Boy* is an account of his boyhood years in Southport, and is recommended reading for those making the trip here. The house is not open to the public.

Bald Head Island Ferry. 6099 Indigo Plantation Marina, Southport 28461. The ferry departs Southport for Bald Head Island daily every hour on the hour from 8:00 A.M. until 6:00 P.M. except at noon. The ferry departs to Bald Head Island daily from 8:00 A.M. to 11:00 P.M. There is no noon ferry Monday through Thursday. No 9:00 P.M. ferry Sunday through Wednesday. Midnight ferry runs on Friday. Reservations must be made before 6:00 P.M. for the evening runs; the cost is $15.00 per person round-trip, $8.00 for children 12 and under. (910) 457-5003.

WHERE TO EAT

The Sea Captain Restaurant. 608 West West Street, Southport 28461. Start here for a hearty breakfast of standard Southern fare: pancakes, eggs, grits, bacon, ham, and sausage. But for something you can't get at home, try the shrimp, gravy, and grits, which consists of a gravy sauce made from onions and shrimp, generously ladled over grits and served with toast. $$. (910) 457-0600.

Dry Street Pub and Pizza. 101 East Brown Street, Southport 28461. Locals say this is the town's best-kept secret for lunch. Located in an old cottage just beneath the water tower, this cozy restaurant offers a range of fresh made sandwiches, salads, and pizza, with indoor and outdoor dining. Favorites include the cheddar bacon ale soup, the baked potato salad, and the chef salad with homemade chunky blue cheese vinaigrette dressing. $$. (910) 457–5994.

The Pharmacy Restaurant. 110 East Moore Street, Southport 28461. The house specialty, Pharmacy Crab Cakes, combines three all-lump-meat crab cakes seasoned with capers, white pepper, salt, and green onion. The crab cakes, each wrapped in phyllo dough, are served on a bed of baby greens. Chive oil, reduced balsamic vinegar, and a mustard dressing are drizzled on the plate to create bright green, dark brown, and gold streams of color. It's the little touches like these that makes dining at the Pharmacy so special, says owner Kelli Menna, noting that herbs are organically grown and hand-picked by the chef. Desserts are made each morning on premises. $$$. (910) 457–5577, www.thepharm-inc.com.

Ship's Chandler Restaurant. 101 West Bay Street, Southport 28461. Located on the site of a ship's chandlery, where the river pilot was situated, Ship's Chandler Restaurant is the best spot in town to sit and watch the river traffic. Noted for its hush puppies, sweet with honey butter for dipping, Ship's Chandler offers generously laden seafood platters, such as the "Chandler's Platter," including fish, shrimp, oysters, clam strips, deviled crabs, and scallops. $$–$$$. (910) 457–6588.

Mr. P's. 317 West Bay Street, Southport 28461. Mr. P's house specialty is Oysters Bienville. Chef Stephen Phipps adds a few touches of his own to this classic New Orleans recipe. Beginning with fresh oysters, he tops them with a white sauce made from chopped shrimp, mushrooms, and sherry. He then sprinkles grated Asiago cheese over the dish and bakes it until the cheese melts. $$$. (910) 457–6595.

Shrimp House Restaurant. 106 Yacht Basin Street, Southport 28461. Fried or broiled, enjoy some fresh local seafood, including shrimp, fish, oysters, and scallops. Try the Shrimp Boat, a large baked potato stuffed with sautéed shrimp, onions, and bell peppers. Also recommended: shrimp and grits. Indoor and outdoor dining are available. $$. (910) 457–1881.

Potter's Steamhouse. 100 Yacht Basin Street, Southport 28461. Potter's has outdoor dining on the waterfront at picnic tables under a screened-in porch. Specialties include steamed jumbo shrimp, local blue crabs, oysters, and crab legs. Try the steam pot, which includes a variety of seafood with steam potatoes, sausage, and corn on the cob. $$. (910) 457–1881.

The Provision Company. 201 Yacht Basin Drive, Southport 28461. If you enjoy sitting out by the water to have lunch, this is the place. The specialty is steamed shrimp. If you're really hungry, order the special, popular among the locals for more than eight years: crab cake, a half pound of shrimp, and cucumber salad. For lighter fare, you can get smaller portions of shrimp alone or the popular grouper salad. Also popular are the conch fritters, made with imported Bahamian conch. $$. (910) 457–0654.

WHERE TO STAY

Brunswick Inn Bed and Breakfast. 301 East Bay Street, Southport 28461. Those seeking a romantic getaway might knock on the door of the Brunswick Inn. The 7,000-square-foot, sixteen-room Federal-style mansion overlooks the Cape Fear. Accommodations include spacious bedrooms with fireplaces and views of the waterway. $$$. (910) 457–5278, www.brunswickinn.com.

Cape Fear Inn. 317 West Bay Street, Southport 28461. This quaint, twelve-unit bed-and-breakfast, located on the second row of streets off the Cape Fear River, is furnished with simple antiques. The inn is adjacent to restaurants and boat harbors, and is a short walk from the center of historic downtown Southport. $$. (910) 457–5278.

Sea Captain Motor Lodge. 608 West West Street, Southport 28461. This family-style hotel has an Olympic-size pool and on-site restaurant. $$. (910) 457–5263, www.seacaptainmotorlodge.com.

BALD HEAD ISLAND

With more than 10,000 of the island's 12,000 acres preserved and protected from development, Bald Head Island has 14 miles of pristine beaches. A meandering creek cuts through acres of salt marsh that border an expanse of maritime forest.

A world-class resort, Bald Head Island offers the vacationer a championship golf course, clubhouse facilities, croquet, a marina, tennis courts, swimming pools, restaurants, snack bars, a full-service grocery store, and hours of peaceful relaxation.

WHERE TO GO

Old Baldy Lighthouse. North Carolina's lighthouses are one of our state's greatest treasures. The oldest still standing is "Old Baldy," built in 1818. Retired in 1935 and recently renovated, Old Baldy is open to the public Tuesday through Saturday 9:00 A.M. until 4:00 P.M., Sunday 11:00 A.M. until 4:00 P.M.; closed Monday. A $3.00 donation is requested.

    Bald Head Island Historic Tours. Guided tours of the island include a visit to Smith Island Museum of History. Tour packages may include lunch or dinner, parking, and ferry tickets. Reservations are required. On–island fares: Adults $16; children 12 and under, $11. Off-island fare includes round-trip ferry passage and lunch: Adults, $36; children 12 and under, $31. Tours depart at 10:30 A.M. Monday through Saturday. (910) 457–5003.

WHERE TO EAT

Bald Head Island Club. A private club for members and accompanied guests or for temporary members staying on the island. Open for lunch (lounge only) and dinner, except on Monday and Tuesday. Offers a *prix fixe* menu and dinner buffets during the summer months and holidays. $$$. (910) 457–7300.

    The Pelicatessen. Located near the Bald Head Island Club pool, the "Peli Deli," as the locals call it, offers deli-style sandwiches, hot dogs, a variety of snacks, and drinks. A phone on the ninth hole allows golfers to call in an order. Open seasonally. $$. (910) 457–7384.

    River Pilot Cafe. Located in the harbor, River Pilot Cafe specializes in Southern cuisine, with the dinner menu offering appetizers such as crabmeat and artichoke dip, and entrees like island seafood Creole pasta or fresh catch grilled daily. Open daily for breakfast and lunch; Monday through Saturday for dinner. The early-bird special offers 20 percent off dinner from 5:30 to 6:15 P.M. $$$. (910) 457–7390.

Eb & Flo's. An open-air waterfront pavilion, Eb & Flo's special-izes in steam pots filled with crab legs, clams, mussels, shrimp, potatoes, and corn. Located harborside, this casual restaurant provides an excellent vantage point for watching boats entering the marina. Open Thursday through Sunday 11:30 A.M. until 10:00 P.M. $$. (910) 457–7390.

WHERE TO STAY

Marsh Harbor Inn. Located in Harbour Village, this New England–style inn's Cape Cod rockers, Shaker beds, and antique wood floors lend each room a simple appeal. All rooms offer tele-vision, VCR, telephone, and private bath. Many of the inn's fifteen rooms have private decks overlooking Bald Head Creek or the Cape Fear River. Included with your stay: breakfast at the nearby River Pilot Cafe, afternoon hors d'oeuvres, use of an electric golf cart, and temporary membership in the Bald Head Island Club. $$$. (800) 432–RENT, www.baldheadisland.com.

Theodosia's Bed and Breakfast. This ten-room bed-and-break-fast provides rooms with a view and a full breakfast. Golf carts and bikes are complimentary with each room, as is temporary Bald Head Island Club membership. Afternoon hors d'oeuvres are included. $$$. (800) 656–1812, www.theodosias.com.

Bald Head Island Resort Sales and Rentals. Listings include a range of accommodations, from cottages to large homes. $$$. (800) 820–0545, www.baldheadresort.com.

Bald Head Island Vacation Rentals. Vacation rentals range from small forest cottages to large oceanfront homes. Included with the rental is temporary membership in the Bald Head Island Club, allowing you access to its celebrated golf course, croquet greens, tennis courts, pool, dining room, and lounge. Also included are round-trip ferry passage and one or more electric carts. $$$. (800) 432–RENT, www.baldheadisland.com.

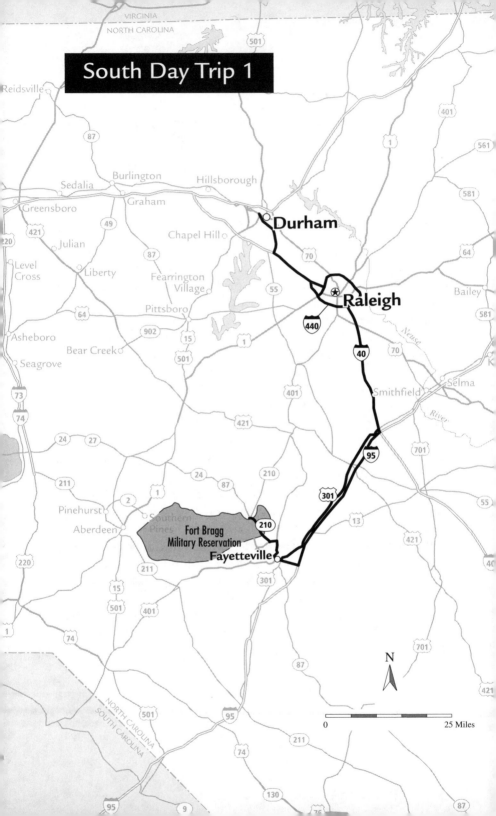

South Day Trip 1

SOUTH DAY TRIP 1

Fayetteville · Fort Bragg

With Fort Bragg and Pope Air Force Base nearby, Fayetteville has had to bear the brunt of being called a military town full of mind-numbing neon, tattoo parlors, and pawn shops. True, you may have to look beyond some of the less attractive development that goes hand-in-hand with the transient trainees who arrive each week at one of the nation's largest military installations. But when you do get past the crass commercialism, Fayetteville has much to offer the day-tripper.

For starters, the town contains four designated historic districts: the downtown Historic District, Haymount Historic District, Liberty Point National Register District, and Market House Square National Register District. And nearly worth the trip alone is the city's new Airborne and Special Operations Museum, the only museum of its kind in the country.

Moreover, Fayetteville's military presence contributes to the city's cultural diversity. Restaurants serving ethnic cuisine, particularly Asian food, are more abundant here than in any other place in the state. It's not unusual to see signs, even city-maintained signs, with Asian script.

Of course, any day trip to Fayetteville should include a tour of Fort Bragg. Visitors may pass freely (albeit through security check-points) through the military installation. The **Fort Bragg Welcome Center** is at Randolph and Knox Streets; phone (910) 907-2026.

A trip through the base will no doubt leave you with a true appreciation for the sacrifices made by our nation's military, and in that regard, Fayetteville and Fort Bragg present a patriotic day trip within an easy drive from Raleigh-Durham along I–40 west to I–95 south.

FAYETTEVILLE

Dozens of U.S. cities and counties have been named after the Revolutionary War hero Marquis de Lafayette, but Fayetteville was the first and, reportedly, the only one he actually visited. The Frenchman arrived here by horse-drawn carriage in 1825 and was welcomed by the residents.

The original settlers of the Fayetteville area were from the Highlands of Scotland. They arrived in 1739 via the Cape Fear River and established two early settlements, Campbellton and Cross Creek. At Liberty Point, in the center of what would become downtown Fayetteville, patriots pledged local support for the Revolutionary War, while nearby, Scottish heroine Flora MacDonald rallied for the loyalist cause.

After the Revolution, with no permanent state capital, the state's legislature periodically met here. It's not unusual to hear a Fayettevillian bitterly claim that Raleigh stole Fayetteville's capital status.

In 1783, Campbellton and Cross Creek converged and were named Fayetteville. In 1789, in a State House that the city built on aspirations of remaining the state capital, North Carolina representatives meeting in Fayetteville ratified the U.S. Constitution; they also chartered the University of North Carolina, America's oldest state university. The Great Fire of 1831 destroyed more than 600 buildings, including the State House, but reconstruction resulted in many of the city's present-day landmark structures. Fayetteville's buildings are some of the oldest in the state.

The area grew as a center of government and commerce because of its location as an inland port and the hub of the early "plank roads" system, key to overland travel from the 1840s to 1850s. During the Civil War, the city found itself in the path of General Sherman's Union troops, who wreaked destruction and burned the North Carolina Arsenal, which had been a munitions center for the Confederacy.

An interesting tidbit about Fayetteville: At the old Cape Fear Fairgrounds, eighteen-year-old George Herman Ruth, the youngest player on the Baltimore Orioles, hit his first professional home run on March 7, 1914. He was dubbed a "babe" in the woods, which Ruth adopted as his nickname.

WHERE TO GO

Fayetteville Area Convention and Visitors Bureau. 245 Person Street, Fayetteville 28301. Stop here for maps and a visitor's guide. In addition to a walk-in facility, the visitors center operates a drive-through window. Open daily. (910) 483–5311 or (800) 255–8217, www.visitfayettevillenc.com.

Cool Spring Tavern. 119 Cool Spring Street, Fayetteville 28301. Built in 1788 and having survived the Great Fire of 1831, Cool Spring Tavern is the oldest structure in the city. The tavern housed the delegates who ratified the U.S. Constitution for North Carolina, and was built in an attempt to entice them to base the state capital here. With Federal-style architecture, it has double porches, a gabled roof, and brick chimneys. The interior is not open to the public.

Kyle House. 234 Green Street, Fayetteville 28301. A victim of the Great Fire of 1831, this house was rebuilt in 1855 in Greek Revival and Italianate style, with 18-inch-thick walls to provide insulation and fireproofing. Open by appointment. (910) 483–7405.

Cape Fear Botanical Garden. 536 North Eastern Boulevard, Fayetteville 28301. The eighty-five-acre garden, at the confluence of the Cape Fear and Cross Creek Rivers, contains an old farmhouse and heritage garden, perennial gardens, wildflowers, majestic oaks in an old-growth forest, nature trails, and numerous species of native plants. Among the 2,000 specimens of ornamental plants are 200 varieties of camellias that keep the garden beautiful year-round. Open Monday through Saturday 10:00 A.M. until 5:00 P.M., Sunday noon until 5:00 P.M. Adults $3.00; children under 12, free. (910) 486–0221.

Airborne and Special Operations Museum. 100 Bragg Boulevard, Fayetteville 28301. Part of the U.S. Army Museum System, this newly opened (2000) museum is the only one of its kind in the nation. It explores the sixty-year history of airborne and special operations units through dramatic, life-size, imaginative exhibits and interactive displays such as a twenty-four-seat simulator that nearly replicates what troopers experience when parachuting or flying at treetop level over rough terrain. Located on six acres in downtown Fayetteville, the museum is open Tuesday through Saturday (and on Federal holiday Mondays) 10:00 A.M. until 5:00 P.M., Sunday noon until 5:00 P.M. Free. (910) 483–3003, www.asomf.org.

Fayetteville Independent Light Infantry Armory and Museum. 210 Burgess Street, Fayetteville 28301. Show by appointment only, the museum houses two centuries of artifacts from the oldest Southern militia unit in continuous existence—serving North Carolina since 1793. (910) 433–1612.

Fayetteville Museum of Art. 839 Stamper Road, Fayetteville 28303. The first structure in North Carolina designed and built as an art museum, it offers a variety of changing exhibits, educational programs, concerts, workshops, and a gift shop. Open Monday through Friday 10:00 A.M. until 5:00 P.M., Saturday and Sunday 1:00 to 5:00 P.M. Free. (910) 485–5121, www.fmoa.org.

Heritage Square. 225 Dick Street, Fayetteville 28301. Owned and maintained by the Fayetteville Woman's Club, Heritage Square has three historic structures listed on the National Register of Historic Places: the Sandford House, built in 1800 and once home to artist Elliott Daingerfield and to the first United States bank in the state; the Oval Ballroom, a freestanding single room built in 1818; and the Baker-Haigh-Nimocks House, constructed in 1804. (910) 483–6009.

Market House. Hay, Gillespie, Person, and Green Streets, Fayetteville 28301. The focal point of downtown Fayetteville, the Market House was built in 1832 on the site of the old State House, where, in 1789, North Carolina ratified the U.S. Constitution, chartered the University of North Carolina, and ceded the state's western lands to Tennessee. The State House was destroyed by fire in 1831. Architecturally unique in North Carolina, the Market House is one of the few structures in America to use this town hall–market scheme found in England. (910) 433–1612.

Liberty Point. Bow and Person Streets, Fayetteville 28301. Here, on June 20, 1775, fifty-five patriots signed a petition declaring independence from Great Britain. The building at this site is the oldest known commercial structure in Fayetteville, constructed between 1791 and 1800. (910) 433–1612.

St. John's Episcopal Church. 302 Green Street, Fayetteville 28301. Reconstructed in 1833, after Fayetteville's Great Fire of 1831, the church has ten pyramidal spires and stained glass windows made in Munich, Germany. (910) 483-7405.

Museum of the Cape Fear Historical Complex. 801 Arsenal Avenue, Fayetteville 28305. Museum exhibits chronicle the history of southern North Carolina from Native Americans to the twentieth century. The 1897 E. A. Poe house examines the lifestyle of upper middle-class families from 1897 to 1917. Arsenal Park reveals the history of a Federal arsenal, commissioned in 1836 by the Federal Government and taken over by the Confederacy at the outset of the Civil War. General Sherman seized Fayetteville in 1865 and ordered the arsenal to be razed by fire. Open Tuesday through Saturday 10:00 A.M. until 5:00 P.M. and Sunday 1:00 to 5:00 P.M. Free. (910) 486-1330.

Arts Center. 301 Hay Street, Fayetteville 28301. Built in 1910 as a U.S. post office, the Arts Center houses the galleries and offices of the Arts Council of Fayetteville/Cumberland County. The galleries feature rotating art exhibits. (910) 323-1776.

Atlantic Coast Line Railroad Station. 472 Hay Street, Fayetteville 28301. Built in 1911, the station is a rare example of Dutch Colonial architecture. The outside passenger and freight platform and shelter date to World War I. The depot serves as an Amtrak passenger station and houses the Atlantic Coast Line Depot Railroad Historical Center. Open alternating Saturdays. (910) 433-1612.

WHERE TO SHOP

Angels and Antiques, 1213 Hay Street, Fayetteville 28301. The owners tell me that their store carries the nation's largest selection of angels. Open Monday through Friday 10:00 A.M. until 5:30 P.M., Saturday 10:00 A.M. until 5:00 P.M. (910) 433-4454.

Eastover Trading Company. 3551 Dunn Road, Fayetteville 28301. A nostalgic old schoolhouse is reborn with antique treasures, collectibles, unique accessories, and specialty gift items. Open Monday through Saturday 9:00 A.M. until 5:00 P.M. (910) 323-1121.

WHERE TO EAT

The Mash House. 4150 Sycamore Dairy Road, Fayetteville 28303. Adjacent to the Wingate Inn (see Where to Stay), the Mash House is known for its award-winning microbrewed beer—with nine varieties on tap when I visited—served in a chilled pint glass with a pretzel on a straw. If you're indecisive about which microbrew to have, try the Mini-Mash (four, 4-ounce glasses of beer) or the larger version (eight 4-ounce glasses). Begin your dinner with "The Wedge," which includes half a head of iceberg lettuce, fried sweet onions, tomatoes, and Gorgonzola dressing. Follow it with one of the delicious entrees, such as wood-oven-roasted filet mignon, served with fried sweet onions, asparagus, roasted potatoes, and béarnaise. Open daily. $$–$$$. (910) 867-9223.

Huske Hardware House. 405 Hay Street, Fayetteville 28301. This restaurant/microbrewery is located in a renovated hardware store, spacious and artfully restored. Its location makes it a good choice for combining a visit with the Airborne and Special Operations Museum; appropriately, the microbrew offers its signature Airborne Ale. The lunch menu offers a variety of soups, salads, and "starters," as well as sandwiches and specialties, including such items as pesto chicken and Cajun shrimp. Dinners include a selection of pasta, seafood, and beef. $$–$$$. (910) 437-9905.

Hilltop House Café. 1240 Fort Bragg Road, Fayetteville .28301. Located in Fayetteville's historic Haymount district, the Hilltop House Cafe serves traditional American cuisine, including steaks, seafood, and the proprietor's Greek specialties. Located in an early twentieth-century home, Hilltop House Cafe is open daily for lunch, dinner, and Sunday brunch. $$. (910) 484-6699, oldmp.com/hilltop/.

New Korea House. 4608 Yadkin Road, Fayetteville 28301. Great Korean cuisine is served daily for lunch and dinner. $$. (910) 864-2772.

Rude Awakenings Coffee House. 227 Hay Street, Fayetteville 28301. In the historic downtown district, this coffee shop offers all varieties of coffees, including specialty cappuccinos, as well as breakfast, lunch, and desserts. Check out the courtyard at the back of this great little coffee shop. Open Monday through Saturday. $. (910) 391-7833, www.rudeawakening.net.

WHERE TO STAY

Wingate Inn. 4182 Sycamore Dairy Road, Fayetteville 28303. The Wingate offers spacious, well-equipped rooms with a desk, coffeemaker (and coffee), refrigerator, safe, ironing board, and free high-speed Internet access. A complimentary continental breakfast features forty-one items. The inn has a fitness club and whirlpool, and is a good base camp for exploring the region. $$. (910) 826–9200 or (800) 228–1000.

Radisson Prince Charles Hotel. 450 Hay Street, Fayetteville 28301. Reminiscent of an Italian palazzo, this 1925 eight-story landmark has Palladian windows and doors, marble floors and staircases, and soaring columns and pilasters. Located in historic downtown Fayetteville, the hotel is listed with Historic Hotels of America, a private nonprofit National Trust. $$–$$$. (910) 433–4444 or (877) 774–6239.

FORT BRAGG

Named for General Braxton Bragg, a native of Warren County who served in the U.S. Army during the Seminole and Mexican Wars and in the Confederate Army during the Civil War, "Camp Bragg" was established by Congress in 1918 as an Army field artillery site. Five years later, the camp was renamed Fort Bragg, and in 1934 the airborne tradition began with the first military parachute jump, which used artillery observation balloons as platforms.

In 1952, Fort Bragg became headquarters for the Army's Special Forces (Green Berets) when the Psychological Warfare Center, now the Special Operations Command, was established here.

With a total area of more than 138,000 acres—three times the size of the District of Columbia—Fort Bragg today is home of XVIII Airborne Corps and the 82nd Airborne Division, as well as of thousands of nonjumping troops. It is one of the largest military reservations in the United States; because of the number of troops there, is considered to be the state's tenth largest city.

WHERE TO GO

John F. Kennedy Special Warfare Museum. Ardennes Street, Building D-2502, Fort Bragg 28307. This museum provides a behind-the-scenes look at unconventional warfare, with an emphasis on Special Forces (Green Berets) and Special Operations from World War II until today. It houses a collection of weapons, military art, and cultural items from all over the world. Open Tuesday through Sunday 11:00 A.M. until 4:00 P.M. Free. (910) 432–4272.

John F. Kennedy Memorial Chapel. Ardennes Street, Fort Bragg 28307. Beautiful stained glass windows are dedicated to Special Forces soldiers. There's also a monument given by John Wayne to the Special Forces for assistance during the filming of *The Green Berets*. (910) 432–2127.

John F. Kennedy Hall of Heroes. Ardennes Street, Fort Bragg 28307. Located across the street from the John F. Kennedy Special Warfare Museum, the JFK Hall of Heroes honors nineteen Special Forces Medal of Honor recipients.

82nd Airborne Division War Memorial Museum. Ardennes and Gela Streets, Fort Bragg 28307. The museum chronicles the history of the 82nd Airborne Division from 1917 to the present through featured photographic exhibits, static displays, and the more than 3,000 artifacts on display. Outdoor equipment displays and an hourly film provide additional insights into this historic unit. Open Tuesday through Sunday. Free. (910) 432–3443.

Main Post Chapel. Half and C Streets, Fort Bragg 28307. Established in 1932, the chapel's stained glass windows were hand-crafted with 14,000 pieces of antique glass from around the world. (910) 396–8016.

Pinehurst · Southern Pines · Aberdeen

The "Golf Capital of the World" is a little more than an hour's drive from the Raleigh-Durham area. A straight shot down US 1 south, Pinehurst, Southern Pines, and Aberdeen provide duffers with action aplenty. The area has more than forty-three championship courses—720 holes. That translates to fewer than one hundred residents per golf hole, making it one of the highest-density golf areas in the country. There are, in fact, more than 165 miles of fairways, and more are scheduled to open soon. Geographically designated as the "Sandhills," for its sandy soil, the golf courses have 2,900 bunkers and no shortage of sand to fill them.

In publications such as *Golf Digest,* the area consistently ranks high among the most popular golf destinations in the United States, but the region has much more to offer. There's also the Spa at Pinehurst, with more than forty services like workouts, body wraps, and massages to replenish body and soul.

Equine enthusiasts and bicyclists favor the rolling sand hills. The region is home to five past Olympic equestrian champions, and Olympic bicycle teams have trained here. If you like to spin, you'll find plenty of quiet roads to roll on.

Speaking of quiet, one of the state's best-kept secrets is the Weymouth Center for the Arts and Humanities in Southern Pines. Weymouth's Writers-in-Residence program offers writers and composers stays of up to two weeks to pursue their work. Not ready to pen your great novel? Stop in to visit North Carolina's Literary Hall of Fame for inspiration.

Nearby, quaint Aberdeen, named for a seaport in Scotland, reflects the strong Scot heritage of this region.

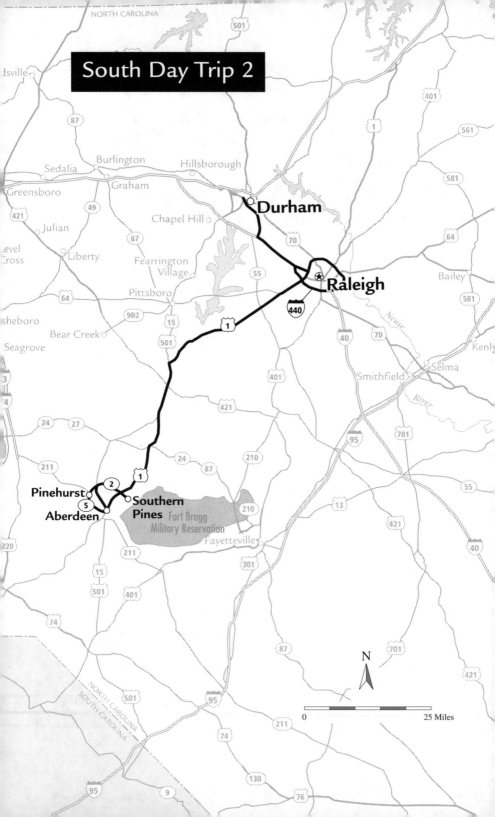

Pinehurst, Southern Pines, and Aberdeen all are charming small towns. Each could pass for a story-book village, and you will enjoy strolling through these easily walkable towns.

PINEHURST

Boston soda fountain magnate James Walker Tufts, who wanted to build a southern winter retreat and a health-driven resort for recovery from the day's maladies, developed Pinehurst in 1895. Tufts purchased 5,000 acres of ravaged timberland in the Sandhills of North Carolina and built an inn and New England–style village he called Tuftstown. He later changed it to Pinehurst, after selecting the name from a runners-up list in a town-naming contest in the New England coastal area. Pinehurst officially opened for its first season on December 31, 1895, and has since hosted some of the most famous athletes, business leaders, philanthropists, government officials, and heroes from America and beyond.

Pinehurst's evolution as a revered golf venue is rooted in the 1898 development of its first golf course. However, it was the hiring of Donald J. Ross as golf professional in 1900 that undeniably altered the focus of Pinehurst Resort forever. His famed Number Two course has laid claim to and continues to serve as the site of some of the most honored amateur and professional golf events in the world. In 1996, Pinehurst was declared a National Historic Landmark, forever protecting its quaintness and ageless quality.

WHERE TO GO

Tufts Archives, Given Memorial Library. 150 Cherokee Road, Pinehurst 28374. James Walker Tufts's dream of Pinehurst unfolds in the displays of letters, pictures, and news clippings dating from 1895. Free. (910) 295–3642.

Sandhills Horticultural Gardens. 2200 Airport Road, Pinehurst 28374. Ten major gardens are featured here, including the Ebersol Holly Collection (the largest on the East Coast), a specialized conifer garden, the Sir Walter Raleigh Garden (a one-and-a-half-acre formal English garden), Hillside Garden, Azalea Garden, and the Desmond Native Wetland Trail Garden. Horticultural students at Sandhills Community College, whose graduates have gone on to find notable horticultural jobs at such places as the White House, maintain the gardens. Free. (910) 695-3882, normandy.sandhills.cc.nc.us/lsg/hort.html.

WHERE TO GOLF

Pinehurst Resort's eight golf courses make it the world's largest golf resort. Pinehurst's course Number Two ranked ninth in *Golf Digest's* biennial 2001 ranking of America's one hundred greatest golf courses. Accordingly, in 2005, the U.S. Open Championship returns to Pinehurst, which hosted the event in 1999. Seldom does the Open return to a golf course so quickly, but Pinehurst Number Two is an exceptional course.

Five of North Carolina's top ten courses, as ranked by *Golf Digest* magazine, are in the Pinehurst and Southern Pines region. Of those, three are public courses at Pinehurst Resort: Ranked first was Pinehurst Number Two, fifth was Pinehurst Number Four, and eighth was Pinehurst Number Eight. Descriptions of each follow. Be forewarned, however, that these courses can cost as much as $225 per person for eighteen holes, and to play those holes properly, you'll want to hire a caddie, for an additional $50 or so per round of golf.

The region does feature lesser-priced golf courses. For more information, order the free *Area Golf Course Guide* from the **Pinehurst, Southern Pines, Aberdeen Area Convention and Visitors Bureau,** 10677 NC 15-501, Southern Pines 28388. Phone (910) 692-3330 or (800) 346-5362, or log on to www.homeofgolf.com.

Pinehurst Number Two Pinehurst Resort and Country Club. Opened in 1901, and the site of the 1999 U.S. Open Championship, architect Donald Ross called this "the fairest test of championship golf I have ever designed." Players have to drive the ball well and hit long irons well. Most of all, players must have a razor-sharp short game because of small greens (by modern standards) that fall off around the edge. Length: back, 6,741 yards (74.1 rating, 131 slope); middle, 6,309 yards (71.4 rating, 127 slope); forward, 5035 yards (74.2 rating, 135 slope). Eighteen holes, par 72/74. (800) 487-4653, www.pinehurst.com.

Pinehurst Number Four Pinehurst Resort and Country Club. Officially opened in April 2000, and dubbed Tom Fazio's "Tribute to Pinehurst," Number Four was built with crowned greens similar to those found on Number Two and complemented by British-style pot bunkers and sand areas planted with native grasses. Although Number Four begins and ends where the old course did and shares some playing corridors, this is a completely new golf course. (800) 487–4653, www.pinehurst.com.

Pinehurst Eight Pinehurst Resort and Country Club. With an Audubon International Signature Sanctuary designation, Number Eight was the site of the 1997 and 1998 PGA Club Professional Championships. Solid, straightforward golf, free from theatrics like artificial earth moments and forced carries. The course was created by Tom Fazio to celebrate the 100th birthday of the resort in 1996. Length: championship, 7,092 yards (74.0 rating, 135 slope); back, 6,698 yards (71.7 rating, 125 slope); middle, 6,302 yards (69.8 rating, 121 slope); forward, 5,177 yards (68.9 rating, 112 slope). Eighteen holes, par 72. (800) 487–4653, www.pinehurst.com.

National Golf Club. One Royal Troon Drive, Pinehurst 28374. Rated by *Golfweek* as one of America's Best Golf Courses in 1995. *Golf Digest* places the National in the top fifteen courses in North Carolina (out of more than 600 courses in the state). This is a straightforward golf course; approach shots and short game are critical. Opened in 1989, the course's architect was Jack Nicklaus. Eighteen holes, par 72. (910) 295–5340 or (800) 471–4339, www.nationalgolfclub.com.

WHERE TO SHOP

The village's boutique shops have storefront windows that invite you to come in and browse. Be sure to stop at **The Theatre Building,** which has graced such luminaries as Helen Hayes, Will Rogers, and Gloria Swanson. It now houses a group of stores, ranging from **G. Monroe's,** a clothing shop, to **King's Gifts & Collectibles.**

WHERE TO EAT

Visitors to Pinehurst typically purchase packages that include modified American meal plans. Golf packages, for example, may include breakfast and lunch. See restaurant descriptions under "Where to Stay."

WHERE TO STAY

Pinehurst Resort. One Carolina Vista, Pinehurst 28374. Nestled among the pines, this four-diamond resort has played host to travelers since 1895. Pinehurst has eight signature golf courses. It was the site of the 1999 U.S. Open, and will host the championship tournament again in 2005.

At Pinehurst Resort, there are opportunities to improve your golf game at Golf Advantage School have "wicket fun" playing croquet at any of the resort's three full-size croquet courts, or play tennis.

Opened in the spring of 2002, a $12 million spa features twenty-eight private treatment rooms and eight salon stations spread throughout 31,000 square feet. The spa also showcases a golf fitness studio.

Also available from the resort are thirty-minute guided carriage tours of the village of Pinehurst for $15 per person.

Pinehurst Resort offers three inns (descriptions follow) as well as condominium and villa rentals. All accommodations in Pinehurst are priced in the $$$ category and can be booked by calling (910) 295-6811 or (800) 487-4653, or visiting www.pinehurst.com.

The **Holly Inn** (2300 Cherokee Road), which originally opened December 31, 1895, was the village's first inn. The newly restored Holly Inn has eighty-five rooms with period furnishings. The inn offers two distinctive dining options in Pinehurst Resort's modified American meal plan. The **1895 Room** ($$$) is the resort's premier dining experience, featuring regional cuisine in an elegant Southern grill, with a buffet breakfast and innovative New American–style cuisine for dinner. The cozy **Tavern** ($$–$$$), with its century-old hand-carved imported Scottish bar, working fireplace, and outdoor patio, is open daily for lunch and dinner.

Built in 1901, the **Carolina** (One Carolina Vista) is one of America's Historic Hotels. This stately Victorian structure is the centerpiece of the resort, housing 210 guest rooms and 12 suites, all recently renovated. The hotel's **Carolina Dining Room** ($$$) serves breakfast, lunch, and dinner, and the **Ryder Cup Lounge** ($$) is for lighter meals and cocktails.

The forty-five-room **Manor Inn** (5 Community Drive) has the intimate feel of a bed-and-breakfast and is a popular choice of golfing groups and families because of its value pricing and room configuration options. **Mulligans** ($$–$$$), an on-location sports-themed restaurant, offers a wide variety of appetizers, sandwiches, and entrees, including English-style fish and chips, made from fresh East Coast cod fillets, hand-dipped in beer batter, fried, and served with fries. Seasonal outdoor dining is available. Open Monday through Sunday 4:00 to 10:00 P.M. (910) 235-8546.

Magnolia Inn. 65 Magnolia Street, Pinehurst 28374. Old South hospitality can be found in this charming inn located in the center of the village of Pinehurst. Enjoy Chef Elliott's gourmet dinners ($$–$$$), particularly the crab cakes, served in the dining room, on the porch in the pub, or poolside. Golf packages are available. $$$. (910) 295-6900 or (800) 526-5562, www.sandhills.org/magnolia.

For the budget-minded, the Southern Pines and Pinehurst region offers a variety of chain hotels. For more information, contact the **Pinehurst, Southern Pines, Aberdeen Area Convention and Visitors Bureau,** 10677 NC 15-501, Southern Pines 28388. Call (910) 692-3330 or (800) 346-5362, or visit www.homeofgolf.com.

SOUTHERN PINES

Incorporated in 1887, Southern Pines was known earlier as Vineland, but the U.S. Postal Service refused to accept the name on the basis that the North Carolina town would be confused with a New Jersey town by the same name. In search of a new name, the popular winter resort chose to identify itself with its geographic location along the edge of the longleaf pine belt.

Southern Pines' downtown is separated by train tracks, mostly hidden by magnolia and pine trees. They divide Broad Street, where you'll find most of the tourist activity—on both sides of the tracks.

WHERE TO GO

Taxidermy Hall of Fame of North Carolina Creation Museum.
156 North West Broad Street, Southern Pines 28387. On exhibit is
every kind of North Carolina wildlife (within the law), state and
national taxidermy ribbon winners, and "the oldest rock on earth."
The museum is located in the Christian Book Store on Broad Street.
(910) 692–3471.

Historic Shaw House Properties. Morganton Road and Broad
Street, Southern Pines 28388. Operated by Moore County Historical Society, these three historic houses (1770–1820) are furnished
with plain-style furniture, depicting life in the early Sandhills. Free.
(910) 692–2051.

Weymouth Center. 555 East Connecticut Avenue, Southern
Pines 28387. This 1920s Georgian mansion, situated on twenty-four
acres with extensive gardens, offers arts and humanities activities.
The former home of author James Boyd, it's listed on the National
Register of Historic Places and is home to the North Carolina
Literary Hall of Fame. (910) 692–6261, www.weymouthcenter.org.

North Carolina Literary Hall of Fame. Weymouth Center,
Southern Pines 28387. At this newly established shrine of the most
distinguished Tarheel men and women of letters, you'll find
displays, photographs, and lists of works for such notable writers as
Thomas Wolfe, O. Henry (William S. Porter), Paul Green, and James
Boyd. (910) 692–6261.

Weymouth Woods Sandhills Nature Preserve. 1024 North
Fort Bragg Road, Southern Pines 28387. Named for Weymouth,
England, the 571-acre nature preserve of longleaf pine forest is
home to the endangered red-cockaded woodpecker, a permanent
resident of the Sandhills. Tour the nature center museum, dedicated to the study of this unique ecosystem; hike the more than 4.5
miles of year-round trails. Guided tours and programs are
presented. (910) 692–2167, ils.unc.edu/parkproject/wewo.html.

WHERE TO SHOP

Campbell House Galleries. 482 East Connecticut Avenue,
Southern Pines 28387. Historic home of the Arts Council of
Moore County, the Campbell House Galleries provide three

spacious exhibit areas that display the work of a featured artist each month. Most artwork is offered for sale. (910) 692–4356, www.artscouncil-moore.org/campbell.html.

WHERE TO EAT

Sweet Basil. 134 Northwest Broad Street, Southern Pines 28387. Sweet Basil is popular for its soups, salads, and sandwiches, particularly the grilled eggplant sandwich with sweet roasted peppers and arugula on focaccia. Another favorite is tuna and fusilli salad with capers, served with la vache bread. Open Monday through Friday 11:00 A.M. until 3:00 P.M., Saturday 11:30 A.M. until 3:00 P.M. $$. (910) 693–1487.

Restaurant 195. 197 Bell Avenue, Southern Pines 28387. Specializing in all-natural cuisine, this restaurant's grilled portabello mushroom sandwich ranks as the favorite menu item. Other popular items include the grilled Angus beef burger with Maytag Blue cheese, and the linguine with grilled shrimp, broccoli, and garlic. Open for lunch and dinner Wednesday through Friday, lunch only on Tuesday. Closed Sunday and Monday. $$. (910) 692–7110.

Chef Warren's. 215 Northeast Broad Street, Southern Pines 28387. This cozy French bistro presents you with mouthwatering menus that feature nightly specials and seasonal dishes. Open for dinner Monday through Saturday. $$$. (910) 692–5240.

Ice Cream Parlor. 176 Northwest Broad Street, Southern Pines 28387. A popular spot among the lunch crowd, the Ice Cream Parlor specializes in old-fashioned hand-pattied burgers served Southern-style with mustard, chili, slaw, and onions. It also serves homemade chicken salad, cakes, and, of course, ice cream. $. Open daily. (910) 692–7273.

WHERE TO STAY

Jefferson Inn. 150 West New Hampshire Avenue, Southern Pines 28387. Established in 1902, the Jefferson inn is located in the historic district of Southern Pines. The Inn has twenty charming rooms and three suites, all newly redecorated. Experience fine dining in the dining room or more casual fare in "T" Patrick's Pub, Steak and Chop House. $$. (910) 692–5300 or (800) 322–1249.

Knollwood House. 1495 West Connecticut Avenue, Southern Pines 28387. Five acres of longleaf pines, dogwoods, magnolias, holly trees, and flowering shrubs surround visitors at this English manor house, appointed with eighteenth-century antiques and the comforts of home. From the back terrace, it's 100 feet to the fifteenth fairway of championship golfing. Enjoy swimming, tennis, and golf. Full breakfast. Knollwood House has five guest rooms and suites with private baths. $$$. (910) 692-9390, www.bbonline.com/nc/knollwood/.

ABERDEEN

Early settlers in this area were predominantly Scottish, and their heritage is still prevalent. Originally known as Blue's Crossing, Aberdeen was renamed in 1887 for a seaport in Scotland.

WHERE TO GO

Malcolm Blue Farm. Bethesda Road, Aberdeen 28315. Built around 1825, this antebellum farm has been recognized by the National Register of Historic Places for its authenticity and uniqueness. Structurally, the site contains the farmhouse and barns, the old gristmill, and a wooden water tower, and stands as a significant preservation of rural history in Moore County. Annual events at the Malcolm Blue Farm include the Historic Crafts and Skills Festival the last weekend of September and the Christmas Open House on the second Sunday of December. Open Wednesday through Saturday 1:00 to 4:00 P.M. Free. (910) 944-7685.

WHERE TO STAY

Inn at Bryant House. 214 North Poplar Street, Aberdeen 28315. A Historic Registry property that has been completely restored to its original 1913 splendor, the inn is located one block east of US 1 in the historic district of downtown Aberdeen, six minutes from Pinehurst. It offers ten guest rooms (all with private baths), a spacious parlor, living and dining areas, and shaded porches and outside areas, as well as a full breakfast. $$. (910) 944-3300 or (800) 453-4019, www.innatbryanthouse.com.

Interstate 40 west takes you to the town that locals call the "Southern Part of Heaven." Although Wolfpack and Blue Devil fans may beg to differ, a day trip to this destination gives you the chance to visit a truly great rival, the University of North Carolina, and the town it inspired.

CHAPEL HILL

Chapel Hill was named after the New Hope Chapel, which stood on a hill at the crossing of two primary roads in the late 1700s. Town lots were auctioned in 1793 when construction began on the university. In 1795, residents occupied permanent homes.

Authorized by the North Carolina Constitution in 1776, the University of North Carolina at Chapel Hill was chartered in 1789, delayed by the Revolutionary War. The cornerstone for Old East, the first state university building in the United States, was laid in 1793. The University of North Carolina at Chapel Hill was the first state university to open its doors when the first student arrived in the winter of 1795 after walking the 170 miles from Wilmington. It was the only public university in the nation to award degrees to students in the eighteenth century.

As part of the sixteen-campus University of North Carolina system, today UNC-CH is ranked among the great institutions of higher education in the nation. The campus covers 740 acres and provides education to more than 24,000 undergraduate, graduate, and professional students.

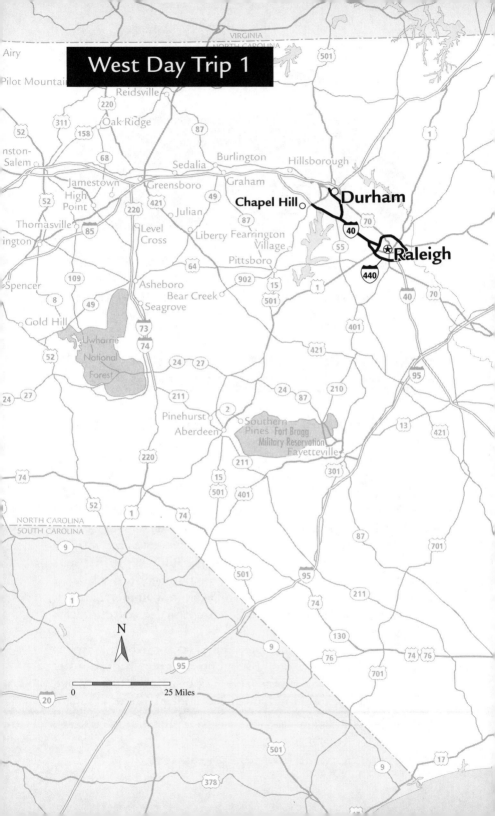

West Day Trip 1

In the early years, Chapel Hill grew along with the university. In 1818, there were twenty-two buildings in Chapel Hill, including eighteen residences, inns, and stores. By 1836 Chapel Hill had one physician, but no lawyer and no schools except for the university. The town was incorporated in 1851.

Chapel Hill, today an idyllic college town, has a population of about 49,000. Its main thoroughfare is Franklin Street (named after Benjamin Franklin), which borders the campus and offers shops and boutiques, restaurants and cafes, movie theaters and houses of worship. The town has historic districts, museums, performing and visual arts activities, a library, parks, malls, and many recreational facilities.

In 1997, *Sports Illustrated* called Chapel Hill "the best college town in America." The city woos visitors with its down-home charm on Franklin Street, where you can sit at the soda fountain at Sutton's Drug Store, and wows them with such attractions as the Morehead Planetarium, where you can gaze at some 8,900 fixed stars on the Star Theater's vast dome, a true celestial treat.

Visit the university, browse the shops, and have lunch or dinner at one of the many "institutions" that are now Chapel Hill landmarks, such as the Rathskeller or Carolina Coffee Shop.

You might want to consider bringing bikes along. Chapel Hill and neighboring Carrboro are extremely bike-friendly towns with dedicated bike paths and good signage.

WHERE TO GO

Chapel Hill/Orange County Visitors Bureau. 501 West Franklin Street, Suite 104, Chapel Hill 27516. The visitors bureau, located downtown has free parking at the rear of the building. Pick up brochures or ask questions of the staff. Open Monday through Friday from 8:30 A.M. until 5:00 P.M. (888) 968–2060, www.chocvb.org.

The UNC Visitors' Center. 250 East Franklin Street, Chapel Hill 27599. Chartered in 1789, the nation's first state university covers more than 700 acres. Start your tour at the visitors center, near Morehead Planetarium, where you can pick up a map and a Sony Walkman, free of charge, for a self-guided tour narrated by Wallace Kuralt, brother of CBS newsman and Chapel Hill alumnus Charles Kuralt. Open Monday through Friday from 9:00 A.M. until 5:00 P.M., Saturdays, 10:00 A.M. until 4:00 P.M. (919) 962–1630.

Horace Williams House. 610 East Rosemary Street, Chapel Hill 27514. As the only historic house in Chapel Hill open to the public, the facility features changing art exhibits in its octagon wing and throughout the house, and hosts chamber music concerts on a regular basis. A weekly historic district bus tour departs from the house every Wednesday from April through November at 2:00 P.M. Tour fee is $5.00 for adults, $3.00 for children 4 to 12. Also offered is a self-guided tour that takes you to a number of Chapel Hill's historic homes, as well as the oldest church in town. Descriptive brochures are available for a token 15 cents. Open Tuesday through Friday 10:00 A.M. until 4:00 P.M.; Sunday 1:00 to 4:00 P.M.; closed on major holidays and the first two weeks in August. (919) 942-7818, www.chapelhillpreservation.com.

North Carolina Botanical Garden. Old Mason Farm Road, Chapel Hill 27514. The largest natural botanical garden in the Southeast, the North Carolina Botanical Garden consists of 600 acres of preserved land, including nature trails, carnivorous plant collections, and aquatic and herb gardens. Collections of North Carolina and Southeastern plants are arranged by habitats in simulated natural settings. Walk from the beach to the mountains, botanically speaking, in just a few minutes. Be sure to visit North Carolina playwright Paul Green's restored cabin, moved here from a site nearby. Group guided tours by advance arrangement and self-guided tours for individuals are available. The facility also presents revolving exhibits of paintings, quilts, and other media, plus sculpture in various sections of the botanical collection. Open year-round, Monday through Friday 8:00 A.M. until 5:00 P.M.; Saturday, 10:00 A.M. until 5:00 P.M. with extended weekend hours during summer. Free. (919) 962-0522, www.unc.edu/depts/ncbg/.

The Blue Heaven Basketball Museum. 1840 Airport Road, Chapel Hill 27514. With the largest public exhibition of Carolina basketball memorabilia in the country, the museum has items such as the 1924 season scorebook, 1957 warm-up uniforms, a 1982 NCAA Championship ring and watches, and 1993 jerseys on display to honor UNC's four national championships. There are also multimedia displays, including the oldest known film and audio of Carolina basketball. Admission is $5.00 for ages 12 and up, $3.00 for those under 12. (919) 929-5877, www.blueheavenmuseum.com.

Dean Smith Center and Carolina Memorabilia Room. Skipper Bowles Drive, Chapel Hill 27514. The Dean E. Smith Center is the third largest on-campus arena in the country, with a seating capacity of 21,572 for basketball games and 20,380 for concerts. Located on the second level of the center is a memorabilia room with artifacts and highlight tapes of some of the greatest moments in the University of North Carolina at Chapel Hill's rich sports history. Championship trophies and exhibits are found throughout the facility. Self-guided tours are available. Open Monday through Friday 8:00 A.M. until 5:00 P.M. except on event and game days. (919) 962–7777, www.tarheelblue.com.

Morehead Planetarium. 250 East Franklin Street, Chapel Hill 27514. The first planetarium in the South, Morehead Planetarium has been teaching space sciences education since 1950. The planetarium features public shows in the Star Theater, educational exhibits, the Rotunda Portrait Gallery, Infinity gift shop, and a sundial rose garden. Self-guided tours are offered. Star Theater admission is $3.50 for children, senior citizens, and students; $4.50 for adults. Building hours: Sunday through Tuesday 12:30 to 5:00 P.M., Wednesday through Saturday 10:00 A.M. until 5:00 P.M. and 7:00 to 9:45 P.M. (919) 549–6863 (Info Line) or (919) 962–1236 (Office), www.morehead.unc.edu.

Chapel Hill Museum. 523 East Franklin Street, Chapel Hill 27514. The museum is a never-ending pursuit to identify and define the special nature of the history and heritage of Chapel Hill and its environs. Self-guided tours are available. Free. Open Thursday through Saturday 10:00 A.M. until 4:00 P.M., Sunday 1:00 to 4:00 P.M., (919) 967–1400, www.chapelhillmuseum.org.

Charles Kuralt Learning Center. UNC School of Journalism, Chapel Hill 27514. The Kuralt Center is on the second floor of Carroll Hall on the UNC campus. Much of Kuralt's TV works, including the famous CBS *On the Road* episodes have been digitized so visitors can watch the programs using touch-screen technology. The contents of Kuralt's three-room office suite on West 57th Street in midtown Manhattan have also been re-created here. (919) 962–1204.

North Carolina Collection Gallery. University of North Carolina at Chapel Hill Louis Round Wilson Library, South Road, Chapel Hill 27599. The gallery presents exhibits on the history of North Carolina and UNC. The world's largest collection of resource materials related to Sir Walter Raleigh is here, including a document signed by Queen Elizabeth I in 1570. Be sure to visit the North Carolina Collection, a treasure trove of historical material relating to the state and the Southern Manuscripts Department, which includes the Charles Kuralt Collection, (the latter is closed on Sunday, so visit this one Saturday if it's high on your list). Standing guided group tours are conducted every Wednesday at 2:00 P.M. Free. Open Monday through Friday 9:00 A.M. until 5:00 P.M., Saturday 9:00 A.M. until 1:00 P.M., Sunday 1:00 to 5:00 P.M. (919) 962-1172, www.lib.unc.edu/ncc/gallery.html.

Governors Club Golf Course. 10100 Governors Drive, Chapel Hill 27514. Nonmembers may play on this private golf course while guests of club cottages. The twenty-seven-hole championship course was designed by Jack Nicklaus and awarded a MetroBravo! for Best Private Golf Course from *MetroMagazine*. (800) 925-0085.

Jordan Lake Educational State Forest. 2832 Big Woods Road, Chapel Hill 27514. Jordan Lake Educational State Forest is the newest of North Carolina's educational state forests. A variety of wildlife can be found here, including birds of prey, deer, songbirds, flying squirrels, and beavers. The 3/4-mile Talking Tree Trail features—you guessed it—"talking trees," each with a recorded message about its history and surroundings. (919) 542-1154 or (800) 468-6242.

University Lake. 400 South Fayetteville Road, Chapel Hill 27516. This 213-acre lake was created in 1932 as a source of drinking water for the university and the communities of Chapel Hill and Carrboro, as well as an outdoor recreation facility. The lake has fishing, picnic, and sunbathing areas; rowboats, canoes, motors, and paddleboats are available for rent. (919) 942-8007.

He's Not Here. 112 1/2 West Franklin Street, Chapel Hill 27516. One of the oldest and best-known nightspots in Chapel Hill, featuring classic rock and blues, He's Not Here is known for big (33 ounce) Carolina blue cups of beer. Cover charge is $2.00 to $3.00 for live entertainment only. (919) 942-7939.

WHERE TO SHOP

Chapel Hill Downtown, University Square, The Courtyard. 133 West Franklin Street, Chapel Hill 27516. East and West Franklin

Street and East and West Rosemary Street offer mostly family-owned and independent shops and restaurants. University Square at 133 and 143 West Franklin Street contains a selection of specialty stores on the concourse level of two midrise office buildings. The Courtyard at 431 West Franklin Street has a small arcade of shops and offices.

Glen Lennox. NC 54 East, Chapel Hill 27514. On the northeast corner of Fordham Boulevard (US 15-501) and Raleigh Road (NC 54), this was Chapel Hill's first shopping center. Built in 1950, it offers a selection of small shops and service businesses.

WHERE TO EAT

Il Palio Ristorante. The Siena Hotel, 1505 East Franklin Street, Chapel Hill, 27514. Enjoy classic Italian cuisine in North Carolina's only AAA four-diamond Italian restaurant. The chef prepares memorable Tuscan cuisine with an emphasis on flavorful infused oils and healthy alternatives, paired with fine Italian wines. Open for breakfast Monday through Friday 6:30 to 10:00 A.M., Saturday and Sunday 7:00 to 10:00 A.M.; for lunch daily, 11:30 A.M. until 2:00 P.M.; and for dinner nightly, 5:30 to 10:00 P.M. $$$. (919) 918-2545.

Michael Jordan's 23. 200 West Franklin Street, Chapel Hill 27516. The menu features contemporary American-style dishes with a nod to good old Southern cooking. The restaurant's decor reflects its namesake's days on the Tar Heel and Chicago Bulls basketball teams. The bar (with three TVs) serves lighter and less expensive fare until late night. Open for lunch and dinner daily except Mondays. $$$. (919) 960-9623.

Weaver Street Market and Cafe. 101 East Weaver Street, Carrboro 27510. Just a short hike or bike from downtown Chapel Hill, this co-op and organic-foods grocery store features a great salad bar, baked goods, sushi, and outdoor seating. The cafe is open 7:30 A.M. to 9:00 P.M. Monday through Friday. $-$$. (919) 929-0010.

The Rams Head Rathskeller. 157-A East Franklin Street, Chapel Hill 27514. Since 1948, this moderately priced Chapel Hill institution has offered great food in an easy-going, fun atmosphere. Traditional specialties include steaks (its signature Gambler), lasagna (a 21-ounce serving that includes nine ounces of cheese!), roast beef dinners, sandwiches, and homemade desserts. Open daily for lunch and dinner. $$. (919) 942-5158.

Top of the Hill Restaurant and Brewery. 100 East Franklin Street, Chapel Hill 27514. Overlooking downtown Chapel Hill from a large third-floor outdoor patio. Top of the Hill offers casual, upscale dining. The restaurant has won fourteen "Best of Triangle" awards, including Best Restaurant in Chapel Hill, Best Microbrew, and Best Outdoor Deck. There's live music Thursday evenings. Open daily 11:00 A.M. until 2:30 A.M. $$-$$$. (919) 929-8676.

Carolina Brewery. 460 West Franklin Street, Chapel Hill 27516. Chapel Hill's first microbrewery and restaurant serves contemporary American cuisine and handcrafted ales and lagers. Many dishes, including desserts, are made with beer. Live blues acts perform every Thursday. Open daily. $$. (919) 942-1800.

W.B. Yeats Irish Pub. 306-G West Franklin Street, Chapel Hill 27516. This Irish pub's menu and lunch buffet offer authentic Irish and American food. There's an outdoor patio, and live entertainment on weekends. Open daily. $$. (919) 960-8335.

Crook's Corner. 610 West Franklin Street, Chapel Hill 27516. Fine seasonal Southern dining and fresh seafood specialties are served inside and on a patio. The menu changes daily at this home of shrimp and grits and vegetarian jambalaya. Open daily 5:30 to 10:00 P.M., Sunday brunch from 10:30 A.M. until 2:00 P.M. $$-$$$. (919) 929-7643.

Mama Dip's Kitchen. 408 West Rosemary Street, Chapel Hill 27516. "Put a little South in your mouth!" Cookbook author "Mama Dip" has been preparing down-home Southern food since she was nine. Her restaurant offers an abundance of traditional American food, especially vegetables, the most popular menu item. Open Monday through Saturday 8:00 A.M. until 3:00 P.M. and 4:00 to 10:00 P.M., Sunday 8:00 A.M. until 9:00 P.M. $$ (919) 942-5837.

Carolina Crossroads. 211 Pittsboro Street, Chapel Hill 27516. Located on the UNC campus in the historic Carolina Inn, this Mobil four-star restaurant serves elegant American cuisine that melds world-class cooking with North Carolina seasonal specialties. It also has an award-winning wine list. British tea service daily at 3:00 P.M. Patio dining is available. Open daily for breakfast, 6:30 to 11:00 A.M.; for lunch, 11:00 A.M. until 2:00 P.M.; for dinner, 5:30 to 10:00 P.M. $$-$$$. (919) 918-2777.

Carolina Coffee Shop. 138 East Franklin Street, Chapel Hill 27514. A Chapel Hill landmark, established in 1922, this dim pub has wooden church pew booths where you can order a cup of coffee or a brew as well as a meal. $$. (919) 942-6875.

WHERE TO STAY

The Siena Hotel. 1505 East Franklin Street, Chapel Hill 27514. This elegant AAA four-diamond boutique hotel offers exceptional service amid fine antique furnishings. Classic Italian cuisine is served in Il Palio, the state's only AAA four-diamond Italian restaurant. Rates include a full buffet breakfast, nightly turndown service, local phone calls, and daily newspaper. On-site services: restaurant, lounge, fitness center, business center, room service, and airport shuttle. $$$. (919) 929-4000 or (800) 223-7379, www.sienahotel.com.

The Carolina Inn. 211 Pittsboro Street, Chapel Hill 27516. A historic AAA four-diamond 184-room hotel with a Mobil four-star restaurant, the Carolina offers gracious Southern hospitality and elegance. Located on the campus of UNC-CH, one block from charming downtown shops and restaurants, the inn has many amenities, including a fitness center, on-command video, room service, nightly turndown service, antiques, and a self-guided history tour. The Carolina Inn is listed on the National Register of Historic Places. $$$. (919) 933-2001 or (800) 962-8519, www.carolinainn.com.

The Inn at Bingham School. 6720 Mebane Oaks Road, Mebane 27302. Situated west of Chapel Hill on ten beautiful country acres, this award-winning historic inn (circa 1790, 1801, and 1835) offers five rooms with private baths, fireplaces, suite with whirlpool, full breakfast, wine and cheese, and free local calls. $$–$$$. (919) 563-5583 or (800) 566-5583, www.chapel-hill-inn.com.

Windy Oaks Inn. 1164 Old Lystra Road, Chapel Hill 27514. Five miles from campus, Windy Oaks offers complimentary extended continental breakfast and evening hors d'oeuvres and beverages. $$$. (919) 942-1001, www.windyoaksinn.com.

Best Western University Inn. 1320 NC 54 East, Chapel Hill 27514. This eighty-four-room property is convenient to UNC campus and Friday Center. Amenities include a free continental breakfast and an outdoor swimming pool. $$. (919) 932-3000 or (800) 528-1234, www.bestwestern.com/universityinnchapelhill.

Days Inn. 1312 North Fordham Boulevard, Chapel Hill 27514. Close to UNC and UNC hospitals and conveniently located near restaurants and shopping, Days Inn's suites feature Jacuzzis, king- and queen-size beds, in-room microwave ovens and fridges, and a complimentary continental breakfast. $$. (919) 929–3090 or (800) 329–7466, www.daysinn.com.

Hampton Inn Chapel Hill. 1740 US 15-501 North, Chapel Hill 27514. Hampton Inn offers a complimentary continental breakfast, an outdoor swimming pool, free local phone calls, free use of a health facility near the hotel, and the convenience of the UNC campus and UNC Hospitals. $$. (919) 968–3000 or (800) 426–7866, www.hampton-inn.com.

Holiday Inn Chapel Hill. 1301 North Fordham Boulevard, Chapel Hill 27514. On-site amenities include Teddy's Restaurant, open for breakfast and dinner, Teddy's Lounge, a fitness center, an outdoor swimming pool, and room service. The hotel provides a free shuttle to downtown and UNC hospitals. $$. (919) 929–2171 or (888) 452–5765, www.holidayinnchapelhill.com.

Chatham County and its county seat, Pittsboro, were named for the first Earl of Chatham, William Pitt (1708–1778). The good Earl reportedly was a staunch defender of American independence, as were the fiercely independent residents of the newly formed Chatham County. Their Court of Pleas and Quarter Sessions abandoned the customary extolling of the King and his titles in 1773, long before the first shot rang out in New England.

PITTSBORO

Located in the heart of North Carolina, Pittsboro offers beautiful rolling landscape, quaint antique stores, pottery shops, and more than fifty art studios and galleries.

Pittsboro is a great day trip to combine with Chapel Hill (see West Day Trip 1). Should you pair the two, plan to stop at Fearrington Village while traveling between Chapel Hill and Pittsboro on US 15-501. Tucked away on farmland dating to the 1700s, Fearrington Village is the anchor to a bustling center of shops and services that serve the 1,500 residents of this special community.

WHERE TO GO

Chatham County Courthouse and Historical Museum. Historic Traffic Circle at the intersection of US 15-501 and US 64, Pittsboro 27312. Built in 1881 and designed by a local lawyer after the roof

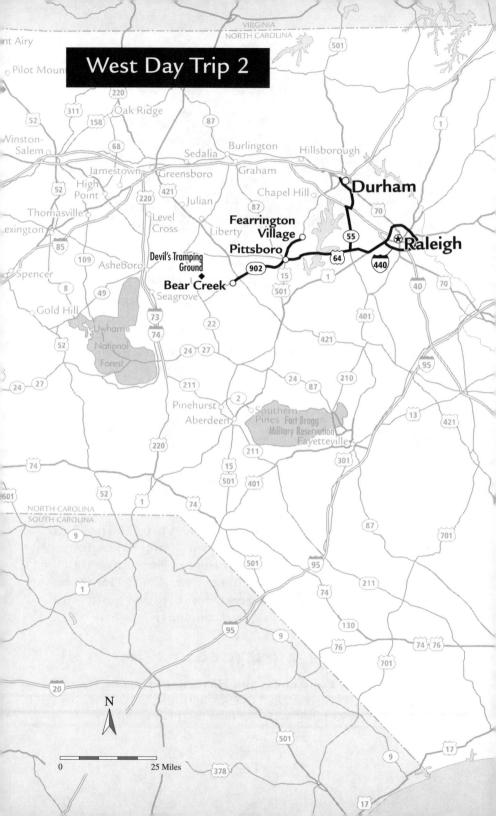

West Day Trip 2

VIRGINIA
NORTH CAROLINA

t Airy

Pilot Moun

501

220

311

52   158

Oak Ridge

87

52   68

Winston-
Salem

Jamestown

Sedalia   Burlington   Hillsborough

Greensboro   Graham

1

52   High
Point

421

Chapel Hill

Durham

70

Thomasville

220   Julian

87

Fearrington
Village

exington

Level
Cross

Liberty

Pittsboro

55

Raleigh

85

Devil's Tramping
Ground

902

64

440

109   Asheboro

15

1

40   70

Spencer

8   49

Bear Creek

Seagrove

501

Gold Hill

73

22

401

52   Uwharrie

74

National

24   27

421

Forest

24   27

211

24   87

210

95

Pinehurst

2

Aberdeen

Southern
Pines Fort Bragg
Military Reservation
Fayetteville

13

421

220

211

301

74

15

501

52   1   74

401

87

701

NORTH CAROLINA
SOUTH CAROLINA

9

501

95

1

74

211

20

N

9

130

95

76

74   76

701

0   25 Miles

501

9

17

378

17

blew off an earlier building during a trial, this is the fourth court-house built in the county since 1771. Listed on the National Register of Historic Places, it was extensively renovated in 1959 and again in the late 1980s. The courtroom is open on weekdays; the Chatham Historical Museum is open on Fridays from 10:00 A.M. until 2:00 P.M. (800) 316–3829, www.chathamhistory.org.

Hall-London House. 206 Hillsboro Street, Pittsboro 27312. Henry Armand London was a lawyer, state senator, and founder-editor of the *Chatham Record,* the local newspaper that has been in continuous publication since 1878. The Winnie Davis chapter of the United Daughters of the Confederacy was founded here in 1898 by London's wife, Bettie Louise Jackson, and others. The home has been converted to offices and is open during normal business hours. Special arrangements for visiting nonpublic areas can be made with Bradshaw, Vernon, and Robinson. (919) 542–2400.

Manly Law Office. Masonic Street, US 15-501, Pittsboro 27312. Charles Manly was governor of North Carolina from 1849 to 1850. A native of Chatham County, Manly had his law office built on Hillsboro Street (US 15-501), calling it Fort Snug. Moved and restored by the Chatham County Historical Association in 1971, the building may be visited by appointment. (919) 542–3603.

Pittsboro Historic District. Listed on the National Register of Historic Places, the district stretches beyond the original four-block center of the town to include Chatham Mills, the Patrick St. Lawrence House, the Pittsboro Community House, the County Courthouse, and other homes and buildings erected between the 1780s and 1949. Visitors may request a Pittsboro Historic District brochure (and a complete visitor information packet) from Chatham County Tourism. (800) 316–3829, www.visitchathamcounty.com.

Pittsboro Presbyterian Church. North East Street, Pittsboro 27312. The pews in Pittsboro's second brick structure (built in 1850) are believed to be the originals. The church bell, imported from London, was offered to and refused by the Confederate government during the Civil War. Open during church services. Arrangements can be made to visit during other times by calling the church office, (919) 542–4702.

Fearrington Garden Tours. 2000 Fearrington Village Center, Pittsboro 27312. Fearrington Garden is a 2000 MetroBravo! winner for Best Public Gardens (*Metro Magazine*). Each Thursday a horticulturist conducts guided group tours with an optional lunch. Stroll through on your own at any time. Be sure to see the Belted Galloways—the black-and-white "Oreo" cows—a rare breed of Scottish beef cattle. Fearrington's Galloways, however, have escaped the butcher, as their role here is strictly to add to the bucolic setting. Fearrington Village is open daily year-round. You can call them at (919) 542-1239 or (800) 316-3829, or check out the Web site at www.fearrington.com.

WHERE TO SHOP

Fearrington Farmers' Market. 2000 Fearrington Village Center, Pittsboro 27312. Stop here for baked goods, eggs, cut flowers, orchids, honey, jams, jellies, soaps, plants of all kinds, poultry, and other meats. Look for the market in the back of the Fearrington Village Center parking lot across from the pond. Open Tuesday 4:00 P.M. until dusk from April through October, rain or shine. (800) 316-3829 or (919) 542-2121, www.fearrington.com.

Pittsboro Antique Walk. Visit twelve great antique shops and five eateries and peruse more than 25,000 square feet of antiques. For more information contact Edwards Antiques, 89 Hillsboro Street, Pittsboro, NC 27312; (919) 542-5649; www.pittsboro-antiques.com.

Cooper Mays Pottery. 4222 US 15-501 North, Pittsboro 27312. Creating hand-thrown pottery, dinnerware, and one-of-a-kind art pottery for more than twenty-five years, the Cooper Mays studio and gallery are located on the banks of the Haw River. Seven cabins and kiln houses built on ten acres contain the production and retail gallery. All pottery made at the Cooper Mays Studio is hand thrown; no other methods are used. (919) 542-1518, www.coopermays.com.

Stone-Crow Pottery. 4269 US 15-501 North, Pittsboro 27312. Stone-Crow has been producing high-fire stoneware and porcelain for twenty-six years. The gallery is a restored 120-year-old log cabin sitting high above a waterfall on the Haw River. (919) 542-4708.

WHERE TO EAT

Fearrington House Country Hotel and Restaurant. 2000 Fearrington Village Center, Pittsboro 27312. The Fearrington House is one of only a handful of AAA five diamond award winners and Mobil five star recipients in the nation. Enjoy gourmet dining

Tuesday through Saturday 6:00 to 9:00 P.M., Sunday until 8:00 P.M. $$$. (919) 542–2121, www.fearringtonhouse.com.

Market Cafe at Fearrington. 2000 Fearrington Village Center, Pittsboro 27312. A full-service restaurant, deli, bar, and grocery store, the Market Cafe serves a wide array of contemporary American cuisine upstairs, while the downstairs grocery department carries the best in gourmet foods and favorite North Carolina products. Drop by for a copy of the *New York Times* and a bagel, or linger over a casual Sunday brunch. $$. (919) 542–5505.

Pitt Stop Cafe and Race Shop. 964 East Street, Pittsboro 27312. Dine and shop while watching NASCAR mechanics on the job. Home of the Busch Team, the Pitt Stop is decorated with nostalgic racing memorabilia, photographs, and track layouts. Suspended from the ceiling are noses and hoods from some of NASCAR's most memorable races. $$. (919) 545–9500, www.premieremotorsports.com.

S & T's Soda Shoppe. 85 Hillsboro Street, Pittsboro 27312. Enjoy good food and reminisce about the past in this nostalgic soda shop. Restored woodwork, a marble counter with bar stools, and several pieces from the past make this place a great stop in between shopping. Open Monday through Saturday 11:00 A.M. until 7:30 P.M. $$. (919) 545–0007.

The Scoreboard. 58 Hillsboro Street, Pittsboro 27312. Home of the "almost famous" cheeseburger, this hometown grill and bar serves good ole American cuisine. Special events, live music, and even shag night add to the fun. Open Monday through Saturday. $–$$. (919) 542–0376.

The General Store Cafe. 39 West Street, Pittsboro 27312. The cafe fare consists of homemade soups and innovatively prepared sandwiches and salads in a cozy, laid-back setting. For vegans, there's the tofu eggless salad sandwich. Enjoy local artwork displayed throughout the place. Open Monday through Saturday. $$. (919) 542–2432.

WHERE TO STAY

Fearrington House Country Hotel and Restaurant. 2000 Fearrington Village Center, Pittsboro 27312. A member of the prestigious Relais & Chateaux organization, Fearrington House is also a recipient of AAA's prestigious five diamond award and Exxon Mobil's five stars; it's the only establishment in North Carolina to

receive both accolades. Rates include gourmet breakfast and afternoon tea. $$$. (919) 542-2121, www.fearringtonhouse.com.

Rosemary Bed and Breakfast. 76 West Street, Pittsboro 27312. This 1912 Colonial Revival home in the heart of Pittsboro offers five guest rooms with private baths, telephones, cable TV/VCR, ceiling fans, fireplaces, two-person whirlpools, and a full gourmet breakfast. $$-$$$. (919) 542-5515 or (888) 643-2017, www.rosemary-bb.com.

BEAR CREEK

One worthwhile side trip is to Bear Creek, located about 20 miles west of Pittsboro on NC 902.

WHERE TO GO

Devil's Tramping Ground. State Road 1100, Bear Creek 27207. This site takes its name from a local legend attached to a circular path said to have been worn down by the devil's pacing as he plotted new forms of mischief.

On January 22, 1898, James I. Morris visited the area, when the Tramping Ground was in an undisturbed condition, and published a good description of it in *The Messenger,* a Siler City weekly newspaper. "On Saturday we visited that noted place known as the 'Devil's Tramping Ground.' This is the most peculiar spot of earth that we remember ever having seen. It is about one and a fourth miles from the X Roads and just a fourth of a mile from the old militia muster ground, known as Rock Spring . . . . The Tramping Ground is, we found to be on measurement, a perfect circle of 36 feet in diameter and resembles a large wheel or circus ring. The path is about 12 inches wide and as smooth and even as if rolled with some heavy iron instrument—nothing growing on this path whatever. It looks as slick as an otter slide. Crossing at right angles are two other paths similar to the outside one; making the whole thing look like a great big wheel. No vegetation whatever grows in these paths. But the strangest thing of it all is that inside of these angles grows the only wire grass that grows perhaps in 400 miles of this spot, and no other vegetation has ever, in the memory of those now living, grown on it, and there are persons nearly if not quite 90 years old living who remember seeing and hearing of it when they were little children, and so far as we can learn this phenomenon or freak or whatever you may call it existed before the knowledge of even their parents."

Follow NC 902 West to Harpers Crossroads and turn right on State Road 1106, then immediately turn left on State Road 1100. Go 1.7 miles until arriving at a gravel parking area on the left. The Tramping Ground is about 150 feet down a small path.

Southern Supreme. 1699 Hoyt Scott Road, Bear Creek 27207. While you're in Bear Creek, stop by for a tour and samples at the state's largest nutty fruitcake factory. (336) 581–3141, www.sosupreme.com.

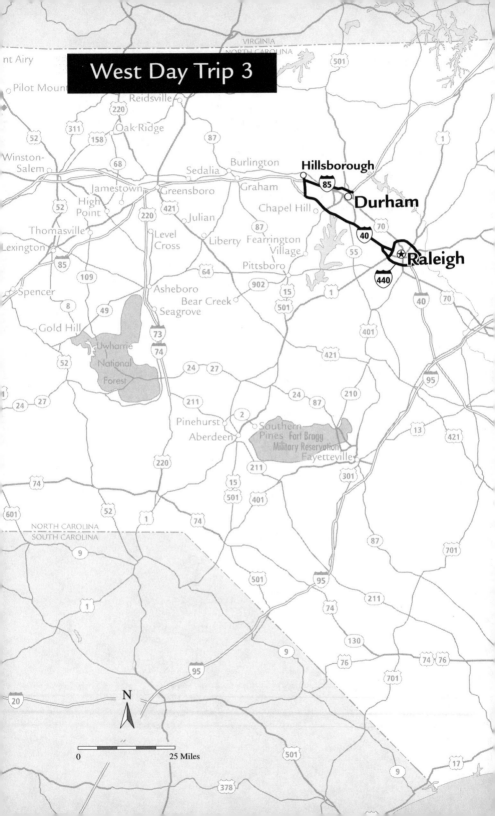

HILLSBOROUGH

Heading south on I-85 or west on I-40 takes you to Hillsborough, a flourishing small town that remains much as it has been since the eighteenth century. True to its heritage, Hillsborough is a refreshing stopover for the traveler interested in Southern and national history.

As a capital of colonial and revolutionary North Carolina, Hillsborough was the scene of many important and dramatic events, including the War of the Regulation (1768–1771), the Third Provincial Congress (1775), and the raising of the royal standard by General Cornwallis (1781).

As the seat of Orange County, Hillsborough remained an important center of politics. It was the final residence of William Hooper, a signer of the Declaration of Independence, and the birthplace of Thomas Hart Benton, who was instrumental in the expansion of the United States during the first half of the nineteenth century. Prominent statesmen and jurists lived here, including William A. Graham, Thomas Ruffin (Senior and Junior), Frederick Nash, James Hogg, Francis Nash, and Alfred Moore.

In 1754 William Churton, surveyor and agent for John Carteret, Earl Granville, laid out Hillsborough as a town near where the Great Indian Trading Path crossed the Eno River. A pleasing mixture of modern convenience and rural charm, Hillsborough's shaded avenues are a virtual record of the passing of two centuries, a combination of Colonial, antebellum, Victorian, and modern styles of architecture.

A living community rather than a reconstructed one, Hillsborough nevertheless has many lovingly restored buildings, both public and private, and the Town Hall is located in a former residence, complete with outbuildings.

Today you'll find more than one hundred sites listed on the National Register of Historic Places, some antedating the Revolutionary War. Gardens, flowering shrubs and trees, and a beautiful historical bed-and-breakfast add to the attractiveness of this small town. Antique shops offer artifacts with a regional emphasis, and the downtown area preserves a village atmosphere.

WHERE TO GO

Alexander Dickson House. Orange County Visitors Center and Office of the Alliance for Historic Hillsborough, 150 East King Street, Hillsborough 27278. This late eighteenth-century Quaker-plan house was moved from its original site nearby and has been restored as the Orange County Visitors Center. An adjacent garden displays traditional eighteenth- and nineteenth-century plants used for cooking, medicine, and dyeing cloth. The site also includes an office used by Confederate General Joseph E. Johnston in April 1865. Open Monday through Saturday 10:00 A.M. until 4:00 P.M., Sunday 1:00 to 4:00 P.M.; closed on major holidays. (919) 732-7741, www.historichillsborough.org.

Ayr Mount. 376 Saint Mary's Road, Hillsborough 27278. One of North Carolina's finest Federal-era plantation homes (circa 1815), Ayr Mount has been carefully restored and exquisitely furnished with period antiques and fine art. Included are many original family pieces of William Kirkland, who built the original 500-acre home for his wife and their fourteen children. The home was occupied by four generations of the family until 1971. Guided tours are offered from mid-March to mid-December, Wednesday through Saturday at 10:00 A.M., Thursday through Sunday at 2:00 P.M., and other times by appointment. The house tour is $6.00 per person, and there's a free one-mile self-guided tour called Poet's Walk around the site. Grounds are open daily 9:00 A.M. until 6:00 P.M. (919) 732-6886.

The Burwell School. 319 North Churton Street, Hillsborough 27278. Site of the Rev. and Mrs. Burwell's School for Young Ladies from 1837 to 1857, it includes a two-story frame house (circa 1821), brick music building (circa 1840), brick necessary house (circa 1840), and formal gardens. A half-hour guided tour focuses on the family, slaves, and the school's students in antebellum Hillsborough. Open Wednesday through Saturday 11:00 A.M. until 3:00 P.M., Sunday 1:00 to 4:00 P.M. Free. (919) 732-7451 or 732-7741.

Colonial Guides of Hillsborough. Experienced guides dressed in Colonial wear will fill you in on the facts, fantasy, and folklore of Hillsborough. The walking tour is held on the last Saturday of the month from May through October at 10:30 A.M. Departing from the Alexander Dickson House at 150 East King Street, tours are $5.00 for adults, $2.00 for children. (919) 732-0858.

Montrose Gardens. 320 Saint Mary's Road, Hillsborough 27278. These nationally known gardens were first planted in the nineteenth century by Governor and Mrs. William Alexander Graham. In addition to a large garden, specimen trees, a rock garden, a woods garden, and sunny perennial borders, several nineteenth-century buildings and architectural items remain. Guided tours are $6.00 per person, available by appointment on Tuesday and Thursday at 10:00 A.M., Saturday at 10:00 A.M. and 2:00 P.M. (919) 732-7787.

Occaneechi Indian Village. Foot of South Cameron Street, Hillsborough 27278. This Indian village is being reconstructed with a palisade, huts, a cooking site, and a sweat lodge, just as it was in the general area in the late seventeenth century when native tribes in south central Virginia and western North Carolina used it along a trading path. The Occaneechi-Saponi Spring Cultural Festival is held here each year, along with various Occaneechi Living Village Days. Don your archaeological duds to poke around the old mill sites and dams along the Eno River, where Native American relics are still found. This was once an important trading route that connected native towns for thousands of years before Europeans arrived. Self-guided tours are available. Open daily during daylight hours. (919) 732-7741.

Orange County Historical Museum. 201 North Churton Street, Hillsborough 27278. Museum exhibits illustrate the first hundred years of Orange County's history and include the collection of silversmith William Huntington, Colonial weights and measures (the only complete set in the United States), and portraits of notable Colonial figures. A second-floor gallery features a different local artist each month. Open Tuesday through Saturday 11:00 A.M. until 4:00 P.M.; Sunday 1:00 to 4:00 P.M. Free. (919) 732-2201.

Old Orange County Courthouse. North Churton and East King Streets, Hillsborough 27278. Designed and built by John Berry in 1844–1845 the courthouse is an outstanding example of Greek Revival architecture, with details of woodwork and stair brackets from Asher Benjamins' pattern book. An English Clock (circa 1769), a gift to the town of Hillsborough, is in the courthouse cupola. (919) 732-7741.

WHERE TO SHOP

Daniel Boone Village. South Churton Street, Hillsborough 27278. Look for the Daniel Boone Statue near I–85 to find more than thirty antique shops and a working blacksmith shop. (919) 732-2361.

Bradiggins Gallery and Espresso Bar. 103 West King Street, Hillsborough 27278. Located in historic downtown Hillsborough, this two-story gallery displays an ever-changing collection of fine paintings, folk art, sculpture, African-American arts, ceramics, glass, jewelry, and—most of all—textiles from nationally known artists. Get your caffeine fix here too. (919) 732-7746, www.bradiggins.com.

Hillsborough Farmers' Market. East Margaret Lane, Hillsborough 27278. The finest and freshest locally grown produce, prepared foods, flowers, and crafts can be found here every Saturday from 7:00 A.M. until noon in April, every Wednesday from 5:00 to 8:00 P.M. from June through the first frost. (919) 732-8315.

WHERE TO EAT

Occoneechee Farm Steak House. 378 South Churton Street, Hillsborough 27278. Specializing in steak and seafood, Occoneechee Farm is open Wednesday through Sunday from 5:00 P.M. until 11:00 P.M. $$–$$$. (919) 732-6939.

Kelsey's Cafe. 105 North Churton Street, Hillsborough 27278. The menu here is traditional but varied, including American, Southern, seafood, and ethnic foods. Open daily 7:00 A.M. until 2:30 P.M. for breakfast and lunch; Friday for dinner from 5:00 to 9:00 P.M. $$. (919) 732-1155.

Tupelo's Restaurant. 101 North Churton Street, Hillsborough 27278. Diverse seasonal menu fuses Southern, Creole, Southwestern, and other regional flavors, and includes creative specialty entrees, daily fresh seafood, and sandwiches. Open Monday through Wednesday 11:30 A.M. until 9:00 P.M.; Thursday through Saturday 11:30 A.M. until 10:00 P.M. $$. (919) 643-7722.

Saratoga Grill. 108 South Churton Street, Hillsborough 27278. This charming second-story restaurant in the heart of historic Hillsborough specializes in grilled seafood. Open for lunch Tuesday through Saturday 11:30 A.M. until 3:00 P.M., dinner Tuesday through Thursday 5:00 to 9:00 P.M., and Friday and Saturday until 10:00 P.M. $$. (919) 732-2214.

Lu-E-G's Sandwich Shop. 111 North Churton Street, Hillsborough 27278. A quaint country-style cafe and old-fashioned ice cream parlor with a casual, homey ambience, Lu-E-G's serves an eclectic mix of Greek pockets, hummus, veggie dogs, and homemade spreads, and a wide assortment of beverages and soda fountain specialties. Enjoy live music (folk and bluegrass) Friday from 8:00 to 10:00 P.M. Open Monday through Thursday 8:00 A.M. until 5:00 P.M., Friday until 10:00 P.M., Saturday 9:00 A.M. until 4:00 P.M. $-$$. (919) 732-5453.

WHERE TO STAY

Hillsborough House Inn. 209 East Tryon Street, Hillsborough 27278. This romantic five-room, one-suite B&B features canopy beds, fireplaces, private baths, and porches. It has a huge front porch, a hammock, an outdoor swimming pool, and seven acres of woods, ponds, and gardens. $$$. (919) 644-1600 or (800) 616-1660, www.hillsboroughhouse.com.

Holiday Inn Express. 202 Cardinal Drive, Hillsborough 27278. Amenities include a complimentary continental breakfast, outdoor swimming pool, and fitness center. Kids up to age 17 stay for free. $$. (919) 644-7997 or (800) 465-4329, www.basshotels.com/hiexpress.

Microtel Inn and Suites. 120 Old Dogwood Street, Hillsborough 27278. Nicely furnished rooms have chiropractor-approved mattresses. $$. (919) 245-3102 or (888) 771-7171, www.microtelinn.com.

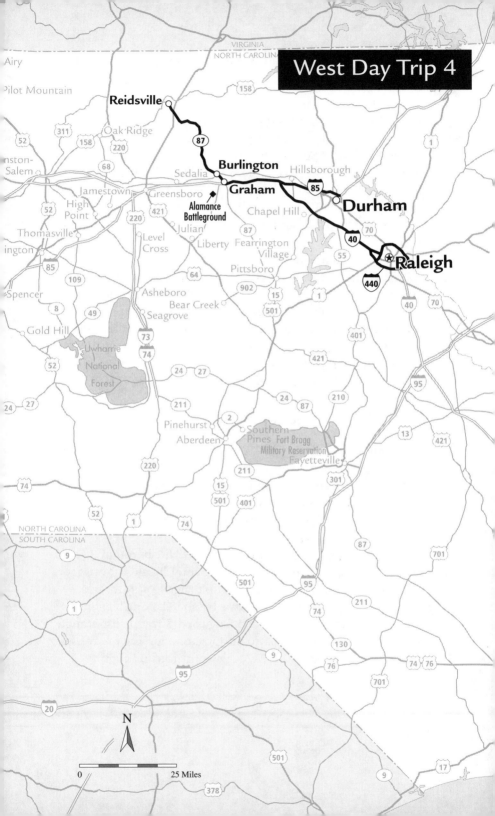

West Day Trip 4

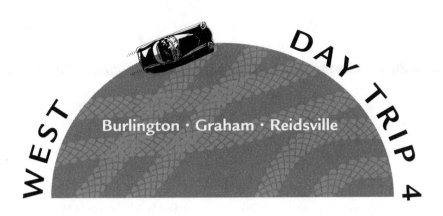

Burlington · Graham · Reidsville

Centrally located on Interstates 85 and 40 between the Blue Ridge Mountains and the Atlantic seashore, Burlington and Graham can be reached from Raleigh by car, bus, train, or plane (and, if you were really ambitious, by boat or canoe). Two trains daily, operated by Amtrak, chug between Raleigh and Burlington and beyond. Call (800) USA–RAIL or visit www.amtrak.com for rates and schedules.

As a side trip, travel north on NC 87 to Reidsville, where you'll visit Chinqua-Penn Plantation, a twenty-seven-room mansion that was the home of Jeff and Betsy Penn. Penn's father and uncle started the Penn Tobacco Company, which they later sold to the American Tobacco Company. Jeff subsequently purchased several hundred acres of land in Rockingham County and called the new tract Corn Jug Farm, which later became Chinqua-Penn Plantation, named for the chinquapin, a dwarf chestnut tree.

BURLINGTON

In 1851 the North Carolina Railroad built its repair shops here and dubbed the community—what else?—Company Shops. Wanting a real name, citizens submitted a list of suggestions in 1887. Katherine Scales, daughter of the governor, suggested Burlington.

Burlington's attractions include a Revolutionary War battleground, museums of local history, special events like hot air ballooning, and an abundance of outlet shopping. Relax at a park with a restored carousel or at a working historical farm. The performing arts are presented at local outdoor dramas and theaters. If you decide to spend the night, rest your head in a pre-Civil War cabin, an upscale bed-and-breakfast, or one of Burlington's many hotels or motels.

WHERE TO GO

Burlington/Alamance County Convention and Visitor's Bureau. 610 South Lexington Street, Burlington 27216. Located in downtown Burlington, the county's visitors bureau is a good place to begin your visit. Pick up brochures and maps and ask questions of the friendly staff. In fact, you can start from the office to visit downtown Burlington attractions. (800) 637-3804, www.burlington-area-nc.org.

Paramount Theater. 128 East Front Street, Burlington 27215. This renovated theater in Historic Downtown Burlington has an Art Deco motif. The theater is home to such groups as the Gallery Players, the Alamance Children's Theater, and its own Paramount Acting Company. Hours and admission vary with events. (336) 222-5001.

Dentzel Menagerie Carousel. South Church Street (NC 70), Burlington 27215. The centerpiece of the seventy-six-acre Burlington City Park is a restored 1910 Dentzel Menagerie Carousel with forty-six hand-carved animals. Worldwide, only fourteen Dentzel Menagerie Carousels remain intact. Dentzel carvers were renowned for their realism, apparent in the facial expressions and muscle definition of the animals. The horses have real horsehair tails, and all the animals have shiny, round glass eyes. No two animals are alike. Hours vary by season, so call ahead. Admission is 50 cents. (336) 222-5030.

Alamance Battleground. 5803 South NC 62, Burlington 27215. This battle site is where Royal Governor William Tryon led the North Carolina militia against the Regulators on May 16, 1771. Located on the grounds is the Allen House, a log dwelling characteristic of those lived in by frontier settlers. Constructed around 1780, the Allen House has been restored and refurbished with its original furnishings. Hours vary. Free. (336) 227-4785, www.ah.dcr.state.nc.us/sections/hs/alamance/alamanc.htm.

ACE Speedway/NASCAR Racing. 3401 Altamahaw-Race Track Road, Altamahaw 27202. Seven miles north of Burlington, this

NASCAR-sanctioned speedway hosts weekly races in season. See stock car racing on a newly expanded 4/10-mile asphalt track every Friday night from April to September. Racing divisions include late-model stock, modifieds, super stock, and mini stock. Pits open at 5:00 P.M.; grandstands open at 5:30 P.M.; race begins at 8:00 P.M. Admission is $12.00 for adults, $8.00 for ages 13 to 16 and seniors, $4.00 for ages 6 to 12, under 6 free. (336) 585–1200 (office) or (336) 584–6354 (race nights), www.acespeedway.com.

Glencoe Mill Village, River Road. Burlington 27215. Travel back in time to when a cotton mill was the center of a community. The Glencoe Mill Village consists of a cotton mill complex and associated worker housing community built on a 105-acre site along the Haw River between 1880 and 1882. Two sons of Edwin M. Holt, arguably the most influential textile pioneer in the nineteenth-century South, developed the mill. Glencoe remains one of the best-preserved mill villages in North Carolina, providing a picture of the social and commercial organization of a late nineteenth-century water-powered Southern cotton mill village. The village, currently undergoing restoration, welcomes drive-by visitation. (336) 228–6644, www.presnc.org.

Ballooning. The Hospice League Balloon Festival and Airshow is held in the spring, annually except in 2002. For private balloon trips, the following pilots are commercially rated by the FAA: Aerial Impressions, Ken Draughn, 2834 McKinney Street, Burlington 27215, (336) 227–5414; Balloon Promotions of NC Inc., Chip Groome/Beverly Ray, 4265 Shepherd Drive, Burlington 27215, (336) 584–7473 (features a balloon that will fly five people); John Jr. and Joyce, 1104 East Willowbrook Drive, Burlington 27215, (336) 227–0218.

WHERE TO SHOP

Burlington Manufacturers Outlet Center. 2389 Corporation Parkway, Burlington 27215. Burlington Manufacturers Outlet Center features quality name brands, selection, and value at its more than seventy-five outlet and designer stores. (336) 227–2872, www.save-at-bmoc-outlets.com.

WHERE TO EAT

Hursey's Pig-Pickin' Bar-B-Q. 1834 South Church Street, Burlington 27215. Recognized by *USA Today* as serving some of the best barbecue in the country, Reporter Jerry Shriver describes Hursey's barbecue as "hickory-smoked shoulder meat, laced with just the right amount of vinegar and a little sweetener, and tomato in the sauce on the side." Seafood and chicken are also available. Open Monday through Saturday 11:00 A.M. to 9:00 P.M. $-$$. (336) 226-1694.

The Blue Ribbon Diner. 2465 South Church Street, Burlington 27215. Designed to replicate a 1950s diner, the Blue Ribbon serves a daily blue plate special, hamburgers, cheeseburgers, and grilled chicken platters or baskets. Be sure to save room for an old-fashioned milk shake or dessert. Haw River Mud is an oversize, fresh-baked brownie topped with Breyers vanilla ice cream, Hershey's chocolate syrup, whipped cream, and a cherry; the Peach Cobbler Sundae is homestyle peach cobbler topped off with vanilla ice cream. Open daily for lunch and dinner. $$. (336) 570-1120, www.bestfoodintown.com.

B. Christopher's. 2260 South Church Street, Burlington 27215. Because this restaurant fronts an office complex, it's easy to overlook B. Christopher's as just another law office or staffing company. Inside you'll find great food, including Chicken Savannah, herb-marinated chicken breasts served with mashed potatoes and a cucumber relish, along with tenderloin medallions and the restaurant's most requested entree, shrimp and grits. Open Monday through Saturday 5:00 to 10:00 P.M. $$-$$$. (336) 222-1177.

Seventy West Cheesecakes. 1048 South Church Street, Burlington 27215. Choose from fifteen flavors of cheesecake, or try the Southern-style cheese biscuits, pie mixes, or muffin and bread pots. Open Monday through Friday 9:00 A.M. until 7:00 P.M., and Saturday 11:00 A.M. until 5:00 P.M. (takeout only). (800) 753-2884.

WHERE TO STAY

Morrow-Barnwell House. 426 West Front Street, Burlington 27215. Located in Burlington's historic district, this 1892 bed-and-breakfast features two bedrooms, a meal plan, a large formal garden, a goldfish pond, a veranda, and a wraparound porch. The National Wildlife Federation has certified the grounds as an official backyard habitat for more than thirty species of birds. $$. (336) 228-1340.

Courtyard by Marriott. 3211 Wilson Drive, Burlington, NC, 27215. The Marriott has a lounge with fireplace, an outdoor pool, an exercise room and Jacuzzi, and a restaurant with a full breakfast buffet. $$. (800) 321–2211.

Hampton Inn. 2701 Kirkpatrick Road, Burlington 27215. The Hampton Inn offers a complimentary continental breakfast, free local calls, fitness center, spa, sauna, and outdoor pool. $$. (800) HAMPTON.

Holiday Inn Outlet Center. 2444 Maple Avenue, Burlington 27215. The Holiday Inn has an outdoor pool, fitness center, business center, restaurant, lounge, and Jacuzzi suites. $$. (800) HOLIDAY.

Burke Manor Inn Bed and Breakfast. 303 Burke Street, Gibsonville 27249. Although it's 20 miles from Greensboro, this upscale, elegant retreat decorated in period furniture is worth the drive. The inn has an on-site restaurant and an outdoor pool. $$–$$$. (336) 449–6266 or (888) 287–5311, www.bbonline.com.nc/burkemanor.

GRAHAM

Formerly part of Orange County, Alamance County was formed in 1849; Graham was designated as the new county seat. In the act providing for the town, Graham was first named Gallatin, then Montgomery, Berry, and finally Graham, after Governor William A. Graham (1845–1849). An equal distance from the coastal region in the east and the Blue Ridge Mountains in the west, Graham is the second largest city in Alamance County.

WHERE TO GO

Alamance County Arts Council/Captain James and Emma Holt White House. 213 South Main Street, Graham 27253. Through adaptive restoration, the Alamance County Arts Council has turned the 1871 Queen Anne–style mansion of Captain James and Emma Holt White into an art gallery and a home for the Arts Council office. The gallery's changing exhibits showcase artists of local, regional, and national acclaim, and the sales gallery carries handmade gifts and crafts by North Carolina artisans. The house offers formal reception rooms and garden. Open Monday through Saturday 9:00 A.M. to 5:00 P.M. Free. (336) 226–4495.

Alamance County Courthouse. 1 Court Square, Graham 27253. The neoclassic Revival Alamance County Courthouse is a three-story stone building located on a hexagonal plot in the center of Graham's commercial district. Designed in 1925 by Harry Barton, a noted architect of the period, the structure replaced the original brick courthouse built in 1849. Sophisticated and richly detailed, the Alamance County Courthouse is the major landmark in Graham. Its scale, style, and materials blend well with the town's commercial buildings, many of which are contemporaries of the courthouse. (336) 570–6860.

City of Graham Historical Museum. 135 West Elm Street, Graham 27253. The museum is the home for Graham Fire Department's Engine 1, a 1930 Seagraves fire truck. Other firefighting equipment is on display, along with local pottery, weapons, military artifacts, and other historical pieces that are related to the history of the citizens of Graham. (336) 570–6700.

Graham Cinema. 119 North Main Street, Graham 27253. According to the owners, the Graham Cinema offers "one theater with one big screen, not a bunch of little bitty screens back in a corner somewhere." With rocking-chair seats, free refills on popcorn and drinks, and first-run movies, the Graham Cinema also features amusing synopses of current flicks. Give a call to learn what's playing. Admission is $6.00 for adults; $4.00 for kids and seniors. Saturday and Sunday matinees are $4.00 for all. (336) 226–1488.

Sesquicentennial Park. Court Square, Graham 27253. Relax in this pleasant park that was developed to commemorate Alamance County's 150th birthday, celebrated on April 24, 1999. The 2,500-square-foot park has a garden, an arbor for vines, park benches, brick walls, and a 10,600-pound bell that sat atop the original courthouse in Graham. (336) 570–1444.

WHERE TO EAT

Carver's on Elm. 106 West Elm Street, Graham 27253. With daily specials of good home cooking, Carver's on Elm is a great restaurant for families. Selections range from prime rib to chicken tenders to oysters. Open Sunday through Friday for lunch, Tuesday through Saturday for dinner. $$. (336) 229–0641.

Barrister's Cafe. 28 Northwest Court Square, Graham 27253. Located in the Paris Building on the Graham Courthouse Square,

Barrister's Cafe offers wonderful sandwiches, soups, and salads. With choices such as the turkey bacon club, blackened chicken salad, and hot house chili, Barrister's is a great place for lunch or dinner. Open Monday through Thursday 11:00 A.M. until 9:00 P.M., Friday and Saturday until 10:00 P.M. $$. (336) 221–1112.

WHERE TO STAY

The Victorian Rose Bed and Breakfast Inn. 407 Graham Road, Graham 27253. Restored to its former grandeur, this 1885 historic mansion has six romantic guest rooms, including a Victorian bridal suite and a four-room suite with whirlpool bath. $$–$$$. (888) ROSE–841, www.bbonline.com.nc/vicrose.

REIDSVILLE

In May 1814, farmer Reuben Reid moved his family to a 700-acre farm on the ridge between Wolf Island and Little Troublesome Creeks in south Rockingham County. Reid became a successful farmer, operated a store and a public inn maintained in a private home, and served the county as a constable and justice of the peace. When the family secured a post office in 1829, sixteen-year-old David Reid was appointed its first postmaster. He later became a state senator (1835–42), a U.S. congressman (1843–47), governor of North Carolina (1850), and a U.S. senator (1854).

The town was incorporated in 1873 by the North Carolina State Legislature. Tobacco was a mainstay of the local economy for many years, and the history of the city was tightly woven with that of American Tobacco Company, which was sold and moved from Reidsville in 1994.

WHERE TO GO

Chinqua-Penn Plantation. 2138 Wentworth Street, Reidsville 27320. The 1920s come alive at this remarkable, historic twenty-seven-room mansion surrounded by award-winning gardens. Stroll through twenty-two acres of historic landscape that reflects the original splendor of Jeff and Betsy Penn. Take a guided tour of the mansion, and see an amazing collection of art and artifacts representing more than thirty countries. Open Tuesday through Saturday 9:00 A.M. until 5:00 P.M., Sunday noon until 5:00 P.M. Open in January and February by appointment only; closed Thanksgiving and Christmas. (336) 349–4576, www.chinquapenn.com.

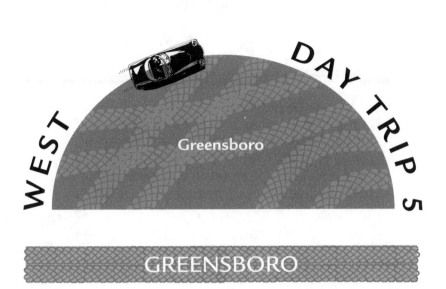

GREENSBORO

Travel back in time as you head west on I-40 to Greensboro. This Triad city allows you to relive history from the Revolutionary War battle to the sit-ins that helped launch a national civil rights movement.

The Saura and Keyauwee Indians were the earliest inhabitants of the region. Germans, Quakers of Welsh and English descent, and Scotch-Irish from the northern colonies were the first European settlers in the Greensboro area. These pioneers worked the land and shaped the future for generations to come. Permanent settlement began around 1740.

In 1767, a Presbyterian minister, David Caldwell, started a local school known as the Log College to educate young men for the ministry. One of his students was John Motley Morehead, governor of North Carolina from 1841 to 1845.

North Carolina's Colonial assembly created Guilford County in 1771. Three years later, a log courthouse and jail were built in a place called Guilford Courthouse, the site of a fierce battle on March 15, 1781. That day, American Major General Nathanael Greene deployed 4,400 rebels at the Battle of Guilford Courthouse to thwart the invasion of North Carolina by 1,900 redcoats under Lord Cornwallis. Cornwallis held the field after an intense fight, but he lost a quarter of his army, which hastened his defeat at Yorktown seven months later.

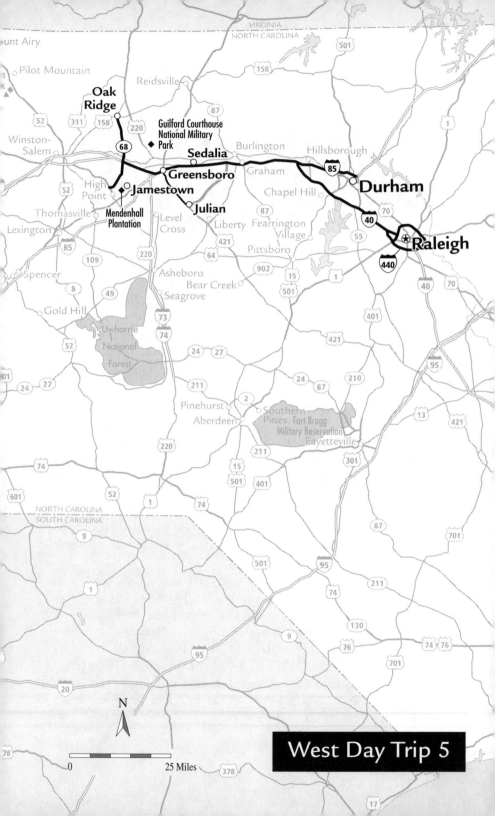

West Day Trip 5

In 1807, the residents of the area voted to create a new, more centrally located seat of government. The following year, elected officials mapped out a forty-two-acre tract of land, paid $98 to purchase it, and suggested that it be named Greensborough in honor of General Greene.

The railroad was a key factor in Greensboro's prosperity and industrial growth. John Motley Morehead, a North Carolina governor, campaigned for two decades to have Greensboro included as a stop on the North Carolina Railroad. Finally, in 1856, a special east-west line of tracks was completed.

During the Civil War, Greensboro was both a storehouse and a railroad center for the Confederacy, a vital source of supplies and troops for Robert E. Lee's Army of Northern Virginia. Civilian refugees and wounded soldiers were transported and sheltered here. Greensboro became the seat of the Confederacy on April 11, 1865, as Confederate President Jefferson Davis arrived here after Lee's surrender at Appomattox to discuss the military situation of General Joseph E. Johnston and the weakened Army of the Tennessee.

A reluctant Davis was advised by Johnston that the Confederate situation was untenable and that he should enter into surrender negotiations with Sherman. These negotiations led to Johnston's surrender to Sherman on April 26, 1865, at Bennett Place outside Durham. Later, all Confederate forces in North Carolina were mustered out and paroled in Greensboro.

William Sydney Porter was an eyewitness to the occupation of Greensboro by Union troops. Years later, using his pen name, O. Henry, he recounted these experiences in some of his short stories. Porter's uncle ran a successful town drugstore in the 1890s. Lunsford Richardson, one of the store's investors, later developed a line of "Vick's Family Remedies." Vicks VapoRub was one of his successful creations.

Textiles were important in Greensboro as early as 1828, when Henry Humphreys built North Carolina's first steam-powered cotton mill. In 1895, Moses and Caesar Cone selected Greensboro for their Southern Finishing and Warehouse Co., forerunner of Cone Mills. By 1920, Blue Bell was a successful maker of bib overalls. In 1935, attracted by the city's railroad and airport, Burlington Industries moved its headquarters to Greensboro. Guilford Mills began operations in 1946.

Greensboro was again a military center during World War II when railroads brought thousands of soldiers here for army training. In 1944, the training facility became the Overseas Replacement Depot (ORD) for the Army Air Corps in the Eastern United States.

Today, Greensboro is a vibrant Piedmont city with much to offer the visitor.

WHERE TO GO

Greensboro Area Convention and Visitors Bureau. 317 South Greene Street, Greensboro 27401. Stop here for free guides, maps, and information on area attractions, accommodations, shopping, restaurants, golf, and a wide variety of activities and special events. (800) 344-2282 or (336) 274-2282, www.greensboronc.org.

Blandwood Mansion and Carriage House. 47 West Washington Street, Greensboro 27401. This elegant nineteenth-century Italian villa was home to former North Carolina Governor John Motley Morehead. The 1844 addition by renowned architect Alexander Jackson Davis contributed to Blandwood's designation as a National Historic Landmark. Today, it still displays many of its original furnishings, and is operated as a museum by Preservation Greensboro Inc. and the Blandwood Guild. Open Tuesday through Saturday 11:00 A.M. until 2:00 P.M., Sunday 2:00 to 5:00 P.M. The last tour begins thirty minutes before closing. Closed during the month of January. (336) 272-5003.

Greensboro Children's Museum. 220 North Church Street. Greensboro 27401. Hands-on exhibits and activities are designed for 1- to 10-year-olds. Fly in an airplane, dig for buried treasure, or wrap yourself in a gigantic bubble. Stroll through "Our Town," complete with a grocery store and bank, then take in the transportation, theater, and early childhood exhibit areas. Open Tuesday through Saturday 9:00 A.M. until 5:00 P.M., Friday until 9:00 P.M., and Sunday 1:00 to 5:00 P.M. Open on Monday in the summer. Admission charged. (336) 574-2898, www.gcmuseum.com.

Greensboro Historical Museum. 130 Summit Avenue, Greensboro 27401. Discover American history through the stories of Piedmont people and events in twelve galleries and two restored houses. You'll learn about the 1960 Greensboro sit-ins that made a difference across the nation, Dolley Madison's lasting legacy as first lady, and the charming short stories written by O. Henry. See the city through twentieth-century photography, imagine travel in a Model T, and marvel at furniture created by Piedmont craftsmen. You'll also have the chance to see a world-class collection of Civil War firearms, stroll through a historic cemetery, and check out the merchandise of an old-fashioned general store. Open Tuesday through Saturday 10:00 A.M. until 5:00 P.M., Sunday 2:00 to 5:00 P.M. Closed on City of Greensboro holidays except the Fourth of July. Free. (336) 373-2043, www.greensborohistory.org.

Carolina Theatre. 310 South Greene Street, Greensboro 27401. First opened in 1927, this restored vaudeville theater serves as one of Greensboro's principle performing arts centers, showcasing theater, dance, concerts, and films. The theater is listed on the National Register of Historic Places. (336) 333-2600, www.carolinatheatre.com.

The International Civil Rights Center and Museum/Sit-in Movement. 134 South Elm Street, Greensboro 27401. See the original counter where four North Carolina A&T State University students sat down and began the National Civil Rights Sit-in Movement. Located in the architecturally significant and historic Art Deco-style historic Woolworth Building, the counter will be the centerpiece of a three-level cultural center and museum when completed in 2007. Open Monday through Friday 10:00 A.M. until 5:00 P.M., Saturday and Sunday by appointment. Free. (336) 274-9199, www.sitinmovement.org.

Mattye Reed African Heritage Center. 1601 East Market Street, Greensboro 27411. Located in the Dudley Building on the North Carolina A&T State University campus, the museum houses one of the best collections of African culture in the country. See more than 3,500 art and craft items from more than thirty African nations, New Guinea, and Haiti. Open Monday through Friday 10:00 A.M. until 5:00 P.M. Free. (336) 334-3209.

O. Henry Statues. Corner of North Elm and Bellemeade Streets, Greensboro 27401. This three-piece outdoor sculpture group honors Greensboro's best-known writer, William Sydney Porter (O. Henry). It features a bronze likeness of the author, a 7-by-14-foot open book of his renowned short stories, and a statue of his small dog, Lovey. An exhibit of the life and times of O. Henry may be seen at the Greensboro Historical Museum. (336) 373-2043.

The Broach Theatre. 520 South Elm Street, Greensboro 27401. A professional theater company offers a full season of adult and children's theater in the heart of the Old Greensborough Historic District. Originally built in 1927 as the Salvation Army, this intimate theater is within walking distance of five of Greensboro's finest restaurants. Adult season runs February through July and September through December. Children's theater runs September through June. (336) 378-9300, www.broachtheatre.org.

Triad Stage. 232 South Elm Street, Greensboro 27401. Featuring classic, contemporary, and new theatrical works, both drama and comedy are presented in a 300-seat live performance theater with two spacious lobbies and many other amenities in the newly renovated, former Montgomery Ward store in Greensboro's downtown historic district. No performances in August and September. Box office, (336) 272-0160.

Old Greensborough and The Downtown Historic District. 47 Arlington Street, Greensboro 27401. This revitalized century-old commercial, residential, and industrial district features antique, art, and other unique shops and restaurants. The Antique and Art Festival is held each May on South Elm Street, providing antique appraisals, entertainment, and more than fifty invited antique and art vendors and food. Be sure to pick up the free downtown shopping guide available at most merchant locations, the Greensboro Area Convention and Visitors Bureau, Greensboro Historical Museum, and the Downtown Greensboro Incorporated office. (336) 379-0060.

Walkway of History. South Elm Street at February One Plaza, Greensboro 27401. Sidewalk markers chronicle six chapters in local African-American history, ranging from the first fugitive slave on the Underground Railroad to the first African-American state Supreme Court justice. The walkway was unveiled on the thirty-fourth anniversary of the Woolworth civil rights sit-ins by the "Greensboro Four."

Weatherspoon Art Museum. Spring Garden and Tate Streets, Greensboro 27413. On the campus of UNC-Greensboro, this fine museum houses a nationally recognized collection, outstanding special exhibitions, and educational activities. With six galleries and a sculpture courtyard, the museum has a collection of more than 5,000 objects, including paintings, sculptures, drawings, prints, and photographs, and objects in miscellaneous media. Highlights include the Dillard Collection of art on paper and the Cone Collection of prints and bronzes by Henri Matisse. Call for hours of operation. Free. (336) 334–5770, weatherspoon.uncg.edu.

Fordham's Drug. 514 South Elm Street, Greensboro 27406. Order a Coke, a cherry smash, or a root beer float made the old-fashioned way at the century-plus-old drugstore. Its flooring, ceiling, soda fountain counter, backdrop, and shelves are all original. (336) 272–5431.

Greensboro Cultural Center at Festival Park. 200 North Davie Street, Greensboro 27401. Browse through this architectural showplace housing fifteen visual and performing arts organizations, five art galleries, rehearsal halls, a sculpture garden, a privately operated restaurant with outdoor cafe-style seating and an outdoor amphitheater. Open Monday through Friday 8:00 A.M. until 10:00 P.M., Saturday 9:00 A.M. until 5:00 P.M., Sunday 2:00 to 5:00 P.M. Free. (336) 373–2712, www.ci.greensboro.nc.us/culture.

Tannenbaum Historic Park. 2200 New Garden Road, Greensboro 27410. Operated by the City of Greensboro's Parks and Recreation Department, this seven-and-a-half-acre park was the eighteenth-century farmstead of Joseph Hoskins, who served the Guilford County community as a constable, tax collector, and sheriff. During the Revolutionary War Battle of Guilford Courthouse, Hoskins's land served as a staging area for British troops under Cornwallis's command. The Colonial Heritage Center offers a variety of exhibits depicting life in colonial Guilford County. Living history programs are scheduled throughout the year. The park also offers a museum store and picnic area. Call for hours of operation. Free. (336) 545–5315, www.ci.greensboro.nc.us/leisure/tannenbaum.

Guilford Courthouse National Military Park. 2332 New Garden Road, Greensboro 27401. On more than 200 acres, twenty-eight monuments of soldiers, statesmen, and patriots of the American Revolution honor the site of the March 15, 1781, battle. Visitors can enjoy recently premiered projects telling the park story. Park activities include a self-guided auto tour (audiotape tour available) and colorful, informational on-site exhibits. In the visitor center, see a dramatic thirty-minute live-action film (shown on the hour), an animated battle map program, and information-packed museum exhibits featuring original Revolutionary War weaponry and artifacts. The park also provides paved walking trails and a bookstore. Open daily 8:30 A.M. until 5:00 P.M. Closed New Year's Day, Thanksgiving, and Christmas. Free. (336) 288–1776, www.nps.gov/guco.

Natural Science Center of Greensboro. 4301 Lawndale Drive, Greensboro 27455. At this hands-on museum, zoo, and planetarium, roam through the Dinosaur Gallery, learn about gems and minerals, see the lemurs, and enjoy touch labs. Visit snakes and amphibians in the Jaycee Herpetarium, pet animals in the zoo's petting area, explore Kids Alley, and interact with exciting traveling exhibits. Find unusual gifts in the Thesaurus Shoppe, as well as educational toys for imaginative minds. Open Monday through Saturday 9:00 A.M. until 5:00 P.M., Sunday 12:30 to 5:00 P.M. Admission is charged. (336) 288–3769, www.naturalsciencecenter.org.

Bicentennial Park and David Caldwell Historic Park. Hobbs Road just north of Friendly Avenue, Greensboro 27403. This beautiful garden has flowering and deciduous trees, shrubs, and annual beds, and **the Bog Garden,** a marsh of ferns, bamboo, and other plants. (336) 373–2199, www.greensborobeautiful.org.

The Greensboro Arboretum. Near Wendover Avenue at West Market Street, Greensboro 27402. Nine different labeled plant collections, special garden displays, and distinctive features are contained within a seventeen-acre portion of Lindley Park. The natural beauty of this area is inviting, and the planted collections provide appeal throughout the year. Open daily, sunrise to sunset. (336) 373–2199, www.greensborobeautiful.org.

Ice House. 6119 Landmark Center Boulevard, Greensboro 27407. This 36,000-square-foot structure houses a standard 200-by-85-foot ice surface. You'll find bilevel seating, four enclosed locker rooms with showers, three large multipurpose rooms, a full-service snack bar, and a pro shop. The Ice House is the official practice facility for the Generals, an East Coast Hockey League team, and home to the Greensboro Youth Hockey Association (GYHA). A wide variety of programs and events is available, including adult and youth hockey leagues and tournaments, figure skating lessons, clinics, and daily public skating sessions. Open daily 6:00 A.M. until midnight. (336) 852–1515, www.icechaletgso.com.

Celebration Station. 4315 Big Tree Way, Greensboro 27409. Enjoy a great collection of attractions designed to entertain the whole family, with miniature golf, go-carts, bumper boats, arcade games, batting cages, and two theme restaurants. Birthday and group party packages are available. Call for hours. (336) 316–0606, www.celebrationstation.com.

Wet 'n Wild Emerald Pointe Water Park. 3910 South Holden Road, I-85 exit 121, Greensboro 27406. The largest water park in the Carolinas and one of the top twelve in the United States offers more than thirty-five rides and attractions. The park provides incredible, exciting summer fun. Thunder Bay, one of only four tsunami (giant wave) pools in the country, makes massive, perfect waves. The Hydra Fighter II is an awesome interactive water coaster that lets you have as much fun on the ground as in the air. Enclosed slides, drop slides, tube rides, and cable glides provide thrills for all ages and sizes. Two great children's areas and a drifting lazy river complete the fun for everyone. Call for seasonal hours of operation. (336) 852-9721 or (800) 555-5900, www.emeraldpointe.com.

Castle McCulloch and The Crystal Garden. 3925 Kivett Drive, Jamestown 27282. Just a ten-minute drive south of Greensboro, the castle is a restored gold refinery listed on the National Register of Historic Places. Built in 1823 and restored in the 1980s, the granite structure has a drawbridge, a moat, and a 70-foot tower. The Crystal Garden, built in 1997, is reminiscent of Victorian times, with beveled glass walls, a crystal chandelier, and a lovely veranda with a commanding view of the castle across the lake. Open Monday through Friday 9:00 A.M. until 5:00 P.M. Free. (336) 887-5413, www.castlemcculloch.com.

Mendenhall Plantation. 603 West Main Street, Jamestown 27282. This early nineteenth-century Quaker plantation includes many unique outbuildings, a museum, and one of two existing false-bottom wagons used to transport runaway slaves during the time of the Underground Railroad. Call for hours of operation. (336) 454-3819, www.thedepot/com.groups-mendenhall.

Old Mill of Guilford. 1340 NC 68 North, Oak Ridge 27310. This water-powered working gristmill with the sights and smells of another era is listed on the National Register of Historic Places. The gift shop has a wide variety of stone-ground meals, honey, ham, and North Carolina pottery and crafts. Open daily 9:00 A.M. until 6:00 P.M. Free. (336) 643-4783.

Piedmont Dragway. 6750 Holt's Store Road, Julian 27283. If you live for the smell of scorched rubber, the whine of a turbo-charger, and the roar of a high-performance engine, then this popular drag strip is your ticket for one-on-one racing excitement. During its busy March through December season, you'll see funny car, Harley-Davidson motorcycle, and souped-up dragster competitions. Call for specific dates and ticket prices. The dragway is 6 miles southeast of Greensboro off I-85 exit 132. (336) 449-7411, www.piedmontdragway.com.

Charlotte Hawkins Brown Memorial State Historic Site. 6136 Burlington Road, Sedalia 27342. Ten miles east of Greensboro off I-85 exit 135, this is North Carolina's first official historic site to honor an African-American and a woman. The site is the former location of the Palmer Institute, an African-American preparatory school established by Brown in 1902. Open April through October, Monday through Saturday 9:00 A.M. until 5:00 P.M., Sunday 1:00 to 5:00 P.M.; November through March, Tuesday through Saturday 10:00 A.M. until 4:00 P.M., Sunday 1:00 to 4:00 P.M. Free. (336) 449-4846, www.ah.dcr.state.nc.us/sections/hs/chb/chb.htm.

WHERE TO SHOP

Friendly Center. Friendly Avenue near the Wendover Avenue overpass, Greensboro 27409. This shopping center, originally opened in 1957, is a telling example of how to manage a retail shopping establishment successfully. "The secret of our success is that we have not stood still," says Bill Hansen, director of property management for Friendly Center. Renovations began in 1992 and have continued since. New shops include an Ann Taylor Loft and Chicos. Also new is a multiplex theater, The Grande. Other shops include Barnes & Noble Booksellers, Old Navy, Banana Republic, Eddie Bauer, Victoria's Secret, The Gap, and more. Friendly Center also boasts several restaurants, including Harpers and the ever popular Jay's Deli. Open Monday through Saturday 10:00 A.M. until 9:00 P.M., Sunday 1:00 to 6:00 P.M. (336) 292-2789, www.friendlycenter.com.

Four Seasons Town Centre. 400 Four Seasons Town Centre, I-40 at High Point Road/Koury Boulevard, Greensboro 27407. Newly renovated, the Centre's three levels include more than 200 specialty stores and eateries, as well as Belk, CompUSA, Dillard's, and JC Penney. Stop by for a bite to eat in the Food Court, or enjoy free and regularly scheduled entertainment in the new performing arts amphitheater. Open Monday through Saturday 10:00 A.M. until 9:00 P.M., Sunday 12:30 to 6:00 P.M. (336) 292-0171, www.shopfourseasons.com.

Greensboro Farmers' Curb Market. 501 Yanceyville Street, Greensboro 27405. The best in home-grown vegetables, fruits, and produce is only half the story: Fresh-cut herbs and flowers, baked goods, pottery, and crafts also are available. Linger, chat with the crowd as goods are unloaded, and shop the old-fashioned way. Open January through April, Saturday 6:00 A.M. until noon; May through December, Tuesday and Thursday 2:00 to 6:00 P.M., Saturday 6:00 A.M. until noon. (336) 574–3547.

Piedmont Triad Farmers' Market. 2914 Sandy Ridge Road, Greensboro 27235. Visit North Carolina's fourth state-owned farmers' market. Get to know some of the South's friendliest people while shopping for local Piedmont fruits, vegetables, flowers, baked goods, jams, honey, crafts and more. Make sure you visit the garden center and restaurant while you're there. Open daily 6:00 A.M. until 6:00 P.M. (336) 605–9157, www.agr.state.nc.us/markets/facilit/farmark/triad/ index.htm.

Replacements, Ltd. Knox Road off I–85/40 exit 132 at Mt. Hope Church Road, Greensboro 27420. The world's largest retailer of old and new china, crystal, flatware, and collectibles has more than eight million pieces of inventory in 150,000+ patterns. During the free daily tours of the showrooms, museum, warehouse, and restoration facility, patrons can inquire about patterns and shop Replacements' 13,000-square-foot showroom for giftware, dinnerware, one-of-a-kind items, antiques, and collectibles. Open daily 8:00 A.M. until 9:00 P.M.; closed Christmas Day. Tours start every thrity minutes. (336) 697–3000 or (800) REPLACE, www.replacements.com.

Shopping in Old Greensborough. Browse more than a dozen antique shops, including old-fashioned clothing stores, a grocery and seed store, and a haven of bookstores, to name a few of the downtown treasures. A free downtown shopping guide is available at most merchant locations, the Greensboro Area Convention and Visitors Bureau, Greensboro Historical Museum, and Downtown Greensboro Incorporated. The district is located in and around South Elm Street from the 100 block south through the 600 block. It also includes the 300 blocks of South Davie and South Greene Streets, as well as portions of East and West Washington Street. For more information, call Downtown Greensboro Incorporated, (336) 379–0060.

State Street Station. Between North Elm and Church Streets, just north of Wendover Avenue. Stroll through a cordial, relaxed neighborhood of thirty-five unique shops, restaurants, and boutiques housed in elegantly refurbished 1920s vintage buildings. (336) 230–0623, www.statestreetstation.com.

WHERE TO EAT

The Green Valley Grill. 622 Green Valley Road, Greensboro 27408. Adjacent to the O. Henry Hotel, enjoy internationally elegant dining with an "Old World" influence. Changing menus feature regional European recipes that may be from Provence one month and Tuscany the next. For appetizers, try the "Expensive Mushrooms and Fancy Grits." The grits resemble polenta and are topped with chopped tomatoes and portabello mushrooms. Follow up with steak salad, topped with Gorgonzola crumbles. $$–$$$. (336) 854–2015.

Restaurant Pastiche. 223 South Elm Street, Greensboro 27401. International cuisine is served in a restored century-old building in downtown Greensboro. With a seasonally reflective menu and a 140-item artisan wine list, Pastiche was recently rated best new restaurant in Greensboro. Serving lunch and dinner Monday through Friday, dinner on Saturday. $–$$$. (336) 272–3331.

Red Oak Brew Pub. Guilford College Road at Friendly Avenue, Greensboro 27410. North Carolina's largest microbrewery offers a twenty-minute tour of the Bavarian-built brewhouse and fermentation cellar. See how lagers are brewed according to the 1516 Law of Purity. Taste samples of Red Oak, Battlefield Black, and other smooth beers. Red Oak raises its own free-range Angus beef and uses only all-natural, fresh ingredients in homemade specialties. Brewery tours are by reservation. Outdoor dining is available. Open daily. $$. (336) 299–3649.

Revival Grill. 604 Milner Drive, Greensboro 27410. The Revival Grill offers casual atmosphere, relaxing dining, and great food. Outdoor dining is available. Open daily. $$–$$$. (336) 297–0950.

Barn Dinner Theatre. 120 Stage Coach Trail, Greensboro 27409. Enjoy a popular Broadway-style play after sampling a traditional buffet at what is reportedly the oldest dinner theater in the country. Performances are Wednesday through Sunday evenings year-round. $$$. (336) 292–2211 or (800) 668–1764, www.barndinner.com.

Bert's Seafood. 2419 Spring Garden Street, Greensboro 27403. Specializing in fresh, nonfried seafood, Bert's has a *Wine Spectator* "Award of Excellence" wine list. Open daily for dinner. $$. (336) 854–2314.

Anton's Restaurant. 1628 Battleground Avenue, Greensboro 27408. A family restaurant serving Greensboro for more than forty years, Anton's specializes in Italian, steaks, seafood, salads, and sandwiches. Dine underground in the cellar. Open Monday through Friday for lunch and dinner, Saturday for dinner only. $$. (336) 273-1386.

Cafe Europa. Greensboro Cultural Center at Festival Park, 200 North Davie Street, Greensboro 27401. At this informal but stylish cafe, you can enjoy a full menu or dine lightly on a variety of hors d'oeuvres or appetizers. Enjoy wines from around the world, reasonably priced by the bottle or glass. Outdoor dining is available. Open Monday through Saturday for lunch and dinner, Sunday for brunch and dinner. $-$$. (336) 389-1010.

Di Valletta Restaurant. Grandover Resort and Conference Center, 1000 Club Road, Greensboro 27407. As the most elegant dining room in the Triad, this AAA four-diamond restaurant overlooks the golf course and offers unique Mediterranean dishes to suit all tastes. Outdoor dining is available. Open daily for breakfast, lunch, and dinner. $$-$$$. 336-834-4877.

Liberty Oak. 100 West Washington Street, Greensboro 27401. Rated four stars by Greensboro's *News & Record,* Liberty Oak offers casual elegance, a changing menu, extensive wines by the glass, and outdoor dining. Open Monday through Saturday for lunch and dinner. $-$$. (336) 273-7057.

Lucky 32. 1421 Westover Terrace, Greensboro 27408. Different menus every month or so relate to American regional cuisine. Menus might feature recipes from the Pacific Northwest one month and from New Orleans the next. Open daily for lunch and dinner, Sunday for brunch. $$-$$$. (336) 370-0707.

Rearn Thai Restaurant. 5109 West Market Street, Greensboro 27409. This restaurant serves great Thai food and offers lunch specials. Open Monday through Saturday for lunch and dinner. $-$$. (336) 292-5901.

Ruth's Chris Steak House. 800 Green Valley Road, Suite 100, Greensboro 27408. Ruth's Chris specializes in corn-fed aged Midwestern beef that is broiled at 1,800 degrees. Open daily. $$$ (336) 574-1515.

Saigon Cuisine Restaurant. 4205 High Point Road, Greensboro 27407. This small, intimate restaurant serves Vietnamese cuisine. Highly rated, it was featured in the January/February 2001 issue of

Saveur magazine as one of the one hundred best food finds in the country. Open Monday through Saturday. $$–$$$. (336) 294–9286.

White Oak Restaurant on Buffalo Lake. 699 East Cone Boulevard, Greensboro 27405. Located on the southern shore of Buffalo Lake, White Oak offers comfortable and innovative menu options. Dining rooms provide scenic views of the lake in a country house setting. Outdoor dining is available. Open daily. $$–$$$. (336) 358–1525.

Yum Yum Better Ice Cream Co. 1219 Spring Garden Street, Greensboro 27403. A Greensboro institution located near UNC-G, Yum Yum serves ice cream and hot dogs. Open Monday through Saturday. $. (336) 272–8284.

WHERE TO STAY

Grandover Resort and Conference Center. One Thousand Club Road, Greensboro 27407. Located on 1,500 acres, this AAA four-diamond resort has 247 guest rooms in an eleven-story tower, men's and women spa facilities, a four-court tennis complex, two racquetball courts, an indoor/outdoor swimming pool, five food and beverage outlets, and lush gardens, as well as the rolling terrain of the resort's top-rated golf courses. The resort has a spa with five treatment rooms and an 1,800-square-foot fitness center. $$$. (336) 294–1800 or (800) 472–6301, www.grandover.com.

O. Henry Hotel. 624 Green Valley Road, Greensboro 27409. Look for the rise of red brick conveniently located near Friendly Center. The stately AAA four-diamond hotel evokes the grandeur of the original O. Henry, which stood in downtown Greensboro from 1919 until it was demolished in 1978. The new hotel was designed, as were hotels at the turn of the twentieth century, to be a part of the community. Great restaurant and lounge are on premises (see Green Valley Grill under "Where to Eat"). $$$. (800) 965–8259, www.o.henryhotel.com.

Sheraton Greensboro Hotel/Joseph S. Koury Convention Center. 3121 High Point Road, Greensboro 27407. Rooms have 13-foot ceilings, extra-large bathrooms complete with whirlpool tubs, and a separate living area with pull-down bed. Six restaurants, four lounges, indoor/outdoor pool, health club, racquetball court, sauna and whirlpool, in-room voice mail with two-line telephone, in-room high-speed Internet access, satellite TV, pay-per-view movies, and nonsmoking and handicapped-accessible rooms are available. The Sheraton is adjacent to the Four Seasons Town Centre Shopping Mall. $$$. (336) 292–9161 or (800) 242–6556, www.sheratongreensboro.com.

Greenwood Bed and Breakfast. 205 North Park Drive, Greensboro 27401. A culinary escape where great conversation is "standard fare," this turn-of-the-century "Chalet on the Park" serves a fine-dining breakfast by candlelight. Located in Greensboro's finest historic district, it serves upscale traditional American dishes with New Orleans and European touches and offers private baths and an in-ground pool. $$. (336) 274–6350 or (800) 535–9363, www.greenwoodbb.com.

Biltmore Greensboro Hotel. 111 West Washington Street, Greensboro 27401. Accommodations at this unique European boutique hostelry, conveniently located in historic downtown Greensboro, include a complimentary deluxe continental breakfast. $$$. (336) 272–3474 or (800) 332–0303, www.biltmorehotelgreensboro.com.

Windy Hill Bed and Breakfast. 4719 Groometown Road, Greensboro 27407. Charming three-room bed-and-breakfast includes one room with private bath and two rooms with a shared bath. $$. (336) 294–1498, www.windyhillbb.com.

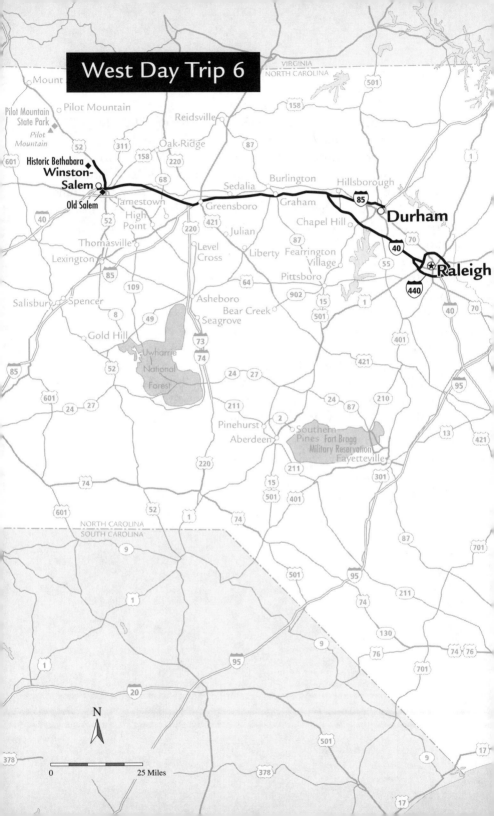

VIRGINIA
NORTH CAROLINA

501

Mount

158

Pilot Mountain
State Park

Pilot Mountain

Reidsville

601

52

Pilot
Mountain

311

Oak-Ridge

87

1

Historic Bethabara

158

220

Hillsborough

Winston-
Salem

68

Sedalia

Burlington

85

Old Salem

Jamestown

Graham

Durham

40

52

High
Point

Greensboro

Chapel Hill

70

Thomasville

220

Julian

87

40

55

Raleigh

Lexington

421

Level
Cross

Liberty

Fearrington
Village

440

85

109

64

Pittsboro

401

Salisbury   Spencer

8

Asheboro

902

15

1

421

Gold Hill

49

Bear Creek
Seagrove

501

85

Uwharrie

73

National

74

24   27

95

52

Forest

211

24   87   210

13   421

601

24   27

Pinehurst

2

Southern
Pines   Fort Bragg
Military Reservation
Fayetteville

74

Aberdeen

301

220

211

15
501   401

601

NORTH CAROLINA
SOUTH CAROLINA

52

1

74

87   701

9

501

95

211

1

74

378

20

130

9

76   74 76

1

95

701

N

501

9   17

378

17

0   25 Miles

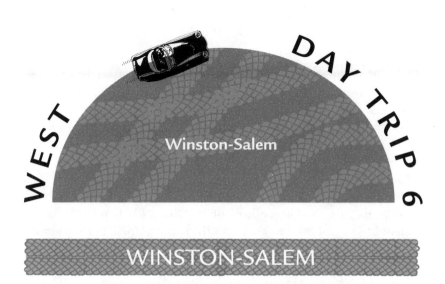

WINSTON-SALEM

In 1874, Richard Joshua Reynolds arrived here on horseback from Virginia to start a tobacco factory, which later became the R. J. Reynolds Tobacco Company. But more than a century before the tobacco baron set up shop here, the region was home to German-speaking Moravians.

The persecuted members of a Protestant sect came from Germany by way of Pennsylvania to settle in an area they called Die Wachau, later called Wachovia, and they established the villages of Bethabara and Bethania. You still can see how these thrifty people lived at Historic Bethabara Park, site of the area's first Moravian settlement, and at Old Salem, founded as a town and backcountry trading center in 1766.

With good reason, Winston-Salem's dominant tourism attraction today is Old Salem, a straight shot from Raleigh-Durham on I–40 west. The historic district near downtown is one of the most authentic restorations in the United States. No visit to Winston-Salem would be complete without a stroll along Old Salem's cobblestone streets, but there is much to see beyond Old Salem as well.

When Forsyth County was formed in 1849, Salem was chosen to be the county seat. Moravian leaders, however, sold the new county a parcel of land for a town a mile north of Salem Square. Two years later, that town was named Winston.

Enter Richard Joshua Reynolds. Tobacco ruled as king, and as it ascended to the throne, the stature of Winston was raised along with it. In 1913, Winston merged with Salem to become the largest city in North Carolina. Tobacco and textiles were huge industries that attracted large populations of people.

But tobacco is no longer king, and textiles are now produced offshore. Although recent census data puts Winston-Salem as the state's fourth largest city, it still has the cultural legacy left by the Moravians and by philanthropists such as Joshua Reynolds.

From the 1960s on, the city billed itself as the "City of the Arts," thanks in part to the goodwill of the Reynolds family. Winston-Salem boasts not only the nation's first arts council, but also ranks first place nationally in per capita contributions to the arts. The city has impressive art galleries, museums, and performance centers. The renowned North Carolina School of the Arts is here, as well as a symphony and even an opera company.

WHERE TO GO

Winston-Salem Visitor Center. 601 North Cherry Street, Winston-Salem 27101. Begin your excursion at the visitors center, either at the physical facility or on the Internet. At either, you can make reservations for accommodations or check out the schedule of performances at the Stevens Center. Pick up maps and ask for recommendations for lunch or dinner. (800) 331–7017, www.visitwinstonsalem.com.

Stevens Center. 405 West Fourth Street, Winston-Salem 27101. A restored 1929 movie palace in downtown Winston-Salem, the center is part of the acclaimed North Carolina School of the Arts and regularly showcases student and faculty work, as well as a host of feature performances that include chamber music, jazz, ballet, the symphony, and films. (336) 721–1945, www.ncarts.edu/Stevens_Center/.

Old Salem. 601 Old Salem Road, Winston-Salem 27101. Founded in 1766 as a Moravian church town and backcountry trading center, Salem has survived to become one of America's most authentic and well-documented Colonial sites. Now a living history town, costumed interpreters demonstrate the household activities and trades that were part of the daily lives of the European-American and African-American residents of Salem in the late eighteenth and early nineteenth centuries. Old Salem, which welcomes visitors into its homes, shops, and gardens year-round, is also home to St. Philips Moravian Church, the state's oldest standing African-American church, along with several museum shops, Salem Tavern restaurant, and the famous Winkler Bakery. An authentic restoration of a Moravian church town and backcountry trading center that began in 1766, Old Salem is the birthplace of modern-day Winston-Salem. The historic district features about one hundred restored and reconstructed buildings. Tours are self-guided, but guides and costumed staff aid in the process of viewing and understanding the town's buildings, operations, and the people who made this community grow and prosper.

Single Brother's House. 600 South Main Street, Winston–Salem 27101. A part of Old Salem, this restored example of a Germanic half-timbered construction (1768–86) in the Moravian planned community of Salem, it was used as a trade school for Moravian boys beginning at around age fourteen and as a dormitory for master craftsmen, journeymen, and apprentices. The first building of the Single Brothers' House (the half-timbered part) was built in 1769; the brick addition was added in 1786. The building has been restored to its original condition.

Salem Tavern. 800 South Main Street, Winston-Salem 27101. Also part of Old Salem, this original Salem Tavern was built in 1771 and was one of the first public buildings built in Salem. In 1784, it was destroyed by fire but quickly rebuilt using materials left over from constructing the Single Sisters' House. It reopened in 1785, and was restored to that condition in 1956. The tavern included two front rooms for gathering, and a gentlemen's room for private dining. Guests could rent rooms upstairs for overnight stays. The tavern's most important guest was President George Washington, who stayed from May 31 to June 2, 1791. He arrived in a cream-colored coach with his secretary, several outriders, and servants, and was greeted by a brass band and a cheering crowd.

The Old Salem Visitor Ticket, which allows two days of unlimited admission to the homes and community buildings on the tour, is $15.00 for adults, $8.00 for children ages 5 to 16. Value-added "All-In-One" tickets that include the Visitor Ticket plus a guided tour of MESDA, an audio walking tour, and the Children's Museum at Old Salem, are $20 for adults, $11 for children ages 5 to 16. Most buildings close for entry at 4:30 P.M. Purchase visitor tickets and watch a brief introduction to the Moravians and their town of Salem at the Old Salem Visitor Center, open Monday through Saturday 9:00 A.M. to

5:00 P.M., Sunday 12:30 to 5:00 P.M. Closed Easter, Thanksgiving, Christmas Eve, and Christmas Day. (888) 348–5420, www.oldsalem.org.

Southeastern Center for Contemporary Art (SECCA). 750 Marguerite Drive, Winston-Salem 27106. SECCA is a series of cascading galleries housed in the 1929 English hunting lodge home of the late industrialist James G. Hanes. The original structure has been enhanced with 20,000 square feet of exhibit space where temporary exhibits change several times a year and represent the finest contemporary art both regionally and nationally. Be sure to visit Centershop at SECCA to browse and purchase handcrafted jewelry, home decor items, unique toys, and more. Open Tuesday through Saturday 10:00 A.M. until 5:00 P.M., Sunday 2:00 to 5:00 P.M., closed Monday and national holidays. Admission: adults, $3.00; students and senior citizens, $2.00; children under 12, free. (336) 725–1904, www.secca.org.

Reynolda House, Museum of American Art. 2250 Reynolda Road, Winston-Salem 27106. An impressive collection of American masterpieces is scattered throughout the gracious sixty-four-room estate where R. J. and Katherine Reynolds lived. The architecture, furnishings, and costume collection reflect the Reynoldses' tastes. The artwork, on the other hand, reflects three centuries of major American paintings, prints, and sculptures by the likes of Jacob Lawrence, Jasper Johns, Stuart Davis, and Georgia O'Keeffe. The works are regarded as one of the finest collections of American art in North America. A National Historic Property, Reynolda House adjoins its original formal gardens and the estate's support buildings, now converted into specialty shops, offices, and restaurants. Open Tuesday through Saturday from 9:30 A.M. until 4:30 P.M., Sunday from 1:30 to 4:30 P.M. Closed on Monday, Thanksgiving, Christmas, and New Year's Day. Admission: adults $6.00; senior citizens $5.00, students and children $3.00. College students with valid identification are admitted free. (888) 663–1149, www.reynoldahouse.org.

Delta Fine Arts Center. 1511 East Third Street, Winston-Salem 27101. The arts center hosts events and activities year-round to emphasize the contributions of African-Americans to the arts and humanities. (336) 722–2625.

The Children's Museum at Old Salem. 924 South Main Street, Winston-Salem 27101. A hands-on "fun space" designed for children ages 4 to 9, the children's museum encourages exploration and play as a pathway to learning about life long ago. Along with a child-size Miksch House, a secret tunnel, and a marble roll, the museum includes a two-story modern climbing sculpture. Children can have a profile drawn, try on costumes from long ago, and build with "bricks." Admission ($4.00) is charged for any children who enter and play and who are old enough to walk. Admission if purchased with an Old Salem or MESDA ticket is $2.00, free with the "All-in-One" ticket. Open Monday through Friday from 9:00 A.M. to 5:00 P.M., Sunday from 1:00 to 5:00 P.M.; closed Easter, Thanksgiving, Christmas Eve, and Christmas Day. (336) 721-7300.

Museum of Early Southern Decorative Art (MESDA). 924 South Main Street, Winston-Salem 27101. Housed in the same building as the Children's Museum, MESDA is the only museum dedicated to exhibiting and researching the regional decorative arts of the early South. With its twenty-four period rooms and seven galleries, MESDA showcases the furniture, paintings, textiles, ceramics, silver, and other metalwares made and used in Maryland, Virginia, the Carolinas, Georgia, Kentucky, and Tennessee through 1820. Guided tours begin on the hour and half hour, and last about eighty minutes. The first and last tours begin at 9:30 A.M. and 3:30 P.M., Monday through Saturday, 1:30 and 3:30 P.M. on Sunday. Closed Easter, Thanksgiving, Christmas Eve, and Christmas Day. Admission is $10.00 for adults, $6.00 for children ages 5 to 16. (888) 348-5420, www.oldsalem.org.

The Gallery at Old Salem. 924 South Main Street, Winston-Salem 27101. Opened in 1996, the Gallery at Old Salem, located in the MESDA building, features changing exhibits. Admission: adults, $5.00; children ages 9 to 16, $3.00; children 8 and under, free. (888) 348-5420, www.oldsalem.org.

Historic Bethabara. 2147 Bethabara Road, Winston-Salem 27106. The first colonial townsite established in the Carolina Piedmont, Bethabara was intended to be a temporary town from which the central Moravian town of Salem and outlying farming communities would be developed within the Moravian lands of Wachovia. However, Bethabara continued in operation as a Moravian community long after Salem was established. Set in a beautiful 175-acre park, Bethabara was the only "House of Passage" built by the Moravians at any of their Colonial settlements in the New World. Archaeological investigations have demonstrated the Bethabara archaeological remains at the townsite are intact; this work has contributed to a significant understanding of the Moravian culture, in particular the manufacture of Moravian pottery. A National Historic Landmark, this 1753 site of the first Moravian settlement in North Carolina was the area's frontier trade and religious center until 1772. Tour the 1788 congregation house known as the Gemeinhaus, visit the archaeological remains in the reconstructed palisade fort, and stroll through the historic gardens. Exhibit buildings are open daily from April through November; grounds are open daily year-round. (336) 924–8191, www.bethabarapark.org.

SciWorks. 400 Hanes Mill Road, Winston-Salem 27105. A 120-seat planetarium, 25,000 square feet of exhibit space, and a multitude of programs and hands-on exhibits such as the Coastal Encounters lab tank, appeal to both the young and the young-at-heart. At SciWorks you'll be able to wish upon a star in the planetarium and learn about the earth and the solar system, watch chemicals fizz and react, and see a dinosaur from millions of years ago. There are picnic areas and an adjacent fifteen-acre environmental park with animals and nature trails. (336) 767–6730, www.sciworks.org.

WHERE TO SHOP

Piedmont Craftsmen Gallery. 1204 Reynolda Road, Winston-Salem 27104. The gallery showcases the work of more than 350 of the Southeast's finest craft artists. Open Tuesday through Saturday 10:00 A.M. until 6:00 P.M. (336) 725–1516, www.piedmontcraftsmen.org.

Hanes Mall. 3320 Silas Creek Parkway, Winston-Salem 27103. The largest mall between Washington D.C. and Atlanta has more than 200 stores. (336) 765–8321, www.shophanesmall.com.

Historic Reynolda Village. 2201 Reynolda Road, Winston-Salem 27106. On the former estate of R. J. Reynolds, this shopping plaza has more than thirty upscale shops, including restaurants, art galleries, jewelry and antiques, fine gifts, and specialty items. Open Monday through Saturday 10:00 A.M. until 5:00 P.M. (336) 758–5584.

erl Originals. 3069 Trenwest Drive, Winston-Salem 27103. Representing more than 400 American artists in 8,000 square feet of gallery space, erl exhibits more than 1,200 paintings, pottery, jewelry, sculpture, and fine contemporary studio glass, plus an extensive library of images. Open Monday through Friday 8:30 A.M. until 5:30 P.M., Saturday 10:00 A.M. until 5:00 P.M. (336) 760–4373, www.erloriginals.com.

Downtown Arts District. Meander along Trade and Sixth Streets near Adams Mark Hotel for the eclectic mix of shops and galleries that make up the resurging arts district. **Snapfingers Gifts and Home Accents,** 217 West Sixth Street, carries a collection of truly unique gifts, greeting cards, and home accessories; (336) 761–1955. **Urban Artware,** 207 West Sixth Street, is an art gallery and retail store with a mix of art and fine-crafted items, including one-of-a-kind artwork by some of the Southeast's finest contemporary artists, handcrafted jewelry, furniture, ceramics, wood, and glass items; (336) 722–2345. **Fiber Company,** 600 North Trade Street, a collective of fiber artist and designers established in 1987, has a working studio complemented by a shop and gallery that offer the works of member artists as well as that of other craftsmen; (336) 725–5277. **Artworks Gallery,** 560 North Trade Street, established in 1984, is an artist-run cooperative that exhibits members' works; (336) 723–5890. **The Bead Bar,** 537-A Trade Street, features beads from around the world; (336) 777–1224. **Earthbound Arts,** 610 Trade Street, which carries only locally made products, bills itself as "a magical world of handcrafted soap, candles, stained glass, copperwork, natural herbs, cards, jewelry, gourmet pickles and jams, and much more"; (336) 773–1043.

WHERE TO EAT

Salem Tavern. 736 Main Street, Winston-Salem 27101. A costumed staff serves lunch and dinner Monday through Saturday (plus lunch on Sunday from March through December) in the 1816 tavern annex. Some menu items are authentic Moravian fare. For lunch, try the Moravian chicken pie or the Moravian beef ragout. From 5:00 to 6:00 P.M., early-bird specials offer reduced rates on Moravian chicken pie and sauerkraut stew, which include a garden salad or cup of soup, vegetables, pumpkin muffins, rolls, and coffee or iced tea. Dinner reservations are recommended. Lunch reservations are only accepted for parties of six or more. $$–$$$. (336) 748–8585.

Winkler Bakery. 525 South Main Street, Winston-Salem 27101. Established in 1800, the bakery still serves up its famous coffee cake hot from the wood-fired oven. Winkler's offers as much history as food. (888) 348–5420, www.oldsalem.org.

Little Richard's Lexington BBQ. 4885 Country Club Road, Winston-Salem 27104. Stop here at "the original" Little Richards for some of the best barbecue this side of Lexington, North Carolina. Richard Berrier, who bills himself as "chef de swine," founded the restaurant with a partner in 1991 (the business appears to be older because the building was erected in 1968). The partner split and opened another Little Richard's just a few miles away. There are no bitter feelings, but Berrier wants folks to know that his location, identifiable by the three smoking chimneys, is the last one in Winston that still pit cooks its barbecue over hickory and hardwood coals. Try the chopped plate for the fullest smoked flavor. It comes with fries, homemade slaw, hush puppies, and rolls. For dessert, pick up a B&G Homemade Pie, made and packaged in Winston-Salem. $-$$. (336) 760–3457.

Zevely House Restaurant. 901 West Fourth Street, Winston-Salem 27101. Located in the historic West End, this oldest house in Winston offers an exquisite dining experience in small, elegant dining rooms or on the covered garden patio. $$$. (336) 725–6666.

Krispy Kreme. 259 South Stratford Road, Winston-Salem 27103. Winston-Salem is home to this doughnut giant, and the Stratford Road location is by far the most popular stop. Try to get there when the HOT DOUGHNUTS NOW sign is flashing and you can watch as these sugary delights come off the conveyor belt. Glazed, cream-filled, or with sprinkles. $. (336) 724–2484.

WestEnd Cafe. 926 West Fourth Street, Winston-Salem 27101. A trendy local favorite, the cafe serves salads, grinders, "heavy hoagies," Reubens, and other sandwiches. Open Monday through Friday 11:00 A.M. until 10:00 P.M., Saturday noon until 10:00 P.M. (336) 723–4774, www.westendcafe.com.

Fourth Street Filling Station. 871 West Fourth Street, Winston-Salem 27101. Originally a gas station, this totally revamped restaurant offers the best patio dining in town, with a fireplace inside for chilly nights. Menu choices range from salads to filet mignon. Try the pan-seared filet mignon with cognac cream sauce over buttermilk mashed potatoes. Also popular is the broiled mahimahi with a crab stuffing. Open 11:00 A.M. until 11:00 P.M. Monday through Thursday, until midnight on Friday and

Saturday. Sunday brunch from 10:00 A.M. until 3:00 P.M. $$–$$$. (336) 724–7600.

Village Tavern. 221 Reynolda Village, Winston-Salem 27106. Enjoy delicious entrees in a warm, casual atmosphere. Treat yourself to a meal on the outdoor patio, and then take a stroll through the many other shops and boutiques that make up Reynolda Village. Try the hot crab dip appetizer, which was created by the owner and hasn't changed in years. The Carolina burger, with homemade chili, is also another popular menu item. Open 11:00 A.M. until 11:00 P.M. Monday through Thursday, until midnight on Friday and Saturday, and Sunday 9:00 A.M. until 10:00 P.M. $$–$$$. (336) 748–0221.

WHERE TO STAY

Adams Mark Winston Plaza. 425 North Cherry Street, Winston-Salem 27101. As North Carolina's second largest hotel, the towering Adams Mark has 603 guest rooms, including 26 spacious suites. Try to book your room on the upper floors with views of the distant mountains, including Pilot Mountain and Hanging Rock. Be sure to ask about specials that put you on the Club Level (available for an extra $25 per night), where you'll receive special upgraded amenities and access to the staffed Club Lounge, which serves a complimentary continental breakfast and evening hors d'oeuvres. This downtown hotel has a glass-enclosed heated swimming pool with outdoor sundeck, a dry sauna, an 1,800-square-foot health club, two lounges, and a restaurant. (800) 444–2326, www.adamsmark.com.

Brookstown Inn. 200 Brookstown Avenue, Winston-Salem 27101. A seventy-one-room property adjacent to the restored village of Old Salem, the Brookstown Inn bills itself as an elegant bed-and-breakfast-style hostelry. On the National Register of Historic Places, the inn was once a warehouse and Winston-Salem's oldest factory. One of the largest historic inns in North America, the Brookstown's guest rooms typically have exposed brick and original beams and/or rafters. Ceilings are 12 to more than 20 feet high, and rooms range from approximately 350 square feet to more than 1,100. Rates include a complimentary wine and cheese reception hosted every evening from 5:00 to 7:00, and a complimentary continental breakfast each morning. $$$. (800) 845–4262, www.brookstowninn.com.

The Augustus T. Zevely Inn. 803 South Main Street, Winston-Salem 27101. As the only lodging in the Old Salem Historic District, this twelve-room bed-and-breakfast has been meticulously and accurately restored to its mid-nineteenth century appearance. The "Winter Kitchen" suite accommodates four, great for families. A continental-plus breakfast is served during the week and a full buffet breakfast on weekends; fresh fruit, fruit juices, and Moravian baked goods are always offered at breakfast. Complimentary wine and cheese are served in the evening. $$-$$$. (800) 928-9299, www.winston-salem-inn.com.

Henry F. Shaffner House. 150 South Marshall Street, Winston-Salem 27101. Built in 1907 by one of the cofounders of Wachovia Loan and Trust Company, this Victorian-style mansion, a restaurant and B&B, is just blocks from historic Old Salem and downtown Winston-Salem. Amenities include evening wine and cheese and a complimentary breakfast. Lunch is available Monday through Friday from 11:00 A.M. until 2:00 P.M.; fine dining seven days a week from 6:30 to 8:00 P.M. The Shaffner House has six rooms with private baths, three suites with private baths. $$-$$$ (800) 952-2256, www.bbonline.com.nc/henry/index.html.

Mount Airy · Pilot Mountain

On this day trip, you're headed to Mayberry. The fictional TV town was fashioned after Mount Airy for *The Andy Griffith Show*. Griffith grew up in a small home here, and although the actor now lives in Manteo, on the coast, it is here in Mount Airy that you will find the world's largest collection of Andy Griffith memorabilia. Other well-known celebrities, including country music singer Donna Fargo and bluegrass legend Tommy Jarrell, are natives of Mount Airy. The original Siamese twins, Eng and Chang Bunker, lived in the nearby White Plains community. You'll learn more about them at the Mount Airy Visitors Center.

Be sure to stop at Pilot Mountain, which Andy referred to as "Mount Pilot" in numerous episodes of *The Andy Griffith Show*. Take a hike to the top of this landmark for gorgeous views of the Piedmont, and to your west, the Blue Ridge Mountains.

MOUNT AIRY

Following I–40 west, exit on I–40 West Business past the Greensboro airport. In Winston–Salem, take US 52 /NC 8 north toward Mount Airy. The town ranked thirty-sixth in the 1996 edition of *The 100 Best Small Towns in America* (Norman Crampton, Hungry Minds, Inc.), recognized for its quality of life.

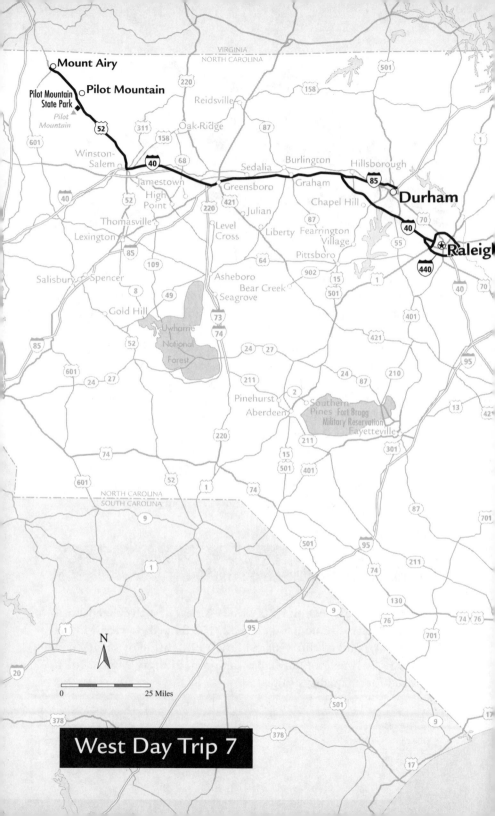

West Day Trip 7

WHERE TO GO

Andy Griffith Museum and Mount Airy Visitors Center. 615 North Main Street, Mount Airy 27030. This historic residence houses the world's largest collection of Andy Griffith memorabilia. Collected by Griffith's childhood friend and Mount Airy resident Emmett Forrest, the artifacts are displayed in three rooms. The collection contains everything from a *Matlock* suit to the chair Andy was rocked in as a baby. Additional exhibits cover topics of local and historical significance. Open daily except Christmas and New Year's Day. Free. (336) 789-4636 or (800) 576-0231, www.visitmayberry.com.

Andy Griffith Playhouse. 218 Rockford Street, Mount Airy 27030. The Andy Griffith Playhouse, circa 1920, is the first known site of a public school in Mount Airy. Andy Griffith attended elementary school and performed on stage when the site was known as the Rockford Street Elementary School. Named for Griffith in the early 1970s, it now houses the Surry Arts Council. (336) 786-7998 or (800) 286-6193, www.surryarts.org.

The Mayberry Jail. 215 City Hall, Mount Airy 27030. At this re-creation of the courthouse seen in episodes of *The Andy Griffith Show,* a vintage 1962 Ford Galaxie squad car sits out front to let you know the defenders of Mayberry are never far away. Open Monday through Friday 8:00 A.M. until 4:30 P.M. Free. (336) 786-6116 or (800) 948-0949.

Moore House. 202 Moore Avenue, Mount Airy 27030. Moore House, circa 1862, is the oldest remaining house in Mount Airy. Located in the front yard of the Moore House is a rustic hexagonal summerhouse constructed around 1865 with wood poles and inter-vening laurel root walls and a wood shingle roof. The furniture inside the summerhouse includes a settee, a chair, and a table with a laurel root base and plank top. (336) 786-6116 or (800) 948-0949, www.visitmayberry.com.

Mount Airy Museum of Regional History. 301 North Main Street, Mount Airy 27030. More than 15,000 square feet of exhibits include a 100-foot mural of the surrounding mountains. Exhibits range from displays about the region's natural history to the world's largest open-face granite quarry, located in Mount Airy, and include an authentic reproduction of a log cabin; a turn-of-the-century general store; a train room with a 70-foot scale model train exhibit;

a gallery on fire fighters that includes a 1916, 1926, and 1946 fire trucks, all used by the City of Mount Airy. The second floor focuses on the early 1900s and changing exhibits. A visit to the observation room, located on the fourth floor of the clock tower, provides an awesome view of the surrounding mountains. The Museum Gift Shoppe, located in the Main Gallery, has gift items related to exhibits, and local and regional history books are for sale. Open Tuesday through Friday 10:00 A.M. until 4:00 P.M., Saturday, 10:00 A.M. until 2:00 P.M. Fee. (336) 786–4478, www.visitmayberry.com.

Siamese Twins Burial Site. 506 Old Highway 601, Mount Airy 27030. Born in Siam (their nationality gave the birth defect in which two people are physically joined together its name), Eng and Chang Bunker became circus performers who fathered twenty-two children. Known as "the original Siamese twins," they are buried outside the Mount Airy city limits in the White Plains Church community. To get there, take NC 601 south from Mount Airy past a Wal-Mart on the left. Turn left onto Old Highway 601, traveling 2 miles to pass over I–74 to White Plains Baptist Church on the right. The cemetery is behind the church. (336) 786–6116 or (800) 948–0949, www.visitmayberry.com.

WHERE TO EAT

Snappy Lunch. 125 North Main Street, Mount Airy 27030. In an early episode of *The Andy Griffith Show*, titled "Andy the Matchmaker," Andy suggested to Barney that they go to the Snappy Lunch to get a bite to eat. Griffith also mentioned the restaurant in his version of the song "Silhouettes." And in a television news interview, Griffith talked about getting a hot dog and a bottle of pop for 15 cents at the Snappy Lunch when he was a boy. This restaurant is famous for the pork chop sandwich, which was created by restaurant owner Charles Dowell, who has been at Snappy Lunch for more than fifty years. Mount Airy's oldest restaurant, circa 1923, Snappy Lunch was featured in the November 1998 issue of *Gourmet*. $$. (336) 786–4931, www.visitmayberry.com.

WHERE TO STAY

Andy's Homeplace. 711 East Haymore Street, Mount Airy 27030. Spend the night in the home where Andy lived with his mother and father until he graduated from high school. Furnished with all the comforts of home, it has two bedrooms, a kitchen, a living room, and one bath. Rollaway beds are available for families or groups. Andy's Homeplace is located near the Andy Griffith Playhouse and Historic Downtown Mount Airy. Enjoy a continental breakfast provided by your host or have breakfast at Snappy Lunch. $$$. (336) 789–5999, www.andyshomeplace.com.

The Merritt House Bed and Breakfast. 618 North Main Street, Mount Airy 27030. Located in Historic Downtown Mount Airy, the Merritt House is a three-story, Victorian-style home with a towerlike front and an inviting wraparound porch. Rates include a complimentary homemade breakfast and an afternoon or evening refreshment. $$–$$$. (336) 786–2174 or (877) 786–2174, www.bbonline.com.nc/merritthouse/.

Mayberry Bed and Breakfast. 329 West Pine Street, Mount Airy 27030. Within walking distance of Historic Downtown Mount Airy, this bed-and-breakfast offers nice rooms and a full breakfast in the private courtyard. Children are welcome. $$. (336) 786–2045.

PILOT MOUNTAIN

Twelve miles south of Mount Airy and 26 miles north of Winston-Salem on US 52, Pilot Mountain offers views of the Winston-Salem skyline and the Blue Ridge Mountains. Stop here on the way to or from Mount Airy to get a feel for the high country.

WHERE TO GO

Pilot Mountain State Park. 1792 Pilot Knob Park Road, Pinnacle 27043. The solitary peak of Pilot Mountain, rising more than 1,400 feet above the rolling countryside of the upper Piedmont plateau, is the centerpiece of the state park. Divided into two sections, with 1,000 acres on the Yadkin River, the park offers hiking trails, scenic overlooks, picnicking, family and group camping, and a climbing area. Pilot Mountain was named a National Natural Landmark in 1976. Free. (336) 325–2355, www.ils.unc.edu/parkproject/visit/pimo/home.html.

WHERE TO STAY

Scenic Overlook Bed and Breakfast. 144 Scenic Overlook Lane, Pilot Mountain 27041. Situated on fifty acres, this bed-and-breakfast has large luxurious suites, all with a view of the lake and Pilot Mountain. Rooms have fireplaces and Jacuzzis; a meal plan, nonsmoking rooms, and boating are available. A complimentary full breakfast is served in suite. $$$. (336) 368–9591, www.scenicoverlook.com.

Flippin's Bed and Breakfast. 203 West Main Street, Pilot Mountain 27041. Situated in the picturesque setting of Pilot Mountain State Park, this Victorian-style bed-and-breakfast is lavishly furnished with antiques. A dog kennel and meal plan are available. $$–$$$. (336) 368–1183, www.bbonline.com.nc/flippins/.

High Point · Thomasville · Lexington

Southeast of Greensboro on I–85, High Point, Thomasville, and Lexington beckon the day visitor with their superlatives. What do we mean? Well, High Point claims the world's largest chest of drawers. Standing 32 feet high, the nineteenth-century dresser was restored to banish any doubt that High Point is the undisputed furniture capital of the world. Thus, one reason to visit High Point is to shop for furniture.

Nearby Thomasville boasts the state's oldest railroad depot and the world's largest chair, a 30-foot-high monument that sits square in the heart of downtown. The Duncan Phyfe chair rises 18 feet above its base and has seated President Lyndon B. Johnson, Robert Redford, and several Miss Americas.

Lexington, farther south on I–85, is famous worldwide for its barbecue. Nearly twenty restaurants serve pork that is cooked in time-honored ways with secret sauces, served chopped or sliced. Lexington-style barbecue, recognized far and wide (except in eastern North Carolina) as the nation's best pork barbecue, is the highlight of the annual Barbecue Festival the last Saturday in October.

HIGH POINT

In 1859, when High Point was named after the "highest point" on the North Carolina Railroad, city founders knew that its central location would attract industry and commerce. Today, High Point draws visitors from all fifty states and more than one hundred

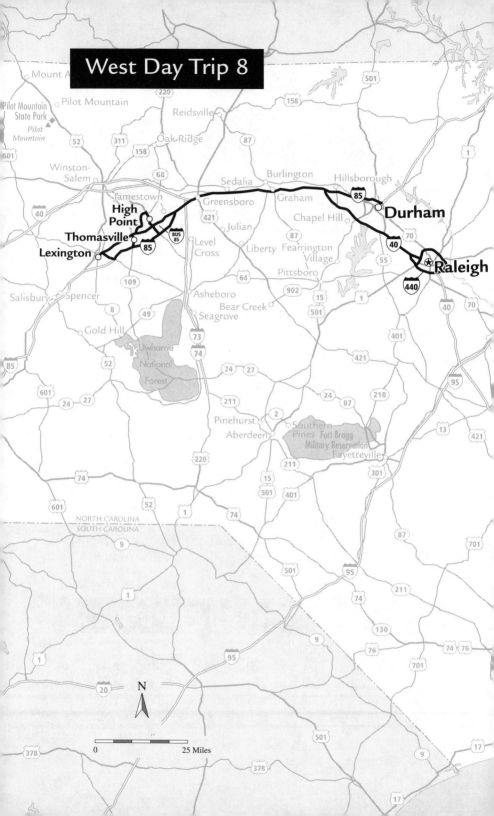

West Day Trip 8

Mount A...
Pilot Mountain State Park
Pilot Mountain
601
52
311
158
220
Reidsville
158
87
501
Winston-Salem
68
Oak-Ridge
Sedalia
Burlington
Hillsborough
85
Jamestown
Greensboro
Graham
40
High Point
421
Chapel Hill
Durham
Thomasville
BUS 85
Julian
87
Level Cross
Liberty
Fearrington Village
70
40
Lexington
85
Pittsboro
55
Raleigh
109
64
902
440
Salisbury
Spencer
Asheboro
15
1
40
70
8
49
Bear Creek
501
401
Gold Hill
Seagrove
73
421
85
52
Uwharrie National Forest
74
24
27
95
601
24
27
211
24
87
210
Pinehurst
2
13
421
Aberdeen
Southern Pines Fort Bragg Military Reservation Fayetteville
74
220
211
301
601
15
501
401
52
1
74
87
NORTH CAROLINA
SOUTH CAROLINA
9
501
95
701
1
130
20
N
9
76
74
76
501
701
378
9
17
0   25 Miles
378
17

countries for the biannual International Home Furnishings Market, the largest event of its kind in the world. Day-trippers come to explore the region's rich history, distinctive cultural events, and diverse shopping selection. For furniture shoppers, High Point offers more than eighty retail furniture outlets.

WHERE TO GO

World's Largest Chest of Drawers. 508 Hamilton Street, High Point 27260. Known as the Bureau of Information in 1926, this beautiful, nineteenth-century dresser is the world's largest. (336) 884–5255 or (800) 720–5255.

Angela Peterson Doll and Miniature Museum. 101 West Green Street, High Point 27260. Among the more than 1,700 dolls and miniatures from around the world is a nativity scene with fifty rare creche dolls, plus a Shirley Temple collection and Bob Timberlake dolls. Open Monday through Friday 10:00 A.M. until 4:30 P.M., Saturday 9:00 A.M. until 4:30 P.M., and Sunday 1:00 to 4:30 P.M. (336) 885–3655.

Furniture Discovery Center. 101 West Green Street, High Point 27260. This interactive hands-on museum shows how furniture is made. Exhibits display case goods and upholstery, miniatures, and the American Furniture Hall of Fame. Admission: adults $5.00, seniors $4.00, ages 5 to 15 $2.00, under age 5 free. Open Monday through Friday 10:00 A.M. until 5:00 P.M., Saturday 9:00 A.M. until 5:00 P.M., and Sunday 1:00 to 5:00 P.M. (336) 887–3876.

City Lake Park. 602 West Main Street, Jamestown 27282. Just a short drive outside the city limits, this 969-acre park, situated along High Point Lake, has picnic areas, amusement rides, miniature golf, fishing and boating, and a swimming pool and water slide. The park's amphitheatre is the site of Jazz Spirit in August. (336) 883–3498.

High Point Museum and Historical Park. 1859 East Lexington Avenue, High Point 27262. Exhibiting the development of High Point from a small Quaker village to the furniture capital of the world, the historical park is home to the Hoggatt House (1754), the Haley House (1786), and a working blacksmith shop. (336) 885–1859, www.highpointmuseum.org.

Piedmont Environmental Center. 1220 Penny Road, High Point 27265. Adjacent to High Point City Lake, the 375 glorious acres include hiking trails, a nature preserve, a nature store, small animal exhibits, the North Carolina Mapscape (large enough so that you can walk across the entire state in a few steps), and access to the 6-mile Greenway Trail. The center is open Monday through Saturday 9:00 A.M. until 5:00 P.M., Sunday 1:00 to 5:00 P.M. Trails are open sunrise to sunset daily. Free. (336) 883–8531.

WHERE TO SHOP

For a free guide to furniture shopping at more than eighty retail furniture outlets in High Point and the surrounding communities, contact the **High Point Convention and Visitors Bureau,** (800) 720–5255, www.highpoint.org.

High Point Farmers' Market. Roy B. Culler Senior Center, High Point 27260. Fresh fruit and vegetables, baked goods, flowers, and plants are available every Wednesday and Saturday through mid-October. (336) 883–3584.

WHERE TO EAT

Kepley's Barbecue. 1304 South Main Street, High Point 27260. The best barbecue north of Lexington, Kepley's serves barbecue sandwiches, plates, trays, hush puppies, and vinegar-based barbecue slaw. Open Monday through Saturday for lunch and dinner. $–$$. (336) 884–1021.

J. Basul Nobles. 101 North Main Street, High Point 27260. Nobles's menu is characterized as Americanized French gourmet. Some of the area's finest chefs have worked here. The menu, which changes nightly, ranges from basic beef dishes to delicious roast half duck to ostrich—for the daring. All entrees are prepared over an open wood fire. Open for dinner only, Monday through Saturday. $$$. (336) 889–3354.

Steak Street. 3915 Sedgebrook Street, High Point 27265. With "outdoor dining inside," according to the owners, the wrought iron furniture, outdoor lighting, and brick inlays on the main dining room floor give this restaurant a cafe feel. The restaurant's Cajun-Creole menu features select cuts of meat, pastas, seafood, and large salads. Open for lunch and dinner daily. $$–$$$. (336) 841–0222.

Vinterra Bistro. 3805 Tinsley Street, High Point 27265. Gourmet specialty foods can be found on a menu that changes weekly, along with a great wine selection. Open for lunch and dinner Monday through Saturday. $$–$$$. (336) 887-0094.

Liberty Steakhouse and Brewery. 1304 North Main Street, High Point 27265. Great beef selections range from prime rib to filet mignon. Enjoy brick-oven specialty pizzas and, with a microbrewery on premises, eight beers on tap all the time. Open for lunch and dinner daily. $$–$$$. (336) 882-4677.

The Dog House. 862 North Main Street, High Point 27260. A local favorite for nearly sixty years, the Dog House features lunch-counter dining for hot dogs and hamburgers. Open for lunch only, Monday through Saturday. $. (336) 886-4953.

Plaza Cafe. 336 South Main Street, High Point 27260. A local favorite for breakfast and lunch, the diner-style cafe specializes in omelettes and fabulous Greek salads. Open daily for breakfast and lunch. $–$$. (336) 886-5271.

WHERE TO STAY

Biltmore Suites Hotel. 4400 Regency Drive, High Point 27265. The Biltmore is an all-suite hotel offering a deluxe continental breakfast, evening reception, fitness center, and surrounding area destination shuttle. $$–$$$. (336) 812-8188 or (888) 412-8188, www.biltmoresuiteshotel.com.

JH Adams Inn. 1108 North Main Street, High Point 27262. Newly restored, the Italian Renaissance–style JH Adams Inn was built in 1918 as a private residence for John Hampton Adams of Adam Millis Hosiery Corporation. Today, the inn serves as a stately reminder of a bygone era. Located in the heart of downtown High Point, the restored home is now a thirty-room property with Jacuzzi tubs, fireplaces, and king-size beds in many rooms. A full breakfast buffet is served. $$$. (336) 882-3267 or (888) 256-1289, www.jhadamsinn.com.

Radisson Hotel City Center. 135 South Main Street, High Point 27260. A full-service hotel, the Radisson Hotel High Point offers guests the convenience of a downtown location. $$–$$$. (336) 889-8888 or (800) 333-3333, www.radisson.com/highpointnc.

Toad Alley Bed and Bagel. 1001 Johnson Street, High Point 27262. This 1924 Victorian home is located in High Point's Johnson Street Historic District. Renovated in 1987, the three-story home has a wraparound front porch with a swing, rocking chairs and private sitting areas. Each of the five charming bedrooms has 9-foot ceilings, ceiling fan, private bath, TV, and VCR. $$–$$$. (336) 889–8349 or (800) 443–1940, www.toadalley.com.

Bouldin House Bed and Breakfast. 4332 Archdale Road, Archdale 27263. This historic bed-and-breakfast inn has four guest rooms, all with private baths. A complimentary gourmet breakfast is served. $$$. (336) 431–4909 or (800) 739–1816, www.bouldinhouse.com.

THOMASVILLE

After North Carolina state senator John W. Thomas helped push through a $3 million state tax to build a railroad system, he settled in an area near the proposed route. Thomas built a depot, general store, and home, and the area became known as "Thomas' Depot." In 1852, the area officially took the name Thomasville by merging Thomas's name with that of local Rounsaville.

WHERE TO GO

North Carolina's Oldest Railroad Depot. 44 West Main Street, Thomasville 27360. The oldest remaining railroad depot in North Carolina, built in 1870, houses the Thomasville Visitors Center. The restored structure is on the National Register of Historic Places. Open 9:00 A.M. until 5:00 P.M. Monday through Friday, 9:00 A.M. until 1:00 P.M. Saturday. Free. (336) 472–4422, www.thomasvilletourism.com.

World's Largest Chair. Intersection of Main Street and NC 109, Thomasville 27361. A symbol of Thomasville's furniture heritage, the fifty-year-old, 30-foot-high monument stands in the heart of downtown Thomasville. The first "big chair" was built in 1922 for the Thomasville Chair Company. In 1936 the old wooden chair was scrapped, and in 1951 ground was broken for a new chair. Recently refurbished, the present structure is a mix of cement, granite dust, and iron, but it appears to be wooden.

WHERE TO EAT

Safari Big Game Steakhouse Restaurant. 15A Laura Lane, Thomasville 27360. The owners claim to offer "big steak food at little steak prices." The 32-ounce porterhouse, for example, goes for $25. The menu also includes such exotic fare as frog legs, alligator meat, buffalo, ostrich, wild boar, pheasant, and venison. $$-$$$. (336) 472-3274.

LEXINGTON

Settled in 1775 and incorporated in 1828, Lexington was named in honor of the revolutionary war battle in Massachusetts. Lexington is the county seat of Davidson County, named for Revolutionary War General William Lee Davidson. The historic uptown is listed on the National Register of Historic Places. Lexington is home to Bob Timberlake, internationally renowned artist and home furnishings designer, and the Bob Timberlake Gallery. But the town is perhaps best known for its pork barbecue.

WHERE TO GO

Lexington Tourism Authority. 305 North Main Street, Lexington 27292. Stop here to begin a self-guided walking tour of Historic Uptown Lexington. The guide highlights forty-one historic properties in a five-block National Register Historic District plus fringe sites dating from 1824 to 1948. (336) 236-4218, www.visitlexingtonnc.org.

Davidson County Historical Museum. 2 South North Main Street, Lexington 27292. The museum's permanent and changing exhibits spotlight the history of the area. It's housed in the old Davidson County Courthouse on the square, which was completed in 1858 and damaged in an 1865 fire during Union General Judson Kilpatrick's occupation. Open daily except Monday. (336) 242-2035.

Richard Childress Racing Shop and Museum. 180 Industrial Drive, Welcome 27374. Tour behind the scenes of NASCAR teams 29 (Kevin Harvick), 31 (Mike Skinner), 30 (Jeff Green), 2 (Kevin Harvick), and 21 (Mike Skinner) with guided shop tours at 10:00 A.M. and 2:00 P.M. on weekdays. Located just ten minutes north of Lexington, the museum and gift shop display a variety of race cars, trophies, and photos of RCR's thirty-plus years in the sport, including the career of the legendary Dale Earnhardt. (336) 731-3389 or (800) 476-3389, www.rcrracing.com.

WHERE TO SHOP

The Bob Timberlake Gallery. 1714 East Center Street, Lexington 27292. This gallery, retail store, and museum that features the art, home furnishings, and accessories of internationally recognized artist and designer Bob Timberlake is located just off I-85 at exit 94 in Lexington. Special events throughout the year highlight Timberlake and other North Carolina artists. (336) 249-4428 or (800) 244-0095, www.bobtimberlake.com.

Historic Uptown Lexington and Visitors Center. 18B West First Avenue, Lexington 27292. Historic Uptown Lexington contains antique stores, the state's largest True Value hardware store (Lanier's), bridal shops, a dress fabric store, an old-fashioned candy store, bakeries, an art and history museum, consignment shops, an old-fashioned grocery store known for homemade pimento cheese and chicken salad, a toy store, restaurants, and more. (336) 249-0383, www.uptownlexington.com.

The Country Store. Old US 52, Welcome 27374. Ten minutes north of Lexington, the Country Store is noted for its handmade quilts, tables, chairs, crafts, and canned foods. Local senior citizens make all the items. Open Thursday through Saturday. (336) 731-2211.

WHERE TO EAT

Lexington Area Barbecue Restaurants. Internationally known for pork shoulders slow-cooked over hot hickory coals, eighteen barbecue restaurants in the small town of Lexington are indeed an attraction for visitors, travel writers, and food editors. The typical cuisine is sliced or chopped pork, served with barbecue slaw (a tomato-vinegar dressing—no mayonnaise), hush puppies, and sweet tea. The following favorites are priced $-$$.

Andy's Barbecue Restaurant. 6043 Old US 52, Lexington 27292; (336) 731-8207.

Back Country BBQ. Linwood-Southmont Road, Lexington 27293; (336) 956-1696.

Bar-B-Q Center. 900 North Main Street, Lexington 27292; (336) 248-4633, www.barbecuecenter.com.

Henry James BBQ. 283 Talbert Boulevard, Lexington 27292; (336) 243-2573.

Jimmy's Barbecue. 1703 Cotton Grove Road, Lexington 27292; (336) 357-2311.

John Wayne's Barbecue. 601 West Fifth Street, Lexington 27292; (336) 249-1658.

Lexington Barbecue. 10 US 70-29 South, Lexington 27292; (336) 249-9814.

Lexington Style Trimmings Barbecue Restaurant. 1515 East Center Street, Lexington 27292; (336) 249-8211.

Smokey Joe's Barbecue Restaurant. 1101 South Main Street, Lexington 27292; (336) 249-0315, www.web.infoave.net/~jcope.

Southern Barbecue Restaurant. 917 Winston Road, Lexington 27292; (336) 248-4528.

Tarheel Q Barbecue Restaurant. 6835 US 64 West, Lexington 27292; (336) 787-4550.

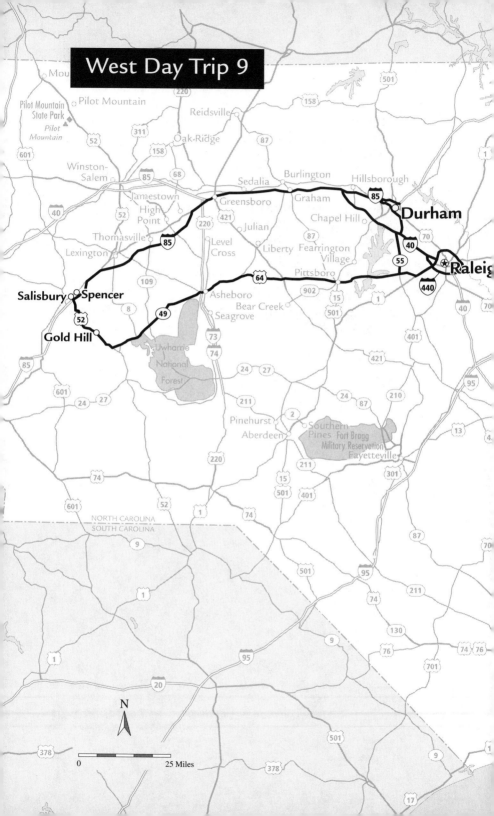

West Day Trip 9

Travel I–40 west to Greensboro to pick up I–85 south for a straight shot into Salisbury. Elizabeth Dole was born here, as was the burgundy-red, bubbly cherry concoction known as Cheerwine, first formulated in 1917 in the basement of L. D. Peeler's wholesale grocery store.

The town of Spencer, just 2 miles north of Salisbury, was once the site of the largest steam locomotive servicing station operated by Southern Railway. Built in 1896 and now known as the North Carolina Transportation Museum, the site presents exhibits on the development of various modes of transport. Here you can see an old roundhouse and ride a steam locomotive.

Complete your day trip by heading to the site of the richest gold mining property east of the Mississippi in the aptly named town of Gold Hill. Once a thriving, rough and rowdy mining town in the eastern part of Rowan County, Gold Hill is now a quaint, restored "Western primitive" village of homes and stores.

On the return trip from Gold Hill to Raleigh, take NC 49 north through Asheboro (see West Day Trip 10 if you'd like to extend your trip), and US 64 east into Raleigh.

SALISBURY

No one knows whether the town was named for Salisbury, England, or for Salisbury, Maryland, where the earliest settlers of Rowan County originated. Nonetheless, Salisbury shares sister-city status with the town in England.

What *is* known about Salisbury is that Daniel Boone once roamed the region, and Andrew Jackson practiced law here. During the conflict that some Southerners still refer to as the "War of Northern Aggression," Salisbury was home to one of the Confederacy's largest prison camps, the only such camp in North Carolina. five-thousand Union troops were buried nearby in a plot of land now designated a National Cemetery.

The thirty-square-block historic district consists of downtown Salisbury and the West Square residential district. Listed on the National Register of Historic Places, this area includes the Dr. Josephus Hall House, which was built in 1820 as the Salisbury Female Academy and later became the home of physician Josephus Hall. Also in the historic district is the Utzman-Chambers House, an 1819 Federal town house built by master builder Jacob Stirewalt.

WHERE TO GO

Rowan County Convention and Visitors Bureau. 204 East Innes Street, Salisbury 28144. Stop here to pick up a narrative cassette tape for touring the Historic National Cemetery and Confederate Prison Site. The tape and player are loaned for free. Also pick up maps and brochures. Open Monday through Friday 9:00 A.M. until 5:00 P.M., Saturday 10:00 A.M. until 4:00 P.M., and Sunday 1:00 to 4:00 P.M. (800) 332–2343 or (704) 638–3100, www.visitsalisburync.com.

Historic National Cemetery and Confederate Prison Site. 204 East Innes Street, Salisbury 28144. This self-guided driving tour is a must for Civil War buffs. Although nothing remains of the Salisbury Prison, the tour provides insights into this period of history. Three monuments erected by the State of Maine, the Commonwealth of Pennsylvania, and the U.S. Government stand in the Salisbury National Cemetery as a tribute to the 11,700 brave Union soldiers who died while at the prison. Tape players and cassettes for the tour are loaned free of charge at the Rowan County Convention and Visitors Bureau. (800) 332–2343 or (704) 638–3100, www.visitsalisburync.com.

Josephus Hall House. 226 South Jackson Street, Salisbury 28144. This impressive museum was once home to Dr. Josephus Hall, chief surgeon at the Salisbury Confederate Prison during the Civil War. Built in 1820 in the Federal style, additions in 1859 and in 1900 have given the house Greek Revival and Victorian features. The interior has painted ceilings, original fixtures, and an impressive collection of mid-Victorian furnishings and decorative accessories belonging to the Hall family. Docents in period costume conduct guided tours. Open Saturday and Sunday 1:00 to 4:00 P.M. (704) 636–0103, www.historicsalisbury.org.

Salisbury Heritage Walking Tour. A perfect way to see Historic Salisbury at your own pace, this 1.3-mile walking tour provides a personal glimpse into the history and architecture of historic downtown Salisbury and the stately homes of the West Square District. The brochures, tapes, and tape players for the tour are loaned free of charge and can be obtained at the Visitor Information Center. (800) 332–2343 or (704) 638–3100, www.visitsalisburync.com.

Utzman-Chambers House. 116 South Jackson Street, Salisbury 28144. This 1819 Federal town house was built by Jacob Stirewalt, master builder of the period, and reflects the lifestyle of the more affluent citizens of the early 1800s with its unique curved staircase and exquisite interior moldings and details. One of the few surviving Federal period town houses in Piedmont North Carolina, its period rooms are furnished with Hepplewhite and Chippendale as well as furniture made by Rowan County craftsmen. The house and gardens are open Thursday through Sunday from 1:00 to 4:00 P.M. (704) 633–5946.

 Rowan Museum. 202 North Main Street, Salisbury 28144. This 1854 courthouse, which survived Stoneman's raid, is one of the finest examples of pre–Civil War architecture in the state. The museum artifacts and displays depict the life and history of Rowan County. (704) 633–5946.

Dan Nicholas Park and Campground. 6800 Bringle Ferry Road, Salisbury 28146. Located 8 miles southeast of Salisbury, this 425-acre park has a ten-acre lake for paddleboating and fishing, plus live animal exhibits, tennis courts, picnic shelters, a playground, volleyball, horseshoes, ballfields, an outdoor theater, miniature golf, a carousel, gem mining, and a miniature train ride for children. The eighty-site family campground is open year-round. (704) 636–0154, www.co.rowan.nc.us.

Old Stone House. Old Stone House Road, Granite Quarry 28072. Built by German immigrant Michael Braun in 1766, this two-story Georgian-style house is the oldest structure in Rowan County. The dry-stacked stones on the front of the house were carefully shaped and matched, creating an impressive face to visitors. Three miles from downtown Salisbury, the house is open Saturday and Sunday 1:00 to 4:00 P.M. (704) 633–5946.

Waterworks Visual Arts Center. One Water Street, Salisbury 28144. Located in the city's first waterworks building, built in 1913, the Waterworks Visual Arts Center offers regional and national gallery exhibitions, studio classes, workshops, and lectures, as well as outreach programs. The Hamlin Sensory Garden in the Taylor/Johnson courtyard invites visitors to participate in the art experience through touch, sound, fragrance, and sight. Visitors are welcome to do research or read in the Murphy Art Library. Open Monday through Friday 9:00 A.M. until 5:00 P.M., Saturday 10:00 A.M. until 4:00 P.M., Sunday 1:00 to 4:00 P.M. Closed major holidays. (704) 638–1882, www.waterworks.org.

WHERE TO SHOP

O.O. Rufty's General Store. 126 East Innes Street, Salisbury 28144. A third-generation family-owned working store, Rufty's has been in operation since 1905. Located in historic downtown Salisbury, the store's more than 5,000 square feet are packed with old and new merchandise. Rufty's Market has an old-fashioned soda fountain, grocery store, meat market, and buffet restaurant. Open Monday through Friday 8:00 A.M. until 6:00 P.M., Saturday 9:00 A.M. until 5:00 P.M. Breakfast and lunch buffet served Monday through Friday 7:00 A.M. until 6:00 P.M. (800) 611–6055 or (704) 633–4381, www.oorufty.com.

Salisbury Square Antiques and Collectibles. 111 South Main Street, Salisbury 28144. This antique mall in historic downtown Salisbury has more than ninety dealers and more than 43,000 square feet of antiques, glassware, and collectibles. Open daily. (704) 633–0773.

The Salisbury Emporium. 230 East Kerr Street, Salisbury 28144. The Salisbury Emporium is a collection of shops and galleries located in a renovated historic landmark adjacent to the architecturally acclaimed Salisbury Train Station. The Emporium contains more than 15,000 square feet of gifts, antiques, home accessories, Christmas items, fine art, handcrafts, and more. Open Tuesday through Sunday. (704) 642–0039.

The Stitchin' Post and Gifts. 104 South Main Street, Salisbury 28144. This historic 1879 shop has high ceilings, original wood floors, and exposed brick walls. The renovated storefront gives you the warm feeling of walking into history. Unusual gifts for every season can be found here in the heart of downtown Salisbury just off the square. Open 10:00 A.M. until 5:30 P.M. Monday through Saturday. Also open Sunday afternoons between Thanksgiving and Christmas. (704) 637–0708, www.spgifts.com.

WHERE TO EAT

The Wrenn House. 115 South Jackson Street, Salisbury 28144. Pull up a chair for the city's namesake dish, Salisbury steak. The menu also features blue-plate specials that offer a meat and two vegetables. $–$$. (704) 633–9978.

Sweet Meadow Cafe. 118 West Innes Street, Salisbury 28144. Serving contemporary cuisine with a twist, the eclectic menu includes crab cakes—crispy on the outside, nice and soft on the inside—red beans and rice, and other items. Fresh breads are made daily. Works by local artists are displayed. $–$$. (704) 637–8715.

Las Palmas. 122 East Fisher Street, Salisbury 28144. This downtown restaurant serves traditional Mexican food, including the best fajitas in town. A watering hole, the restaurant has a long bar where you may want to dine if tables are filled. $–$$. (704) 636–9475.

The Checkered Flag Barbecue. 1530 South Main Street, Salisbury 28144. Popular among the breakfast crowd, the Checkered Flag also serves barbecue and sandwiches during lunch. $–$$. (704) 636–2628.

WHERE TO STAY

The Mary Steele House. 126 East Steele Street, Salisbury 28144. Built in 1893 by Mary Steele Lord Scales and her husband, Major Nathaniel Eldridge Scales, this wonderful Queen Anne Victorian home provides a quaint, romantic atmosphere for couples. $–$$. (704) 239–1805, www.marysteelehouse.com.

Mama Josephine's Country Cottage. 2106 Old Concord Road, Salisbury 28146. Mama Josephine's has six cozy rooms. $$. (704) 637–2717.

Rowan Oak House Bed and Breakfast. 208 South Fulton Street, Salisbury 28144. An elegant Queen Anne Victorian in the Historic District of downtown Salisbury, Rowan Oak has a wraparound porch, leaded and stained glass windows, original gas and electric fixtures, seven fireplaces, antique-filled oversize rooms, and luxurious bathrooms. A smoke-free property, it's just three blocks from downtown shopping, antiquing, and fine restaurants. (704) 633–2086 or (800) 786–0437, www.rowanoakbb.com.

Turn of the Century Victorian Bed and Breakfast. 529 South Fulton Street, Salisbury 28144. This bed-and-breakfast mixes 1890s elegance with contemporary comforts and amenities. The business suite includes a private office/sitting room. The home has a welcoming wraparound front porch, and complimentary gourmet breakfast is served. $$$. (704) 642–1660 or (800) 250–5349, www.turnofthecenturybb.com.

SPENCER

Because it sat halfway between Atlanta and Washington, D.C., Spencer was chosen as Southern Railway's repair facility location. The town of Spencer and the shops were named for Southern Railway's first president, Samuel Spencer.

WHERE TO GO

North Carolina Transportation Museum. 411 South Salisbury Avenue, Spencer 28159. Located on the site of what was once Southern Railway Company's largest steam locomotive repair facility, the museum has thirteen buildings, including a restored round-house, on 57 acres. Exhibits on early transportation allow you to visit antique automobiles at *Bumper to Bumper* and trace the history of transportation in *Wagons, Wheels & Wings*. Experience days of the working railroad repair shop in the restored 1924 Robert Julian roundhouse. Enjoy seasonal train rides, an audiovisual show, and the visitor center and gift shop. Open April through October Monday through Saturday 9:00 A.M. until 5:00 P.M., Sunday 1:00 to 5:00 P.M.; November through March, Tuesday through Saturday 10:00 A.M. until 4:00 P.M., Sunday 1:00 to 4:00 P.M. Free admission; charge for train rides, turntable rides, and guided tours. (704) 636–2889 or (877) 628–6386, www.NCTrans.org.

Spencer Historic District. Adjacent to the North Carolina Transportation Museum, the Spencer National Historic Register District is the largest contiguous district in North Carolina. It contains 322 residential and commercial buildings primarily constructed between 1905 and 1920 to provide support and housing for the workers of Southern Railway's former steam locomotive repair facility. (704) 633–2231, www.ci.spencer.nc.us.

WHERE TO SHOP

The Little Choo Choo Shop. 500 South Salisbury Avenue, Spencer 28159. Across the street from the North Carolina Transportation Museum, this well-stocked model-railroad shop is a must-see for train enthusiasts. Open Tuesday through Saturday. (704) 637–8717.

WHERE TO EAT

La Dolce Vita. 518 South Salisbury Avenue, Spencer 28159. Across from the transportation museum, this small restaurant is often filled with locals. Authentic Italian food is prepared by the authentic Italian owner. $$. (704) 636–8891.

GOLD HILL

"The richest mining property east of the Mississippi" was the message sent to England after gold was discovered in this part of Rowan County in 1824. Here, vertical shaft mines ran eighty stories deep. With its boardwalks and narrow streets connecting places that were here as early as the 1840s, Gold Hill has the feel of a set for a Western movie.

WHERE TO SHOP

Mauney's 1840 Store and Museum. 775 Saint Stephens Church, Gold Hill 28071. Opened in 1840, Mauney's was the first store in Gold Hill. Offering Victorian-era antiques, the store doubles as a museum that displays photos from the days when Gold Hill was emerging as a mining town. The town was named right inside this store by a group of prospectors. Open Wednesday through Sunday. (704) 279–1632.

E.H. Montgomery Store. 770 Saint Stephens Church, Gold Hill 28071. Aside from being a general store, E.H. Montgomery's has the "best hot dogs in three counties," according to the owner. Order milk shakes or soft drinks or pick up some old-fashioned candy at the counter. The store opened in this building in 1850. Open Wednesday through Sunday. (704) 279–1632.

WHERE TO EAT

Miss Ruby's Restaurant. 840 Saint Stephen's Church Road, Gold Hill 28071. An upscale country inn that offers such items as filet topped with rosemary goat cheese and a balsamic reduction, served with horse-radish, mashed potatoes, and steamed asparagus. Try the "Stick to Your Innards" creamy cheddar cheese grits topped with shrimp and maple country ham. Open Wednesday through Sunday for lunch and dinner, and Sunday for brunch. $$–$$$. (704) 209–6049.

The Gold Hill Mint. 842 Saint Stephen's Church Road, Gold Hill 28071. This bakery and coffee shop is operated by a local baker who supplies many of the desserts for Miss Ruby's. The bakery offers such "comfort food" as pound cake, seasonal pies, and desserts. Open daily. $. (704) 209–3280.

Level Cross · Asheboro · Seagrove

This day trip could be called a transportation day trip, an animal lover's day trip, or a pottery tour. That's because the three towns you will visit on this outing from Raleigh-Durham give you plenty of each. Begin your journey by heading west on I–40 toward Greensboro, where you'll pick up US 220 south toward Asheboro.

The first stop along the way is Level Cross in Randleman, where NASCAR legend Richard Petty and the Petty Racing Team make their home. From Petty's shop and museum, it's only another fifteen minutes to Asheboro, where you'll visit one of the South's finest collections of vintage Harley-Davidson motorcycles. Nearby is the North Carolina Aviation Museum, home to vintage military aircraft.

Of course, Asheboro's big drawing card is the North Carolina Zoo. The nation's largest and perhaps finest walk-through natural-habitat zoo has more than 1,100 animals and 60,000 plants in its African and North American sections. After visiting the zoo, make your way to Seagrove, which bills itself as the "pottery capital of the world." Try to schedule your trip around the kiln openings, traditionally in the spring, or the pottery festival in the fall. Along the way, visit Pisgah Bridge, one of only two covered bridges in North Carolina.

As you head home by way of US 64 north, you could stop at the gravesite of Frances Bavier, who played Aunt Bee in episodes of *The Andy Griffith Show*. Bavier is buried in Siler City's Oakwood Cemetery. If you are a huge fan of the old *Andy Griffith* episodes, be sure to see our West Day Trip 7 to Mount Airy, the town that fictional Mayberry was based on.

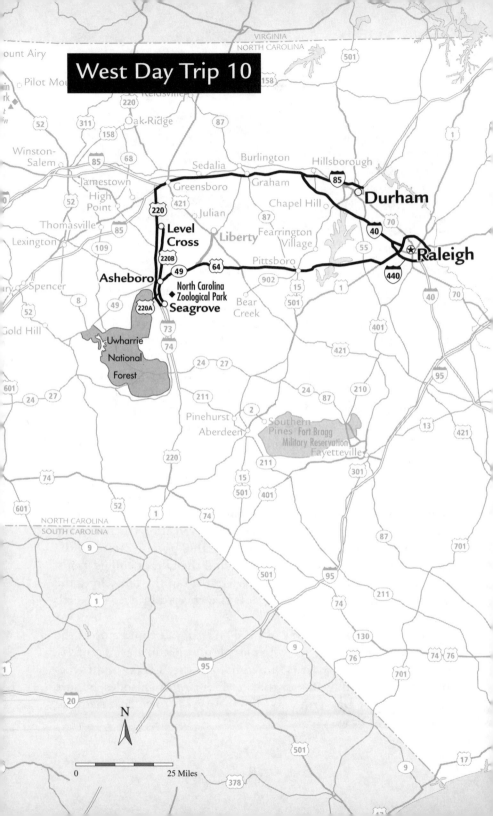

West Day Trip 10

VIRGINIA
NORTH CAROLINA

ount Airy

Pilot Mou
rk
t
in

Reidsville

Oak-Ridge

Winston-Salem

Jamestown
High
Point

Thomasville

Lexington

Spencer

Gold Hill

Level Cross

Asheboro

North Carolina
Zoological Park

Seagrove

Uwharrie
National
Forest

Greensboro

Julian

Liberty

Sedalia

Burlington
Graham

Chapel Hill

Fearrington
Village

Pittsboro

Bear
Creek

Hillsborough

Durham

Raleigh

Pinehurst
Aberdeen

Southern
Pines   Fort Bragg
Military Reservation
Fayetteville

NORTH CAROLINA
SOUTH CAROLINA

N

0   25 Miles

LEVEL CROSS

With Greensboro and Asheboro only 14 miles in opposite directions, Level Cross is a convenient stop for day-trippers visiting either destination. There are two reasons to park your car here: to visit the Richard Petty Museum and to have lunch where the shop mechanics do, at Frank and Larry's Breakfast and Lunch.

WHERE TO GO

Richard Petty Museum. 311 Branson Mill Road, Randleman 27317. Race cars, awards, and photos honor this seven-time Winston Cup Series champion. See highlights of "The King's" thirty-five-year career in a full-length movie in the mini theater, and take home gifts for a favorite race fan. Open Monday through Saturday 9:00 A.M. until 5:00 P.M. Admission is $3.50 for adults, $2.00 for kids. (336) 495–1143, www.pettyracing.com.museum/museum.htm.

WHERE TO EAT

Frank and Larry's Breakfast and Lunch. 5624 Randleman Road, Randleman 27317. This is the spot where the locals and the Petty shop mechanics gather for breakfast and lunch. The restaurant has been here as long as Richard has, the owners proudly boast. Offering daily blue plate lunch specials, Frank & Larry's is popular for hot dogs, hamburgers, and barbecue as well as breakfasts that include homemade biscuits and gravy and homemade sausage. $. (336) 674–9177.

ASHEBORO

In 1701, explorer John Lawson crossed the Uwharrie River into a Keyauwee Indian village. "Nature hath so fortify'd the Town with Mountains, that were it a Great Seat of War, it might easily be made impregnable, having large cornfields joining to their cabins, and a

Savanna near the Town, at the foot of these Mountains, that is capable of keeping some hundreds of heads of Cattle," Lawson wrote in *A New Voyage to Carolina,* published in 1709.

The mountains and rolling hills where the Keyauwee made their home are now the domain of a species more ancient than man, a species whose denizens make up kingdom *Animalia.*

Six miles southeast of Asheboro, the North Carolina Zoological Park sits on 1,450 acres skirting the eastern edge of the Uwharries. Where Native Americans once walked, exotic animals now roam, and they roam more freely here than in most other zoos in the world. That's because Randolph County's rolling hills make for ideal natural habitats, where animals move about unrestricted by fences and steel bars.

Although a visit to the zoo can take the better part of the day, you will want to allow time to visit the other sites in Asheboro. They include the American Classic Motorcycle museum, with its more than six decades of motorcycle history, and for classic aircraft enthusiasts and World War II buffs, the North Carolina Aviation Museum.

Finally, if you just want to get away from it all, there's the Uwharrie National Forest, which occupies 50,189 acres west of Asheboro. You're not likely to run up on any of the Keyauwee that John Lawson encountered in those old mountains, but all that mesmerized him is still there, and almost as pristine as it was when he first laid eyes on it. For more information, call (910) 576–6391 or visit www.cs.unca.edu/nfsnc/recreation/uwharrie/index.htm.

WHERE TO GO

North Carolina Zoological Park. 4401 Zoo Parkway, Asheboro 27203. This facility was the first American zoo designed from its inception around the "natural habitat" philosophy, presenting animals and plants in exhibits that closely resemble the habitats in which they would be found in the wild.

The zoo's African habitats stretch over 300 acres and contain nine large outdoor exhibits for animals such as lions, zebras, ostriches, baboons, chimpanzees, rhinos, and elephants. The North American habitat, with 200 acres, is home to alligators, polar bears, bison, roadrunners, rattlesnakes, and tarantulas. The streamside exhibit re-creates North Carolina's stream wildlife, from the mountains through the Piedmont region and coastal plain.

The best way to see the zoo is on foot, so you can explore the exhibits and trails. An internal tram is available to transport visitors between exhibit areas, but most animals are not visible from the trams. You can enter or exit by either the North American or African gate; a shuttle bus transports visitors to the parking areas. Zoo officials recommend taking a minimum of five hours to explore all that the park offers at a comfortable pace.

Open daily, April through October from 9:00 A.M. until 5:00 P.M.; closes at 4:00 P.M. from November through March. Admission is charged. (336) 879-7000 or (800) 488-0444, www.nczoo.org.

Pisgah Covered Bridge. Take exit 49, just south of Asheboro off US 220 Business. Look for the historical markers that will direct you to the covered bridge, one of only two in North Carolina, which was built around 1910. Hiking trails, picnic tables, and parking are available.

American Classic Motorcycle Museum. 1170 US 64 West, Asheboro 27203. One of the South's finest collections of antique and classic Harley-Davidson motorcycles, the museum has more than thirty bikes dating from 1936 through 1972, and an authentic 1948 Harley dealership/repair shop. Open Monday through Saturday. Free. (336) 629-9564.

North Carolina Aviation Museum. Asheboro Regional Airport, Asheboro 27203. This museum, created for the conservation of military aircraft, is home to an impressive collection of airworthy vintage military aircraft. The museum also houses exhibits of World War II military uniforms and a collection of WW II–era newspaper features. Open Monday through Saturday 10:00 A.M. until 4:00 P.M. and Sunday noon until 4:00 P.M. Fee. (336) 625-0170.

WHERE TO SHOP

Collector's Antique Mall. 211 Sunset Avenue, Asheboro 27203. More than 125 dealers offer antiques and collectibles in more than 35,000 square feet of retail space in the downtown antiques district of Asheboro. Open daily. (336) 629-8105.

WHERE TO EAT

Sir Pizza. 813 East Dixie Drive, Asheboro 27203. Sir Pizza has been an Asheboro favorite for pizza, pasta, and sandwiches since 1969. The locals tell us that when people who have moved from Asheboro return home, this is the first place they want to return to. Open daily. $$. (336) 629-2874. Second location at 724 North Fayetteville Street, (336) 629-9101.

Rock-Ola Café. 1131 East Dixie Drive, Asheboro 27203. This family-oriented, casual dining establishment serves pork, chicken, ribs, certified Angus beef, pastas, and seafood. Try the handmade onion rings or loaded cheese fries for starters. Open daily. $$. (336) 626-4001.

Taste of Asia. 127 East Taft Avenue, Asheboro 27203. Among the more popular Thai and Cambodian dishes are curries, seafood stir-fry, and noodle dishes. Open daily. $$. (336) 626-7578.

Blue Mist Barbecue. 3409 US 64 East, Asheboro 27203. Blue Mist serves the area's finest barbecue plates and sandwiches. Open daily. $$. (336) 625-3980.

WHERE TO STAY

Asheboro has several major chain hotels, including Comfort Inn, Days Inn, Hampton Inn, Holiday Inn Express, Jameson Inn, and Super 8 Hotel. In addition, there is one bed-and-breakfast in downtown Asheboro and another situated on a 128-acre farm, twenty minutes north.

Victorian Country Bed and Breakfast. 711 Sunset Avenue, Asheboro 27203. Offering four guest rooms and complimentary breakfast, this stately Queen Anne home is located in downtown Asheboro. $$-$$$. (336) 626-4706.

The Inn at Rising Meadow Farm. 3750 Williams Dairy Road, Liberty 27298. If animals were your reason for this day trip, then you'd do well to travel twenty minutes north of Asheboro for an overnight stay in this two-guest room bed-and-breakfast. Spend some time fishing in the pond (or just toss some feed in), catch lightning bugs, or acquaint yourself with the sheep (raised for wool products sold here), cows, goats, horses, and donkey that live here. If you want to lend a hand, there may be eggs to gather or kittens to hold. $$. (336) 622-1795, www.risingmeadow.com.

SEAGROVE

Fifteen minutes south of Asheboro, Seagrove, named for a railroad official, invites visitors to discover one of the finest sources of decorative pottery on the East Coast. What you'll find here is not just handmade ashtrays and such. Seagrove pottery passes for museum-quality art, with some pieces going for as much as $12,000. Some of the more than one hundred potters who work in the area have garnered national and worldwide attention.

WHERE TO GO

North Carolina Pottery Center. 250 East Avenue, Seagrove 27341. Seagrove pottery is showcased at the North Carolina Pottery Center's museum, gallery, and learning center. The facility presents permanent and changing exhibits. Open Tuesday through Saturday 10:00 A.M. until 4:00 P.M. Adults $3.00, children $1.00. (336) 873–8430, www.ncpotterycenter.com.

WHERE TO SHOP

For a guide to the potteries and galleries in the Seagrove area, order the free brochure *Raised in Clay* from the **Randolph County Tourism Development Authority,** (800) 626–2672. Two helpful web sites: www.seagrovepotteries.com and www.discoverseagrove.com. Following is a sampling of our some of my favorite potteries.

    King's Pottery. 4905 Reeder Road, Seagrove 27341. Operated by the King family, this pottery specializes in wheel-thrown and hand-built utilitarian pottery. The wood-fired and salt-glazed items include folk art, face jugs, and specialty pieces. Open Monday through Saturday, but the owners suggest calling first if you "are coming some distance." (336) 381–3090, www.kingspottery.com.

    Phil Morgan Pottery. 966 NC 705, Seagrove 27341. Morgan specializes in quality crystalline glazed porcelain, reflecting the 1,500-year-old techniques from the Chung Dynasty. Morgan's pieces are in collections worldwide, including those owned by heads of state in the United States, Argentina, and China. His shop, established in 1973, also sells hand-painted decorative and utilitarian pieces. Open Monday through Saturday. (336) 873-7304.

Pott's Pottery. 630 East Main Street, Seagrove 27341. Opened in 1991, Pott's Pottery specializes in wheel-thrown utilitarian ware. Open Monday through Saturday. (336) 873-9660.

Turn and Burn. 124 East Avenue, Seagrove 27341. Operating since 1985, Turn & Burn specializes in traditional Seagrove salt glaze in utilitarian and decorative pottery, wood-fired stoneware, contemporary and traditional folk art, raku, and fire pit. Open Monday through Saturday. (336) 873-7381.

Seagrove Pottery. 106 North Broad Street, Seagrove 27301. This gallery represents more than thirty potters and artists from the Seagrove region, offering a wide variety of face jugs, utilitarian and decorative pottery, basketry, candles, and hand-painted garden accessories. Open daily. (336) 873-7280.

Southern Visions. 2475 NC 705 South, Seagrove 27301. Featuring functional stoneware and wood-fired, salt-glazed pottery, this shop specializes in traditional folk art, face jugs, and figural pieces. (336) 879-6990.

WHERE TO EAT

Jugtown Cafe. 7042 Old US 220, Seagrove 27341. Stop by for blue plate specials, breakfast with biscuits, gravy, grits and sausage, and great homemade pies. Try the "huge" cookies, reasonably priced at 80 cents each. Open Monday through Wednesday 6:00 A.M. until 2:00 P.M., Thursday through Saturday 6:00 A.M. until 8:00 P.M., Sunday 7:00 A.M. until 2:00 P.M. $-$$. (336) 873-8292.

Westmoore Family Restaurant. 2172 NC 705 South, Seagrove 27341. A full line of fried and broiled seafood, steaks, salads, and sandwiches is available plus pit-cooked barbecue and daily blue plate specials. This place is popular for its charcoal-grilled burgers, clubs, and seafood. $-$$. (910) 464-5222.

WHERE TO STAY

The Duck Smith House Bed and Breakfast. 465 North Broad Street, Seagrove 27341. This beautifully restored historic farm house has four guest rooms. The full country breakfast includes freshly